DATE DUE

GAYLORD 353 CDD

THE COMPONENTS OF LIFE

OF LIFE

From Nucleic Acids to Carbohydrates

THE COMPONENTS OF LIFE

From Nucleic Acids to Carbohydrates

EDITED BY KARA ROGERS, SENIOR EDITOR, BIOMEDICAL SCIENCES

Britannica®
Educational Publishing

IN ASSOCIATION WITH

ROSEN
EDUCATIONAL SERVICES

Published in 2011 by Britannica Educational Publishing
(a trademark of Encyclopædia Britannica, Inc.)
in association with Rosen Educational Services, LLC
29 East 21st Street, New York, NY 10010.

First Edition

Britannica Educational Publishing
Michael I. Levy: Executive Editor
J.E. Luebering: Senior Manager
Marilyn L. Barton: Senior Coordinator, Production Control
Steven Bosco: Director, Editorial Technologies
Lisa S. Braucher: Senior Producer and Data Editor
Yvette Charboneau: Senior Copy Editor
Kathy Nakamura: Manager, Media Acquisition
Kara Rogers: Senior Editor, Biomedical Sciences

Rosen Educational Services
Alexandra Hanson-Harding: Editor
Nelson Sá: Art Director
Cindy Reiman: Photography Manager
Matthew Cauli: Designer, Cover Design
Introduction by Jennifer Capuzzo

Library of Congress Cataloging-in-Publication Data

The components of life : from nucleic acids to carbohydrates / edited by Kara Rogers.—1st ed.
   p. cm.—(Biochemistry, cells, and life)
"In association with Britannica Educational Publishing, Rosen Educational Services."
Includes bibliographical references and index.
ISBN 978-1-61530-324-3 (lib. bdg.)
1. Biochemistry--Popular works. 2. Biomolecules--Popular works. I. Rogers, Kara
QH506C6416 2011
572—dc22

                                                                    2010025747

Manufactured in the United States of America

Cover © www.istockphoto.com / Osuleo

On page x: Scientist Emil Fischer's work on sugars earned him a Nobel Prize for Chemistry
in 1902. *SSPL via Getty Images*

On pages 1, 41, 67, 98, 133, 185, 229, 232, 235: Pairs of chromosomes, close-up. *Sandra
Baker/The Image Bank/Getty Images*

CONTENTS

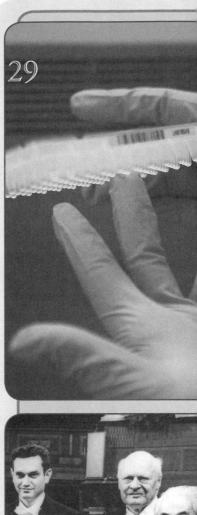

102

110

148

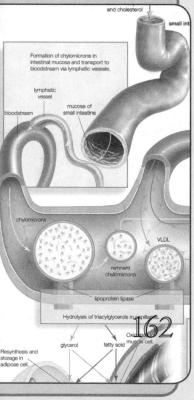

162

204

Introduction

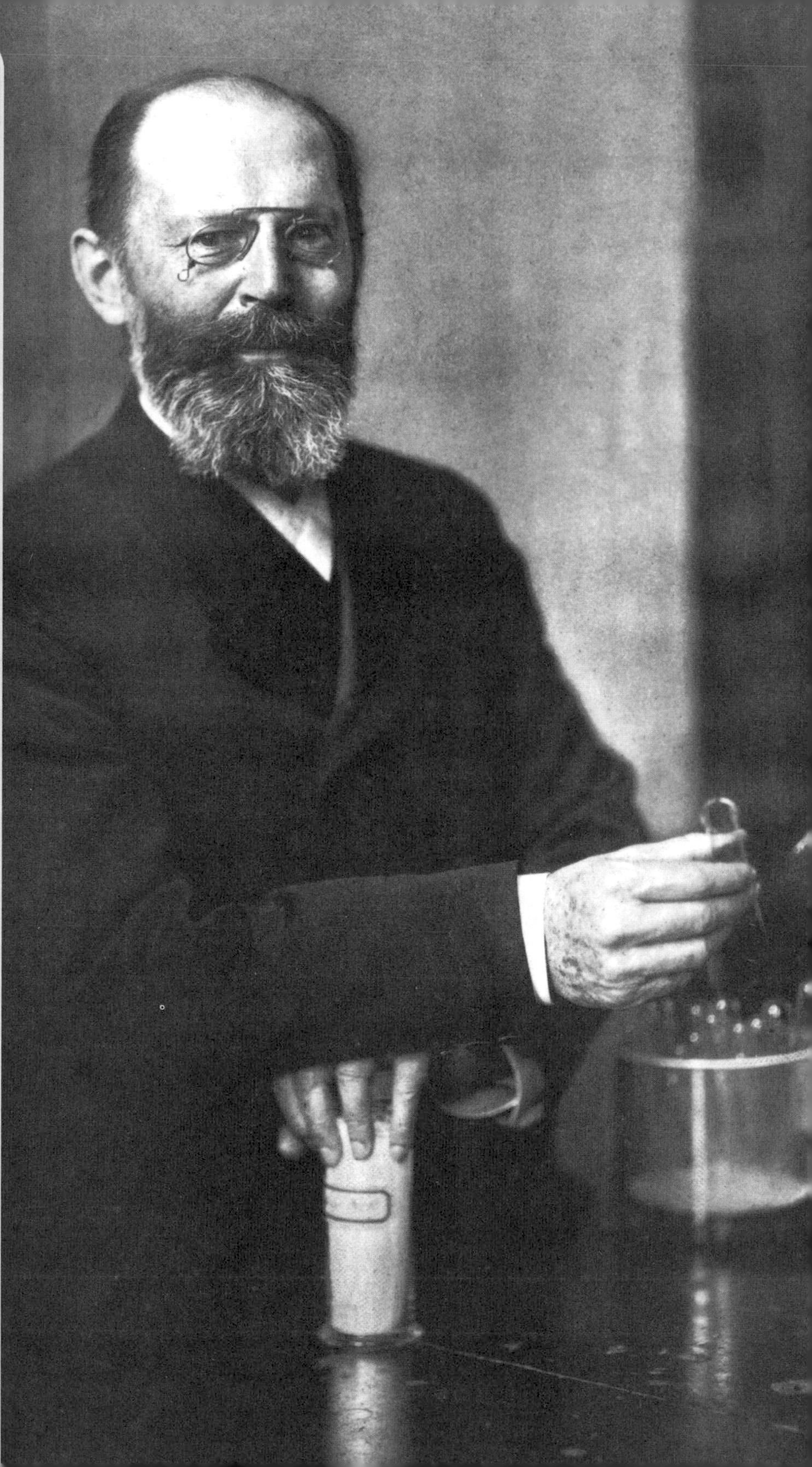

The molecular components of life—nucleic acids, amino acids, proteins, lipids, and carbohydrates—are vital for life. Awareness about the need to fuel the body with protein, to monitor carbohydrate intake, and to maintain a healthy cholesterol level has caused these basic biochemical components to become a part of the mainstream consciousness. Although mass media may simplify the ideas that form the basis of biochemistry, the science behind the headlines is often fascinatingly complex.

A nucleic acid is a large molecule that appears in every cell of living things. The two main nucleic acids, deoxyribonucleic acid (DNA) and ribonucleic acid (RNA), both play a role in determining the inherited characteristics of living things, although the specific form and function of each is different. Nucleic acids are made up of long links of molecules composed of a series of nearly identical building blocks called nucleotides. Thus, nucleic acids are often described as polynucleotides. DNA is the master blueprint for life. It makes up the genetic material in every living organism and in many viruses. Each DNA nucleotide is made up of three parts: (1) a phosphate group, composed of phosphate and hydrogen atoms; (2) a sugar molecule containing five carbon atoms; and (3) one of four different kinds of nitrogen-containing molecules called bases. The four bases have specific pairings with one another. For example, two hydrogen bonds connect adenine (A) to thymine (T), while three hydrogen bonds connect guanine (G) to cytosine (C). The specific sequence of these bases produces the genetic code found within the nucleus of a cell.

The chemical structure of DNA is complex. In 1953 American biophysicist James D. Watson and English biophysicist Francis Crick introduced the idea that the shape of a DNA molecule is a twisted double helix. In their model, the double helix is formed by two strands of polynucleotides that coil around each other. The two phosphate-sugar strands run in opposite directions and form the outside of the helix. The A-T-C-G bases are found on the inside of the helix, with the bonds between them connecting the two strands and resembling the steps of a ladder. The biological structure of DNA can vary from circular molecules in most prokaryotes (organisms such as bacteria that lack a distinct cell nucleus) to the linear DNA molecules called chromosomes found in most eukaryotes (organisms containing a membrane-bound nucleus).

DNA is normally a very stable molecule. But certain natural and unnatural factors can change DNA. Chemical carcinogens, oxidation, and ionizing radiation can alter the intrinsic structure of DNA, causing mutations. Biochemists also know how to artificially manipulate DNA by breaking the hydrogen bonds that hold together DNA's double helix. Through a process called denaturation, heat is applied to a solution containing DNA. The heat breaks the bonds, and the two strands separate. Cooling the solution allows the strands to reassociate in a process called renaturation, or hybridization. Ultraviolet (UV) light is weakly absorbed by double-stranded DNA but is strongly absorbed by single-stranded DNA. Therefore, biochemists can determine to what extent DNA is separated—whether segments are in single-stranded or double-stranded conformation—by observing UV absorption. This provides important information on the biochemical properties of DNA, which is useful for characterizing chemical modifications, including mutations, that occur within the molecule.

Assembled DNA molecules can be further manipulated through methylation and through enzymes called nucleases. Methylation, the process of adding molecules called methyl groups to DNA bases to modify them, has many cellular functions. In bacteria, for example, methylation-can protect DNA from enzymes capable of cutting the molecule into fragments. Methylation also helps to eradicate incorrect base sequences in some organisms and can repress or activate certain genes that control embryonic development in other organisms. Nucleases are enzymes that cleave (cut) and degrade DNA. Endonucleases cleave DNA at specific sites within the middle portions of the molecule, whereas exonucleases degrade DNA from the end of the chain. Some endonucleases cleave specific sequences of DNA that can then be moved from one organism to another. Manipulation and modification of DNA through the use of endonucleases can dramatically alter the function of genetic material.

In contrast to the double-helix structure of DNA, RNA is single-stranded. Similar to DNA, it is also composed of the nucleotides A, C, and G, but thymine (T) is replaced by uracil (U). RNA is the first intermediate in converting the information from DNA into amino acids, which form proteins essential for the working cell.

While DNA is inherently stable and provides the genetic information for the cell, RNA serves multiple roles and is comparatively less stable than DNA. Since RNA is constantly synthesized and degraded, its instability is not a major problem for the cell.

Because RNA is single-stranded, its chemical structure is quite different from that of DNA. It is more flexible, which allows RNA molecules to form various structures that perform different functions. Messenger RNA (mRNA), for example, delivers the information in genes from the DNA to a cellular organelle known as a ribosome. The ribosome then serves as the site where genetic information is decoded into a protein. Ribosomal

RNA (rRNA) molecules help catalyze protein synthesis. Transfer RNA (tRNA) carries amino acids into the ribosome for assembly into a protein.

The three main processes of DNA metabolism (the chemical reactions that produce energy and organic materials necessary for life) are replication, repair, and recombination. In DNA replication, the two strands are separated and new complementary strands are generated independently. The result is two exact copies of the original DNA molecule, with each copy containing one strand that is derived from the parent and one new strand. During the process of recombination, the DNA molecules are nicked to form single strands that then invade the other duplex for base pairing, producing a four-stranded DNA structure. The process of repair varies depending on the damage or error that can occur during recombination. In some cases, enzymes in the cell recognize and repair mismatches. In other cases, the process of recombination functions to repair lesions in DNA by copying information from a healthy chromosome and inserting it in place of information from the damaged chromosome of that pair.

The metabolism of RNA also involves multiple phases. In a complex and controlled process, small segments of DNA are transcribed into RNA by the enzyme RNA polymerase. Only one strand of the DNA is copied, and the RNA molecules produced are single-stranded. When the precursor RNAs become functionally mature RNAs and then mRNAs, they direct the synthesis of a specific protein for use by the cell. Translation takes place on a ribosome and decodes the information within mRNA molecules. After RNAs have been used, they are degraded and their bases are recycled.

Beyond nucleic acids, which are heritable components of life, this volume also explores amino acids. These molecules contain nitrogen, hydrogen, carbon, and oxygen. Most amino acids are chiral molecules, meaning they exist in two asymmetric forms that are mirror images of each other. These molecules join together in special bonds called peptide bonds. Groups of amino acids that are arranged in specific ways make up proteins. The sequence of amino acids determines the physical and chemical properties of proteins, including its shape and function.

Aside from their biological role in making proteins, amino acids are commonly used for other purposes as well. Some active agents found in soaps and shampoos, for example, are derived from amino acids. Aspartame is a sweetener made from combining aspartic acid and phenylalanine. Single amino acids are often used in medicine. For example, therapies based on amino acids are used in the treatment of Parkinson disease, peptic ulcer, and liver disease.

Proteins are involved in many vital cellular chemical reactions. Some proteins provide the cell with its structural elements, whereas others make muscles contract, thereby enabling movement. Scientists have identified 20 amino acids as being the essential pieces that make up all proteins. Proteins, however, are extraorinarily diverse in the structures and functions. Thus, the proteins of one species differ from those of another, and within a single organism, the proteins of one organ differ from those of other organs. A protein molecule is made of many amino acids conjoined in a long, chainlike structure. Whereas plants can synthesize all the amino acids they need for proteins through photosynthesis, animals cannot. Therefore, animals must meet their amino acid requirement by eating large amounts of plant materials or by consuming other animals and their products.

The organization of a protein is described in terms of primary, secondary, tertiary, and quaternary structure.

The primary structure refers to the amino acid sequence, whereas the other three terms refer to the peptide chain's configuration. The molecular weight of a protein varies depending on the protein's amino acid composition. A protein's shape varies in complicated and irregular ways. For instance, globular proteins such as ovalbumin have a closely folded structure, and fibrous proteins such as collagen are elongated and thin.

Scientists have faced several challenges in terms of classifying proteins. First they considered how proteins dissolved in solvents, but when that technique proved too inaccurate, scientists tried to distinguish between proteins based on their biological functions. But this approach also proved problematic. One protein can have more than one function, and definite functions of some proteins are still unknown. Despite these drawbacks, a functional classification system can be used to show the connection between a protein's structure and its function when such a correlation exists. Structural proteins include collagen, which is found in bones, tendons, ligaments, and skin, and keratin, which is found in the outermost layers of the skin. Muscle proteins such as myosin outnumber any other type of protein in mammals.

Enzymes are catalytic proteins that regulate the various biochemical reactions that take place in animals, plants, and microorganisms. All cells contain enzymes, and each enzyme facilitates only one type of chemical reaction. Enzymes promote functions such as the storage and release of energy, the course of reproduction, and the processes of respiration and metabolism. Three properties serve as the basis of enzyme classification: the chemical nature of the enzyme, the chemical nature of the substrate (the substance that is being acted on), and the nature of the catalyzed reaction.

Lipids are considered the hydrophobic ("water-fearing") components of life because they do not interact extensively with water. Fats, oils, hormones, and certain membrane components are organic compounds included in this diverse group. Biological lipids are composed of molecular building blocks homologous (similar) in structure, allowing lipids to be classified as fatty acids, fatty acid derivatives, cholesterol and its derivatives, and lipoproteins. Lipids function as energy-storage molecules, chemical messengers, and structural components of cells.

Triglycerides are the main source of fatty acids in the diet and are stored in different ways in different animals. Sharks store fat in their livers, whereas insects store it in an organ called the fat body. Cholesterol is member of a class of lipids called isoprenoids, which are widely distributed in nature. Cholesterol is absorbed into the cells of the intestinal lining and transported in the blood in lipoproteins to the body's tissues and organs. Lipoproteins facilitate the transport of all lipids throughout the body by the circulatory system. A high concentration of lipoproteins can result in a buildup in and blockage of critical arteries, causing a heart attack or stroke. On the other hand, fatty acids stored as triglycerides are a major source of energy, making it crucial to find the right balance of lipids in the diet to maintain health.

Carbohydrates are another important source of energy. They are formed during photosynthesis in plants and are part of the structure of nucleic acids. Carbohydrates are composed of carbon, hydrogen, and oxygen. They can be divided into four major groups: monosaccharides, disaccharides, oligosaccharides, and polysaccharides. Monosaccharides are simple sugars that include glucose, which indirectly provides organisms with a major part of their energy needs. Disaccharides are double sugars such as table sugar, more commonly referred to as sucrose, which consists of a molecule of fructose and a molecule of glucose. Oligosaccharides consist of three to six simple sugar units and are found in some plant derivatives. Polysaccharides are made up of many sugars and vary in size, structure, and sugar content. The most common polysaccharide is cellulose.

In addition to being a major source of needed nutrition, people use carbohydrates as a vehicle for medicinal and industrial innovation. Some antibiotics are derived from carbohydrates, as are industrial materials, such as paper, wood, and fabrics.

Understanding the components of life is a continuous process, one that tries to link the biochemical discoveries of the past with the scientific advancements of the future.

CHAPTER 1

A ll life on Earth is composed of a basic set of chemical components. The most fundamental of these are water (H_2O), charged particles known as ions, and small molecules, namely, nucleic acids, amino acids, fatty acids, and carbohydrates. Small molecules are of special significance in understanding the structure, function, and behaviour of living things, particularly because they have such enormous influence on the biochemical phenomena—from genetically programmed activities to physical appearance—that characterize organisms. Of the small molecules, nucleic acids are among the most fundamental. They combine to form an organism's genetic code; therefore, they determine an organism's genetic makeup, which in turn governs physical makeup. Nucleic acids are also the molecules of evolution, susceptible to change in response to environmental factors, thereby enabling adaptation and survival.

The information locked in the genetic code of nucleic acids is translated into amino acids, a molecular form that renders genetic information more accessible to cells. Amino acids, which are defined chemically by the presence of an amino group, which is made up of a nitrogen atom and two atoms of hydrogen ($-NH_2$), as well as carbon (C) and oxygen (O), join together to form proteins, with the sequence in which they join being a direct translation of the sequence of the nucleic acids from which they were formed. Proteins, because they inherit the nitrogen (N) molecules of amino acids, are characterized as nitrogenous compounds. They are an extraordinarily diverse group of molecules and serve many different functions within cells, from providing structural support to communicating information about regulatory processes and other cellular activities.

In contrast to proteins, carbohydrates do not contain nitrogens. Rather, they are formed from various arrangements of carbon, hydrogen, and oxygen. While carbohydrates provide important structural functions in cells, they are better known as the primary sources of energy utilized by most life-forms. Fatty acids, or lipids, form a secondary energy source for many organisms. These molecules, although composed of the same basic elements as carbohydrates—carbon, hydrogen, and oxygen—are distinguished by the linkages, or bonds, connecting the elements. The unique bonding and chemical arrangement of fatty acids determines the molecules' function and metabolism.

Nucleic acids, the amino acids of proteins, carbohydrates, and fatty acids all are naturally occurring chemical compounds. Each is also capable of being broken down to yield discrete components. For example, nucleic acids can be broken down into phosphoric acid, sugars, and a mixture of organic bases (purines and pyrimidines). Nucleic acids are the main information-carrying molecules of the cell, and, by directing the process of protein synthesis, they determine the inherited characteristics of every living thing. The two main classes of nucleic acids are deoxyribonucleic acid (DNA) and ribonucleic acid (RNA). DNA is the master blueprint for life and constitutes the genetic material in all free-living organisms and most viruses. RNA is the genetic material of certain viruses, but it is also found in all living cells, where it plays an important role in certain processes such as the making of proteins.

NUCLEOTIDES: BUILDING BLOCKS OF NUCLEIC ACIDS

Nucleic acids are polynucleotides—long chainlike molecules composed of a series of nearly identical building blocks called nucleotides. Each nucleotide consists of a nitrogen-containing aromatic base (a stable organic compound) attached to a pentose (five-carbon) sugar, which is in turn attached to a phosphate group. Each nucleic acid contains four of five possible nitrogen-containing bases: adenine (A), guanine (G), cytosine (C), thymine (T), and uracil (U). A and G are categorized as purines, and C, T, and U are collectively called pyrimidines. All nucleic acids contain the bases A, C, and G; T, however, is found only in DNA, while U is found in RNA. The pentose sugar in DNA (2'-deoxyribose) differs from

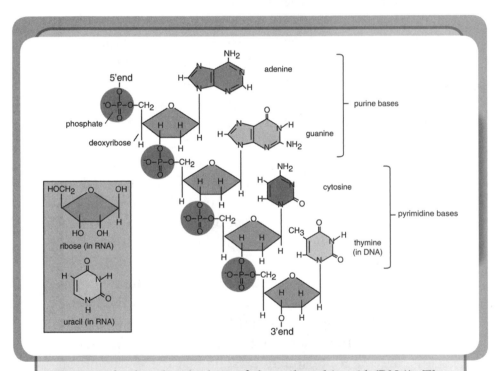

Portion of polynucleotide chain of deoxyribonucleic acid (DNA). The circles indicate phosphate groups, which are made up of three oxygen (O) molecules surrounding one phosphate (P) molecule. Each phosphate group is attached to a pentose (five-sided) sugar. In DNA, this sugar is called deoxyribose. The phosphate-sugar group is then joined with one of four nitrogen (N)-carrying bases, which are either purine or pyramidine molecules. The inset shows the corresponding pentose sugar called ribose and the pyrimidine base uracil in ribonucleic acid (RNA). Copyright Encyclopædia Britannica; rendering for this edition by Rosen Educational Services

the sugar in RNA (ribose) by the absence of a hydroxyl group (-OH) on the 2' carbon of the sugar ring. Without an attached phosphate group, the sugar attached to one of the bases is known as a nucleoside. The phosphate group connects successive sugar residues by bridging the 5'-hydroxyl group on one sugar to the 3'-hydroxyl group of the next sugar in the chain. These nucleoside linkages are called phosphodiester bonds and are the same in RNA and DNA. Without an attached phosphate group, the sugar attached to one of the bases is known as a nucleoside. The phosphate group connects successive sugar residues by bridging the hydroxyl (hydrogen and oxygen) group at the 5' position on one sugar (see diagram) to the position 3'-hydroxyl group of the next sugar in the chain. These nucleoside linkages are called phosphodiester bonds and are the same in RNA and DNA.

Nucleotides are created, or synthesized, from readily available precursors in the cell—i.e., smaller molecules of the right chemical composition. The ribose phosphate portion of both purine and pyrimidine nucleotides is synthesized from the sugar glucose via a chemical process called the pentose phosphate pathway. The six-atom pyrimidine ring is synthesized first and subsequently attached to the ribose phosphate. The two rings in purines are synthesized while attached to the ribose phosphate during the assembly of adenine or guanine nucleosides. In both cases the end product is a nucleotide carrying a phosphate attached to the 5' carbon on the sugar. Finally, a specialized enzyme called a kinase adds two phosphate groups using adenosine triphosphate (ATP), an energy-carrying molecule found in the cells of all living things, as the phosphate donor to form ribonucleoside triphosphate, the immediate precursor of RNA. For DNA, the hydroxyl (OH) group from the 2' position is removed from the ribonucleoside diphosphate to give

Johann Friedrich Miescher

(b. Aug. 13, 1844, Basel, Switz.—d. Aug. 26, 1895, Davos)

Swiss physician and biochemist Johann Friedrich Miescher conducted important investigations into cell metabolism. He is best known for his discovery of nucleic acids.

In 1869, while working under German chemist Ernst Hoppe-Seyler at the University of Tübingen, Miescher discovered a substance containing both phosphorus and nitrogen in the nuclei of white blood cells found in pus. The substance, first named nuclein because it seemed to come from cell nuclei, became known as nucleic acid after 1874, when Miescher separated it into protein and acid components. His work was fundamental to later investigations of DNA.

Upon returning to Basel as a professor, Miescher found nucleic acid and protamine (a protein commonly associated with nucleic acids) in salmon spermatozoa. He was one of the earliest researchers to propose and to collect data supporting the hypothesis that it is the carbon dioxide concentration (rather than the oxygen concentration) in the blood that regulates breathing. In 1885 he founded Switzerland's first physiological institute.

deoxyribonucleoside diphosphate. An additional phosphate group from ATP is then added by another kinase to form a deoxyribonucleoside triphosphate, the immediate precursor of DNA.

During normal cell metabolism, RNA is constantly being made and broken down. The purine and pyrimidine residues are reused by several salvage pathways to make more genetic material. Purine is salvaged in the form of the corresponding nucleotide, whereas pyrimidine is salvaged as the nucleoside.

DEOXYRIBONUCLEIC ACID (DNA)

DNA is a polymer (complex molecule) of the four nucleotides A, C, G, and T, which are joined through a backbone of alternating phosphate and deoxyribose sugar residues. These nitrogen-containing bases occur in complementary pairs as determined by their ability to form hydrogen bonds between them. A always pairs with T through two hydrogen bonds, and G always pairs with C through three hydrogen bonds. The spans of A:T and G:C hydrogen-bonded pairs are nearly identical, allowing them to bridge the sugar-phosphate chains uniformly.

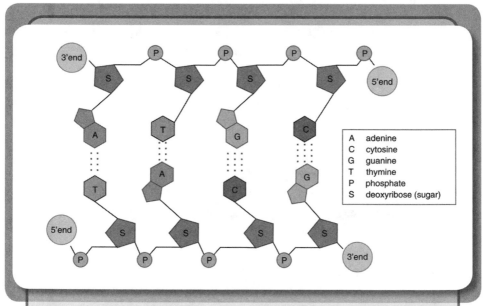

DNA structure, showing the nucleotide bases cytosine (C), thymine (T), adenine (A), and guanine (G) linked to a backbone of alternating phosphate (P) and deoxyribose sugar (S) groups. Two sugar-phosphate chains are paired through hydrogen bonds between A and T and between G and C, thus forming the double-stranded double helix of the DNA molecule. Copyright Encyclopædia Britannica; rendering for this edition by Rosen Educational Services

This structure, along with the molecule's chemical stability, makes DNA the ideal genetic material. The bonding between complementary bases also provides a mechanism for the replication of DNA and the transmission of genetic information.

In 1953 biophysicists James D. Watson and Francis Crick proposed a three-dimensional structure for DNA based on low-resolution X-ray crystallographic data and on Erwin Chargaff's observation that, in naturally occurring DNA, the amount of T equals the amount of A and the amount of G equals the amount of C. Watson and

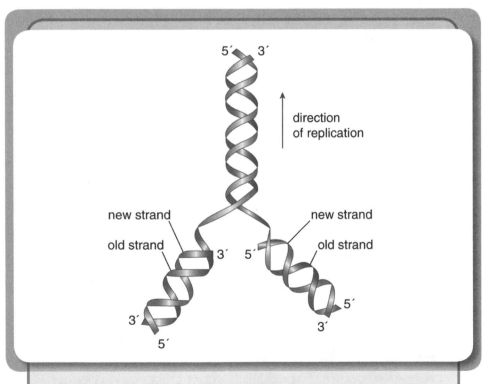

The initial proposal of the structure of DNA by James Watson and Francis Crick, which was accompanied by a suggestion on the means of replication. Copyright Encyclopædia Britannica; rendering for this edition by Rosen Educational Services

Crick, along with biophysicist Maurice Wilkins, whose X-ray diffraction studies proved crucial to understanding DNA's structure, shared the 1962 Nobel Prize for their efforts. An important component of Watson and Crick's work was their hypothesis that two strands of polynucleotides coil around each other, forming a double helix. The two strands, though identical, run in opposite directions as determined by the orientation of the 5' to 3' phosphodiester bond. The sugar-phosphate chains run along the outside of the helix, and the bases lie on the inside, where they are linked to complementary bases on the other strand through hydrogen bonds.

The double helical structure of normal DNA takes a right-handed form called the B-helix. The helix makes one complete turn approximately every 10 base pairs. B-DNA has two principal grooves, a wide major groove and a narrow minor groove. Many proteins interact in the space of the major groove, where they make sequence-specific contacts with the bases. In addition, a few proteins are known to make contacts via the minor groove.

Several structural variants of DNA are known. In A-DNA, which forms under conditions of high salt concentration and minimal water, the base pairs are tilted and displaced toward the minor groove. Left-handed Z-DNA forms most readily in strands that contain sequences with alternating purines and pyrimidines. DNA can form triple helices when two strands containing runs of pyrimidines interact with a third strand containing a run of purines.

B-DNA is generally depicted as a smooth helix; however, specific sequences of bases can distort the otherwise regular structure. For example, short tracts of A residues interspersed with short sections of general sequence result in a bent DNA molecule. Inverted base sequences, on the other hand, produce cruciform structures with four-way junctions that are similar to recombination intermediates.

Most of these alternative DNA structures have only been characterized in the laboratory, and their cellular significance is unknown.

BIOLOGICAL STRUCTURES

Naturally occurring DNA molecules can be circular or linear. The genomes of single-celled bacteria and archaea (the prokaryotes), as well as the genomes of mitochondria and chloroplasts (certain functional structures within the cell), are circular molecules. In addition, some bacteria and archaea have smaller circular DNA molecules called plasmids that typically contain only a few genes. Many plasmids are readily transmitted from one cell to another. For a typical bacterium, the genome that encodes all of the genes of the organism is a single contiguous circular molecule that contains 0.5 million to 5 million base pairs. The genomes of most eukaryotes (organisms with a clearly defined nucleus) and some prokaryotes contain linear DNA molecules called chromosomes. Human DNA, for example, consists of 23 pairs of linear chromosomes containing 3 billion base pairs.

In all cells, DNA does not exist free in solution but rather as a protein-coated complex called chromatin. In prokaryotes, the loose coat of proteins on the DNA helps to shield the negative charge of the phosphodiester backbone. Chromatin also contains proteins that control gene expression and determine the characteristic shapes of chromosomes. In eukaryotes, a section of DNA between 140 and 200 base pairs long winds around a discrete set of eight positively charged proteins called a histone, forming a spherical structure called the nucleosome. Additional histones are wrapped by successive sections of DNA, forming a series of nucleosomes like beads on a string. Transcription and replication of DNA is more complicated in eukaryotes

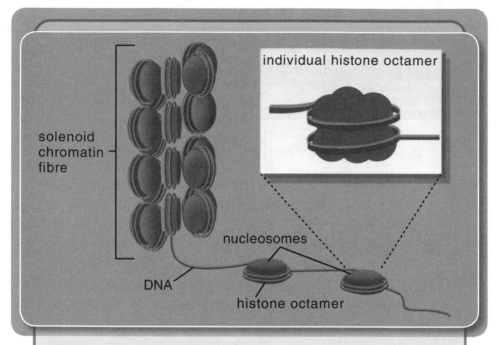

individual histone octamer

solenoid chromatin fibre

nucleosomes

DNA

histone octamer

DNA wrapped around clusters of histone proteins to form nucleosomes, which are coiled to form solenoids, the basis of the chromatin fibre that makes up chromosomes. Copyright Encyclopædia Britannica; rendering for this edition by Rosen Educational Services

because the nucleosome complexes have to be at least partially disassembled for the processes to proceed effectively.

Although viruses are not organisms, they do contain DNA or RNA. Most viruses that infect prokaryotes contain linear genomes that typically are much shorter and contain only the genes necessary for viral propagation. Bacterial viruses called bacteriophages (or phages) may contain both linear and circular forms of DNA. For instance, the genome of bacteriophage λ (lambda), which infects the bacterium *Escherichia coli*, contains 48,502 base pairs and can exist as a linear molecule packaged in a protein coat. The DNA of phage λ can also exist in a circular form that is able to integrate into the circular genome of the host bacterial cell. Both circular and linear genomes are also found among viruses that infect eukaryotes such as plants and humans, but these viruses commonly use RNA as the genetic material.

BIOCHEMICAL PROPERTIES

The biochemical properties of nucleic acids are characterized by the molecules' behaviour under certain environmental and biological conditions. The most important factors determining these characteristics include the response of nucleic acids to heat and the extent to which they absorb ultraviolet (UV) radiation. These properties are particularly useful in biochemical research and in understanding the chemical activities of nucleic acids in the context of biological systems.

DENATURATION

The strands of the DNA double helix are held together by hydrogen bonding interactions between the complementary base pairs (such as guanine and cytosine). Heating DNA in solution easily breaks these hydrogen bonds, allowing the two strands to separate—a process called denaturation or melting. The two strands may reassociate when the solution cools, re-forming the starting DNA duplex—a process called renaturation or hybridization. These processes form the basis of many important techniques for manipulating DNA. For example, a short piece of DNA called an oligonucleotide can be used to test whether a very long DNA sequence has the complementary sequence of the oligonucleotide embedded within it. Using hybridization, a single-stranded DNA molecule can capture complementary sequences from any source. Single strands from

RNA can also reassociate. DNA and RNA single strands can form hybrid molecules that are even more stable than double-stranded DNA. These molecules form the basis of a technique that is used to purify and characterize messenger RNA (mRNA) molecules corresponding to single genes.

ULTRAVIOLET ABSORPTION

DNA melting and reassociation can be monitored by measuring the absorption of UV light at a wavelength of 260 nanometres (billionths of a metre). When DNA is in a double-stranded conformation, absorption is fairly weak, but when DNA is single-stranded, the unstacking of the bases leads to an enhancement of absorption called hyperchromicity. Therefore, the extent to which DNA is single-stranded or double-stranded can be determined by monitoring UV absorption.

CHEMICAL MODIFICATION

After a DNA molecule has been assembled, it may be chemically modified—sometimes deliberately by special enzymes called DNA methyltransferases and sometimes accidentally by oxidation, ionizing radiation, or the action of chemical carcinogens. DNA can also be cleaved and degraded by enzymes called nucleases.

METHYLATION

Three types of natural methylation have been reported in DNA. (A methyl group is a structural unit of organic compounds consisting of three hydrogen atoms bonded to a carbon atom [CH_3].) Cytosine can be modified either on the ring to form 5-methylcytosine or on the exocyclic amino group to form N^4-methylcytosine. Adenine may be modified to form N^6-methyladenine. N^4-methylcytosine and N^6-methyladenine are found only in bacteria and archaea, whereas 5-methylcytosine is widely distributed. Special enzymes called DNA methyltransferases are responsible for this methylation. These enzymes recognize specific sequences within the DNA molecule so that only a subset of the bases is modified. Other methylations of the bases or of the deoxyribose are sometimes induced by carcinogens. These usually lead to mispairing of the bases during replication and have to be removed if they are not to become mutagenic.

Natural methylation has many cellular functions. In bacteria and archaea, methylation forms an essential part of the immune system by protecting DNA molecules from fragmentation by enzymes called restriction endonucleases. In some organisms, methylation helps to eliminate incorrect base sequences introduced during DNA replication. By marking the parental strand with a methyl group, a cellular mechanism known as the mismatch repair system distinguishes between the newly replicated strand where the errors occur and the correct sequence on the template strand. In higher eukaryotes, 5-methylcytosine controls many cellular phenomena by preventing DNA transcription. Methylation is also believed to signal imprinting, a process whereby some genes inherited from one parent are selectively inactivated. Correct methylation may also repress or activate key genes that control embryonic development. On the other hand, 5-methylcytosine is potentially mutagenic because thymine produced during the methylation process converts C:G pairs to T:A pairs. In mammals, methylation takes place selectively within the dinucleotide sequence CG—a rare sequence, presumably because it has been lost by mutation. In many cancers, mutations are found in key genes at CG dinucleotides.

NUCLEASES

Nucleases are enzymes that hydrolytically split the phosphodiester backbone of DNA. (Hydrolysis occurs when a molecule is cleaved through reaction with water, with insertion of the elements of water into the final products.) Endonucleases cleave in the middle of chains, while exonucleases operate selectively by degrading from the end of the chain. Nucleases that act on both single- and double-stranded DNA are known.

Restriction endonucleases are a special class that recognize and cleave specific sequences in DNA. Type II restriction endonucleases always cleave at or near their recognition sites. They produce small, well-defined fragments of DNA that help to characterize genes and genomes and that produce recombinant DNAs. Fragments of DNA produced by restriction endonucleases can be moved from one organism to another. In this way it has been possible to express proteins such as human insulin in bacteria.

MUTATION

Chemical modification of DNA can lead to mutations in the genetic material. Anions such as bisulfite can deaminate (remove an amine from)cytosine to form uracil. This change can alter the genetic message by causing C-to-T transitions. Exposure to acid causes the loss of purine residues, though specific enzymes exist in cells to repair these lesions. Exposure to UV light can cause adjacent pyrimidines to dimerize, while oxidative damage from free radicals or strong oxidizing agents can cause a variety of lesions that are mutagenic if not repaired. Halogens such as chlorine and bromine react directly with uracil, adenine, and guanine, giving substituted bases that are often mutagenic. Similarly, nitrous acid reacts with primary amine groups—for example, converting adenosine into inosine—which then leads to changes in base pairing and mutation. Many chemical mutagens, such as chlorinated hydrocarbons and nitrites, owe their toxicity to the production of halides and nitrous acid during their metabolism in the body.

SUPERCOILING

Circular DNA molecules such as those found in plasmids or bacterial chromosomes can adopt many different topologies. One is active supercoiling, which involves the cleavage of one DNA strand, its winding one or more turns around the complementary strand, and then the resealing of the molecule. Each complete rotation leads to the introduction of one supercoiled turn in the DNA, a process that can continue until the DNA is fully wound and collapses on itself in a tight ball. Reversal is also possible. Special enzymes called gyrases and topoisomerases catalyze the winding and relaxation of supercoiled DNA. In the linear chromosomes of eukaryotes, the DNA is usually tightly constrained at various points by proteins, allowing the intervening stretches to be supercoiled. This property is partially responsible for the great compaction of DNA that is necessary to fit it within the confines of the cell. The DNA in one human cell would have an extended length of between 2 and 3 metres (6.5 to 9.8 feet), but it is packed very tightly so that it can fit within a human cell nucleus that is 10 μm (1 μm = 3.9 × 10^{-5} inch) in diameter.

RIBONUCLEIC ACID (RNA)

RNA is a single-stranded nucleic acid polymer of the four nucleotides A, C, G, and U joined through a backbone of alternating phosphate and ribose sugar residues. It is the first intermediate in converting the information from DNA into proteins essential for the working of a cell.

Some RNAs also serve direct roles in cellular metabolism. RNA is made by copying the base sequence of a section of double-stranded DNA, called a gene, into a piece of single-stranded nucleic acid. This process, called transcription, is catalyzed by an enzyme called RNA polymerase.

Whereas DNA provides the genetic information for the cell and is inherently quite stable, RNA has many roles and is much more reactive chemically. RNA is sensitive to oxidizing agents such as periodate that lead to opening of the 3'-terminal ribose ring. The 2'-hydroxyl group on the ribose ring is a major cause of instability in RNA, because the presence of alkali leads to rapid cleavage of the phosphodiester bond linking ribose and phosphate groups. In general, this instability is not a significant problem for the cell, because RNA is constantly being synthesized and degraded.

Interactions between the nitrogen-containing bases differ in DNA and RNA. In DNA, which is usually double-stranded, the bases in one strand pair with complementary bases in a second DNA strand. In RNA, which is usually single-stranded, the bases pair with other bases within the same molecule, leading to complex three-dimensional structures. Occasionally, intermolecular RNA/RNA duplexes do form, but they form a right-handed A-type helix rather than the B-type DNA helix. Depending on the amount of salt present, either 11 or 12 base pairs are found in each turn of the helix. Helices between RNA and DNA molecules also form. These structures adopt the A-type conformation and are more stable than either RNA/RNA or DNA/DNA duplexes. Such hybrid duplexes are important species in biology, being formed when RNA polymerase transcribes DNA into mRNA for protein synthesis and when reverse transcriptase copies a viral RNA genome such as that of the human immunodeficiency virus (HIV).

Single-stranded RNAs are flexible molecules that form a variety of structures through internal base pairing and additional non-base pair interactions. They can form hairpin loops such as those found in transfer RNA (tRNA), as well as longer-range interactions involving both the bases and the phosphate residues of two or more nucleotides. This leads to compact three-dimensional structures. Most of these structures have been inferred from biochemical data, since few crystallographic images are available for RNA molecules. In some types of RNA, a large number of bases are modified after the RNA is transcribed. More than 90 different modifications have been documented, including extensive methylations and a wide variety of substitutions around the ring. In some cases these modifications are known to affect structure and are essential for function.

MESSENGER RNA

mRNA delivers the information encoded in one or more genes from the DNA to the ribosome, a specialized structure, or organelle, where the genetic information is decoded into a protein. In prokaryotes, mRNAs contain an exact transcribed copy of the original DNA sequence with a terminal 5'-triphosphate group and a 3'-hydroxyl residue. In eukaryotes the mRNA molecules are more elaborate. The 5'-triphosphate residue goes through a chemical process called esterification, forming a structure called a cap. At the 3' ends, eukaryotic mRNAs typically contain long runs of adenosine residues (polyA) that are not encoded in the DNA but are added enzymatically after transcription. Eukaryotic mRNA molecules are usually composed of small segments of the original gene and are generated by a process of cleavage and rejoining from an original precursor RNA (pre-mRNA) molecule, which is an exact copy of the gene. In general, prokaryotic mRNAs are degraded very rapidly, whereas the cap structure and the polyA tail of eukaryotic mRNAs greatly enhance their stability.

Ribosomal RNA

Ribosomal RNA (rRNA) molecules are the structural components of the ribosome. The rRNAs form extensive secondary structures and play an active role in recognizing conserved portions of mRNAs and transfer RNAs (tRNAs). They also assist with the catalysis of protein synthesis. In the prokaryote *Escherichia coli*, seven copies of the rRNA genes synthesize about 15,000 ribosomes per cell. In eukaryotes the numbers are much larger. Anywhere from 50 to 5,000 sets of rRNA genes and as many as 10 million ribosomes may be present in a single cell. In eukaryotes these rRNA genes are looped out of the main chromosomal fibres and coalesce in the presence of proteins to form an organelle called the nucleolus. The nucleolus is where the rRNA genes are transcribed and the early assembly of ribosomes takes place.

Transfer RNA

tRNA carries individual amino acids into the ribosome for assembly into the growing polypeptide chain. The tRNA molecules contain 70 to 80 nucleotides and fold into a characteristic cloverleaf structure. Specialized tRNAs exist for each of the 20 amino acids needed for protein synthesis, and in many cases more than one tRNA for each amino acid is present. The nucleotide sequence is converted into a protein sequence by translating each three-base sequence (called a codon) with a specific protein. The 61 codons used to code amino acids can be read by many fewer than 61 distinct tRNAs. In *E. coli* a total of 40 different tRNAs are used to translate the 61 codons. The amino acids are loaded onto the tRNAs by specialized enzymes called aminoacyl tRNA synthetases, usually with one synthetase for each amino acid. However, in some organisms, less than the full complement of 20 synthetases is required because some amino acids, such as glutamine and asparagine, can be synthesized on their respective tRNAs. All tRNAs adopt similar structures because they all have to interact with the same sites on the ribosome.

Robert William Holley

(b. Jan. 28, 1922, Urbana, Ill., U.S.—d. Feb. 11, 1993, Los Gatos, Calif.)

American biochemist Robert William Holley performed research that helped explain how the genetic code controls the synthesis of proteins. He shared the 1968 Nobel Prize in Physiology or Medicine with American biochemists Marshall Warren Nirenberg and Har Gobind Khorana.

Holley obtained his Ph.D. in organic chemistry from Cornell University, Ithaca, N.Y., in 1947. He investigated a variety of biochemical questions at the state and federal agricultural experiment stations at Cornell (1948–64). He began his research on RNA after spending a year studying with American molecular biologist James F. Bonner at the California Institute of Technology (1955–56).

By 1960 Holley and others had shown that small molecules of ribonucleic acids, called transfer RNAs (tRNAs), were involved in the assembly of amino acids into proteins. Holley and his collaborators developed techniques to separate the different tRNAs from the mixture in the cell. By 1965 he had determined the composition of the tRNA that incorporates the amino acid alanine into protein molecules. This feat—the first determination of the sequence of nucleotides in a nucleic acid—required digesting the molecule with enzymes, identifying the pieces, then figuring out how they fit together. It has since been shown that all tRNAs have similar structures.

In 1968 Holley became a resident fellow at the Salk Institute for Biological Studies in La Jolla, Calif. There he studied both the normal and the abnormal functions of the growth of cells in mammals, primarily focusing on the timing of cell division. The latter was crucial to understanding the growth of cancer and aided in diagnosis and treatment of that disease and others.

RIBOZYMES

Not all catalysis within the cell is carried out exclusively by proteins. Molecular biologists Thomas Cech and Sidney Altman, jointly awarded a Nobel Prize in 1989, discovered that certain RNAs, now known as ribozymes, showed enzymatic activity. Cech showed that a noncoding sequence (intron) in the small subunit rRNA of protozoans, which had to be removed before the rRNA was functional, can excise itself from a much longer precursor RNA molecule and rejoin the two ends in an autocatalytic reaction. Altman showed that the RNA component of an RNA protein complex called ribonuclease P can cleave a precursor tRNA to generate a mature tRNA. In addition to self-splicing RNAs similar to the one discovered by Cech, artificial RNAs have been made that show a variety of catalytic reactions. It is now widely held that there was a stage during evolution when only RNA catalyzed and stored genetic information. This period, sometimes called "the RNA world," is believed to have preceded the function of DNA as genetic material.

ANTISENSE RNAS

Most antisense RNAs are synthetically modified derivatives of RNA or DNA with potential therapeutic value. In nature, antisense RNAs contain sequences that are the complement of the normal coding sequences found in mRNAs (also called sense RNAs). Like mRNAs, antisense RNAs are single-stranded, but they cannot be translated into protein. They can inactivate their complementary mRNA by forming a double-stranded structure that blocks the translation of the base sequence. Artificially introducing antisense RNAs into cells selectively inactivates genes by interfering with normal RNA metabolism.

VIRAL GENOMES

Many viruses use RNA for their genetic material. This is most prevalent among viruses that infect eukaryotes, but a few RNA viruses that infect prokaryotes are also known. Some common examples of RNA viruses include poliovirus, HIV, and influenza virus, all of which affect humans, and tobacco mosaic virus, which infects plants. In some viruses the entire genetic material is encoded in a single RNA molecule, while in the segmented RNA viruses several RNA molecules may be present. Many RNA viruses such as HIV use a specialized enzyme called reverse transcriptase that permits replication of the virus through a DNA intermediate. In some cases this DNA intermediate becomes integrated into the host chromosome during infection. The virus then exists in a dormant state and effectively evades the host immune system.

OTHER RNAS

Many other small RNA molecules with specialized functions are present in cells. For example, small nuclear RNAs (snRNAs) are involved in RNA splicing, and other small RNAs that form part of the enzymes telomerase or ribonuclease P are part of ribonucleoprotein particles. The RNA component of telomerase contains a short sequence that serves as a template for the addition of small strings of oligonucleotides at the ends of eukaryotic chromosomes. Other RNA molecules serve as guide RNAs for editing, or they are complementary to small sections of rRNA and either direct the positions at which methyl groups need to be added or mark U residues for conversion to the isomer pseudouridine (an isomer is one of two or more compounds that contain the same number of atoms and elements but have different structural arrangements).

RNA PROCESSING

Following synthesis by transcription, most RNA molecules are processed before reaching their final form. Many rRNA molecules are cleaved from much larger transcripts and may also be methylated or enzymatically modified. In addition, tRNAs are usually formed as longer precursor molecules that are cleaved by ribonuclease P to generate the mature 5' end and often have extra residues added to their 3' end to form the sequence CCA. The hydroxyl group on the ribose ring of the terminal A of the 3'-CCA sequence acts as the amino acid acceptor necessary for the function of RNA in protein building.

In prokaryotes the protein coding sequence occupies one continuous linear segment of DNA. However, in eukaryotic genes the coding sequences are frequently "split" in the genome—a discovery reached independently in the 1970s by molecular biologists Richard J. Roberts and Phillip A. Sharp, whose work won them a Nobel Prize in 1993. The segments of DNA or RNA coding for protein are called exons, and the noncoding regions separating the exons are called introns. Following transcription, these coding sequences must be joined together before the mRNAs can function. The process of removal of the introns and subsequent rejoining of the exons is called RNA splicing. Each intron is removed in a separate series of reactions by a complicated piece of enzymatic machinery called a spliceosome. This machinery consists of a number of small nuclear ribonucleoprotein particles (snRNPs) that contain small nuclear RNAs (snRNAs).

Some RNA molecules, particularly those in protozoan mitochondria, undergo extensive editing following their initial synthesis. During this editing process, residues are added or deleted by a posttranscriptional mechanism under the influence of guide RNAs. In some cases as much as 40 percent of the final RNA molecule may be derived by this editing process, rather than being coded directly in the genome. Some examples of editing have also been found in mRNA molecules, but these appear much more limited in scope.

NUCLEIC ACID METABOLISM: DNA

Replication, repair, and recombination—the three main processes of DNA metabolism—are carried out by specialized machinery within the cell. DNA must be replicated accurately in order to ensure the integrity of the genetic code. Errors that creep in during replication or because of damage after replication must be repaired. Finally, recombination between genomes is an important mechanism to provide variation within a species and to assist the repair of damaged DNA. The details of each process have been worked out in prokaryotes, where the machinery is more streamlined, simpler, and more amenable to study. Many of the basic principles appear to be similar in eukaryotes.

BASIC MECHANISMS OF REPLICATION

DNA replication is a semiconservative process in which the two strands are separated and new complementary strands are generated independently, resulting in two exact copies of the original DNA molecule. Each copy thus contains one strand that is derived from the parent and one newly synthesized strand. Replication begins at a specific point on a chromosome called an origin, proceeds in both directions along the strand, and ends at a precise point. In the case of circular chromosomes, the end is reached automatically when the two extending chains meet, at which point specific proteins join the strands. DNA polymerases cannot initiate replication at the end of a DNA strand; they can only extend preexisting oligonucleotide fragments called primers. Therefore, in linear chromosomes, special mechanisms initiate and terminate DNA synthesis to avoid loss of information. The initiation of DNA synthesis is usually preceded by synthesis of a short RNA primer by a specialized RNA polymerase called primase. Following DNA replication, the initiating primer RNAs are degraded.

The two DNA strands are replicated in different fashions dictated by the direction of the phosphodiester bond. The leading strand is replicated continuously by adding individual nucleotides to the 3' end of the chain. The lagging strand is synthesized in a discontinuous manner by laying down short RNA primers and then filling the gaps by DNA polymerase, such that the bases are always added in the 5' to 3' direction. The short RNA fragments made during the copying of the lagging strand are degraded when no longer needed. The two newly synthesized DNA segments are joined by an enzyme called DNA ligase. In this way, replication can proceed in both directions, with two leading strands and two lagging strands proceeding outward from the origin.

ENZYMES OF REPLICATION

DNA polymerase adds single nucleotides to the 3' end of either an RNA or a DNA molecule. In the prokaryote *E. coli*, there are three DNA polymerases. One is responsible for chromosome replication, and the other two are involved in the resynthesis of DNA during damage repair. DNA polymerases of eukaryotes are even more complicated. In human cells, for instance, more than five different DNA polymerases have been characterized. Separate polymerases catalyze the synthesis of the leading and lagging strands in human cells, and a separate polymerase is responsible for replication of mitochondrial DNA. The other polymerases are involved in the repair of DNA damage.

A number of other proteins are also essential for replication. Proteins called DNA helicases help to separate the two strands of DNA, and single-stranded DNA binding proteins stabilize them during opening prior to being copied. The opening of the DNA helix introduces considerable strain in the form of supercoiling, a movement that is subsequently relaxed by enzymes called topoisomerases. A special RNA polymerase called primase synthesizes the primers needed at the origin to begin transcription, and DNA ligase seals the nicks formed between individual fragments.

The ends of linear eukaryotic chromosomes are marked by special sequences called telomeres that are synthesized by a special DNA polymerase called telomerase. This enzyme contains an RNA component that serves as a template for the exact sequence found at the ends of chromosomes. Multiple copies of a short sequence within the telomerase-associated RNA are made and added to the telomere ends. This has the effect of preventing shortening of the DNA chain that would otherwise occur during replication.

Mitochondrial genomes and some viral genomes are replicated in specialized ways. Several viruses such as adenovirus use a nucleotide covalently bound to a protein as a primer. (A covalent bond is one in which two atoms share a link that results from the sharing of an electron pair.) The protein remains covalently bound to the DNA after replication. Many single-stranded viruses use a rolling circle mechanism of replication whereby a double-stranded copy of the virus is first made. The replicating machinery then copies the nonviral strand in a continuous fashion, generating long single-stranded DNA from which full-length viral DNA strands are excised by specialized nucleases.

RECOMBINATION

Recombination is the principal mechanism through which variation is introduced into populations. For example, during meiosis, the process that produces sex cells (sperm or eggs), homologous chromosomes— one derived from the mother and the equivalent from the father—become paired, and recombination, or crossing-over, takes place. The two DNA molecules are fragmented, and similar segments of the chromosome are shuffled to produce two new chromosomes, each being a mosaic of the originals. The pair separates so that each sperm or egg receives just one of the shuffled chromosomes. When sperm and egg fuse, the normal set of two copies of each chromosome is restored.

There are two forms of recombination, general and site-specific. General recombination typically involves cleavage and rejoining at identical or very similar sequences. In site-specific recombination, cleavage takes place at a specific site into which DNA is usually inserted. General recombination occurs among viruses during infection, in bacteria during conjugation, during transformation whereby DNA is directly introduced into cells, and during some types of repair processes. Site-specific recombination is frequently involved in the parasitic distribution of DNA segments throughout genomes. Many viruses, as well as special segments of DNA called transposons, rely on site-specific recombination to multiply and spread. The two processes are described in greater detail in the following sections.

GENERAL RECOMBINATION

General recombination, also called homologous recombination, involves two DNA molecules that have long stretches of similar base sequences. The DNA molecules are nicked to produce single strands, which subsequently invade the other duplex, where base pairing leads to a four-stranded DNA structure. The cruciform junction within this structure is called a Holliday junction, named after British geneticist Robin Holliday, who proposed the original model for homologous recombination in 1964. The Holliday junction travels along the DNA duplex by "unzipping" one strand and re-forming the hydrogen bonds on the second strand. Following this branch migration, the two duplexes can be nicked again, allowing them to separate. Finally, the nicks are repaired by DNA ligase. The result is two DNA duplexes in which the segment between the two nicks has been replaced. The enzymes involved in recombination have been characterized best in the prokaryote *E. coli*. A key enzyme is RecA, which catalyzes the strand invasion process. RecA coats single-stranded DNA and facilitates its pairing with a double-stranded DNA molecule containing the same sequence, which produces a loop structure.

Another protein, known as RecBC, is important for the recombination process. Functioning at free ends of DNA, RecBC catalyzes an unwinding-rewinding reaction as it traverses the length of the molecule. Since unwinding is faster than rewinding, a loop is produced behind the enzyme that facilitates subsequent pairing with another DNA molecule. A number of other proteins are also important for recombination, including single-stranded DNA binding proteins that stabilize single-stranded DNA, DNA polymerase to repair any gaps that might be formed, and DNA ligase to reseal the nicks after recombination is complete. The details of eukaryotic recombination are expected to parallel those found in *E. coli*, although the highly compact chromatin structure in eukaryotes makes the process more complicated.

It is important to note that the initial product of recombination between two regions of DNA that are similar but not identical will be a "heteroduplex"— that is, a molecule in which mismatched bases will be present at some positions in the helix. Thus, in the specialized recombination that takes place during meiosis, one round of replication is necessary before the mosaic chromosomes produced by recombination are properly matched. Enzymes are present in cells that specifically recognize and repair mismatches, so that the initial products of recombination can sometimes be repaired before they are replicated. In such cases the final products of replication will not be true reciprocal events, but rather one of the original parental molecules will appear to have been maintained to the exclusion of the other—a process called gene conversion.

Recombination also functions occasionally to repair lesions in DNA. If one chromosome of a pair becomes irreversibly damaged, the information from the other chromosome can be copied and inserted by recombination

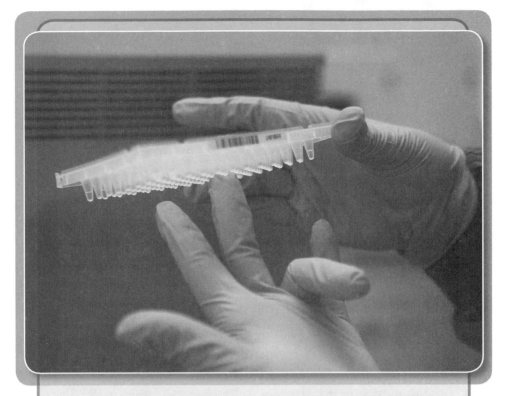

In Berlin, Germany, a scientist operates an RT-PCR machine as it converts the nucleic acid RNA into its complementary DNA in order to analyze an influenza virus. Andreas Rentz/Getty Images

to provide a correct replacement of the damaged section. The key idea here is that sequences flanking the damage from a sister chromosome can base-pair with the corresponding sequences on the damaged chromosome, thus allowing replication to copy the correct sequence and repair the lesion.

SITE-SPECIFIC RECOMBINATION

Site-specific recombination involves very short specific sequences that are recognized by proteins. Long DNA sequences such as viral genomes, drug-resistance elements, and regulatory sequences such as the mating type locus in yeast can be inserted, removed, or inverted, having profound regulatory effects. More than any other mechanism, site-specific recombination is responsible for reshaping genomes. For example, the genomes of many higher organisms, including plants and humans, show evidence that transposable elements have been constantly inserted throughout the genome and even into one another from time to time.

One example of site-specific recombination is the integration of DNA from bacteriophage λ into the chromosome of *E. coli*. In this reaction, bacteriophage λ DNA, which is a linear molecule in the normal phage, first forms a circle and then is cleaved by the enzyme λ-integrase at a specific site called the phage attachment site. A similar site on the bacterial chromosome is cut by integrase to give ends with the identical extension. Because of the complementarity between these two ends, they can be rejoined so that the original circular λ chromosome is inserted into the chromosome of the *E. coli* bacterium. Once integrated, the phage can be held in an inactive state until signals are generated that reverse the process, allowing the phage genome to escape and resume its normal life cycle of growth and spread into other bacteria. This site-specific recombination process requires only λ-integrase and one host DNA binding protein called the integration host factor. A third protein, called excisionase, recognizes the hybrid sites formed on integration and, in conjunction with integrase, catalyzes an excision process whereby the λ chromosome is removed from the bacterial chromosome.

A similar but more widespread version of DNA integration and excision is exhibited by the transposons, the so-called jumping genes. These elements range in size from fewer than 1,000 to as many as 40,000 base pairs. Transposons are able to move from one location in a genome to another, as first discovered in corn (maize) during the 1940s and '50s by American scientist Barbara McClintock, whose work won her a Nobel Prize in 1983. Most, if not all, transposons encode an enzyme called transposase that acts much like λ-integrase by cleaving the ends of the transposon as well as its target site. Transposons differ from bacteriophage λ in that they do not have a separate existence outside of the chromosome but rather are always maintained in an integrated site. Two types of transposition can occur—one in which the element simply moves from one site in the chromosome to another, and a second in which the transposon is replicated prior to moving. This second type of transposition leaves behind the original copy of the transposon and generates a second copy that is inserted elsewhere in the genome. Known as replicative transposition, this process is the mechanism responsible for the vast spread of transposable elements in many higher organisms.

The simplest kinds of transposons merely contain a copy of the transposase with no additional genes. They behave as parasitic elements and usually have no known associated function that is advantageous to the host. More often, transposable elements have additional genes associated with them—for example, antibiotic resistance factors. Antibiotic resistance typically occurs when an infecting bacterium acquires a plasmid that carries a gene encoding resistance to one or more antibiotics. Typically, these resistance genes are carried on transposable elements that have moved into plasmids and are easily transferred from one organism to another. Once a bacterium picks up such a gene, it enjoys a great selective advantage because it can grow in the presence of the antibiotic. Indiscriminate use of antibiotics actually promotes the buildup of these drug-resistant plasmids and strains.

REPAIR

It is extremely important that the integrity of DNA be maintained in order to ensure the accurate workings of a cell over its lifetime and to make certain that genetic information is accurately passed from one generation to the next. This maintenance is achieved by repair processes that constantly monitor the DNA for lesions and activate appropriate repair enzymes. Serious lesions in DNA such as pyrimidine dimers (a compound of two simpler molecules) or gaps can be repaired by recombination mechanisms, but there are many other repair mechanisms.

One important mechanism is that of mismatch repair, which has been studied extensively in *E. coli*. The system is directed by the presence of a methyl group within the sequence GATC on the template strand. Comparable systems for mismatch repair also operate in eukaryotes, though the template strand is not marked by methyl groups. In fact, lesions within the genes for human mismatch repair systems are known to be responsible for many cancers. Loss of the mismatch repair system allows mutations to build up quickly and eventually to affect the genes that cause cells to divide. As a result, cells divide in an uncontrolled manner and become cancerous.

Once replication is complete, the most common kind of damage to nucleic acids is one in which the normal A, C, G, and T bases are changed into chemically modified bases that usually differ significantly from their natural counterparts. The only exceptions are the deamination of cytosine to uracil and the deamination of 5-methylcytosine to thymine. In these cases the product is a G:U or G:T mismatch. Specific enzymes called DNA glycosylases can recognize uracil in DNA or the thymine in a G:T mismatch and can selectively remove the base by cleaving the bond between the base and the deoxyribose sugar. Many of these enzymes are specific for the different chemically modified bases that may be present in DNA.

Another common means of repairing DNA lesions is by an excision repair pathway. Enzymes recognize damage within DNA, probably by detecting an altered conformation of DNA, and then nick the strand on either side of the lesion, allowing a small single-stranded DNA to be excised. DNA polymerase and DNA ligase then repair the single-stranded gap. In all of these systems, the presence of an abnormal base signifies which strand is to be repaired, and the complementary strand is used as the template to ensure the accuracy of repair.

NUCLEIC ACID METABOLISM: RNA

RNA provides the link between the genetic information encoded in DNA and the actual workings of the cell. Some RNA molecules such as the rRNAs and the snRNAs become part of complicated ribonucleoprotein structures with specialized roles in the cell. Others such as tRNAs play key roles in protein synthesis, while mRNAs direct the synthesis of proteins by the ribosome. Three distinct phases of RNA metabolism occur. First, selected segments of the genome are copied by transcription to produce the precursor RNAs. Second, these precursors are processed to become functionally mature RNAs ready for use. When these RNAs are mRNAs, they are then used for translation. Third, after use the RNAs are degraded, and the bases are recycled. Thus, transcription is the process where a specific segment of DNA, a gene, is copied into a specific RNA that encodes a single protein or plays a structural or catalytic role. Translation is the decoding of the information within mRNA molecules that takes place on a specialized structure called a ribosome. There are important differences in both transcription and translation between prokaryotic and eukaryotic organisms.

TRANSCRIPTION

Small segments of DNA are transcribed into RNA by the enzyme RNA polymerase, which achieves this copying in a strictly controlled process. The first step is to recognize a specific sequence on DNA called a promoter that signifies the start of the gene. The two strands of DNA become separated at this point, and RNA polymerase begins copying from a specific point on one strand of the DNA using a ribonucleoside 5'-triphosphate to begin the growing chain. Additional ribonucleoside triphosphates are used as the substrate, and, by cleavage of their high-energy phosphate bond, ribonucleoside monophosphates are incorporated into the growing RNA chain. Each successive ribonucleotide is directed by the complementary base pairing rules of DNA. Thus, a C in DNA directs the incorporation of a G into RNA, G is copied into C, T into A, and A into U. Synthesis continues until a termination signal is reached, at which point the RNA polymerase drops off the DNA, and the RNA molecule is released. In some cases this RNA molecule is the final mRNA. In other cases it is a pre-mRNA and requires further processing before it is ready for translation by the ribosome. Ahead of many genes in prokaryotes, there are signals called "operators" where specialized proteins called repressors bind to the DNA just upstream of the start point of transcription and prevent access to the DNA by RNA polymerase. These repressor proteins thus prevent transcription of the gene by physically blocking the action of the RNA polymerase. Typically, repressors are released from their blocking action when they receive signals from other molecules in the cell indicating that the gene needs to be expressed. Ahead of some prokaryotic genes are signals to which activator proteins bind that positively induce transcription.

Transcription in higher organisms is more complicated. First, the RNA polymerase of eukaryotes is a more complicated enzyme than the relatively simple five-subunit enzyme of prokaryotes. In addition, there are many more accessory factors that help to control the efficiency of the individual promoters. These accessory proteins are called transcription factors and typically respond to signals from within the cell that indicate whether transcription is required. In many human genes, several transcription factors may be needed before transcription can proceed efficiently. A transcription factor can cause either repression or activation of gene expression in eukaryotes.

During transcription, only one strand of the DNA is usually copied. This is called the template strand, and the RNA molecules produced are single-stranded. The DNA strand that would correspond to the mRNA is called the coding or sense strand, and it is not unusual for this to change from one gene to the next. In eukaryotes the initial product of transcription is called a pre-mRNA, which is extensively spliced before the mature mRNA is produced, ready for translation by the ribosome.

TRANSLATION

The process of translation uses the information present in the nucleotide sequence of mRNA to direct the synthesis of a specific protein for use by the cell. Translation takes place on the ribosomes—complex particles in the cell that contain RNA and protein. In prokaryotes the ribosomes are loaded onto the mRNA while transcription is still ongoing. Near the 5' end of the mRNA, a short sequence of nucleotides signals the starting point for translation. It contains a few nucleotides called a ribosome binding site, or Shine-Dalgarno sequence. In *E. coli* the tetranucleotide GAGG is sufficient to serve as a binding site. This typically lies five to eight bases upstream of an initiation codon. The mRNA sequence is read three bases at a time from its 5' end toward its 3' end, and one amino acid is added to the growing chain from its respective aminoacyl tRNA, until the complete protein chain is assembled. Translation stops when the ribosome encounters a termination codon, normally UAG, UAA, or UGA. Special release factors associate with the ribosome in response to these codons, and the newly synthesized protein, tRNAs, and mRNA all dissociate. The ribosome then becomes available to interact with another mRNA molecule.

Marshall Warren Nirenberg

(b. April 10, 1927, New York, N.Y., U.S. — d. Jan. 15, 2010, New York)

American biochemist Marshall Warren Nirenberg was known for his role in deciphering the genetic code. He demonstrated that, with the exception of "nonsense codons," each possible triplet (called a codon) of four different kinds of nitrogen-containing bases found in DNA and, in some viruses, in RNA ultimately causes the incorporation of a specific amino acid into a cell protein. Nirenberg was a corecipient, with Robert William Holley and Har Gobind Khorana, of the 1968 Nobel Prize for Physiology or Medicine. Nirenberg's work and that of Holley and Khorana helped to show how genetic instructions in the cell nucleus control the composition of proteins.

Nirenberg earned a B.S. (1948) in zoology and chemistry and an M.S. (1952) in zoology at the University of Florida. He received a Ph.D. in biological chemistry from the University of Michigan in 1957 and that year joined the staff of the National Institutes of Health (NIH) in Bethesda, Md. His research earned him the National Medal of Science in 1965, and the following year he was elevated to director of biochemical genetics at the NIH, a position he held for the remainder of his career. In 1968 Nirenberg and Khorana were recognized with an Albert Lasker Basic Medical Research Award and the Louisa Gross Horowitz Prize for Biology or Biochemistry.

In the late 1960s Nirenberg's research shifted from genetics to neurobiology. He began investigating neuroblastomas—tumours involving masses of neurons, known as ganglia—and eventually developed a neuroblastoma model that served as the basis for a broad range of neurobiological research. In the 1970s Nirenberg used his model as a platform for explorations into morphine's effects on the nervous system and neural synapse formation in chicken retinas. During this time scientists discovered that under the influence of certain factors normal genes could be "switched on," becoming overactive in the form of oncogenes (cancer-causing genes). This finding, which demonstrated that gene activity could change and that these changes could affect cell growth, stimulated Nirenberg's interest. His research had begun to focus on nervous system growth and development, but how these processes were controlled was unknown. Nirenberg reasoned that to further understand the development of the nervous system, it was necessary to understand the genes that had the greatest influence on neurological development in the embryo. By the late 1980s a set of genes, known as homeobox genes (discovered in 1983), had become central to his studies. His experiments concerning homeobox genes and the assembly of the nervous system in *Drosophila* (fruit fly) were crucial to the advancement of the field of neurobiology. Much of Nirenberg's work on nervous system development in *Drosophila* proved relevant to studies on the development of the nervous system in humans.

In eukaryotes the essence of protein synthesis is the same, although the ribosomes are more complicated. As with prokaryotic initiation, the signal sequence interacts with the 3' end of the small subunit rRNA during formation of the initiation complex.

The issue of fidelity is important during protein synthesis, but it is not as crucial as fidelity during replication. One mRNA molecule can be translated repeatedly to give many copies of the protein. When an occasional protein is mistranslated, it usually does not fold properly and is then degraded by the cellular machinery. However, proofreading mechanisms exist within the ribosome to ensure accurate pairing between the codon in the mRNA and the anticodon in the tRNA.

Har Gobind Khorana

(b. Jan. 9, 1922, Raipur, India)

Indian-born American biochemist Har Gobind Khorana shared the Nobel Prize in Physiology or Medicine in 1968 with Marshall Warren Nirenberg and Robert William Holley for research that helped to show how the nucleotides in nucleic acids control the cell's synthesis of proteins.

Khorana was born into a poor family and attended Punjab University at Lahore and the University of Liverpool, England, on government scholarships. He obtained his Ph.D. at Liverpool in 1948. He began research on nucleic acids during a fellowship at the University of Cambridge (1951) under Sir Alexander Todd. He held fellowships and professorships in Switzerland at the Swiss Federal Institute of Technology, in Canada at the University of British Columbia (1952–59), and in the United States at the University of Wisconsin (1960–70). In 1966 Khorana became a naturalized citizen of the United States, and in 1971 he joined the faculty of the Massachusetts Institute of Technology, where he remained until he retired in 2007. In addition to the Nobel

Prize, Khorana received the Albert Lasker Basic Medical Research Award (1968) and the National Medal of Science (1987).

In the 1960s Khorana confirmed Nirenberg's findings that the way the four different types of nucleotides are arranged on the spiral "staircase" of the DNA molecule determines the chemical composition and function of a new cell. The 64 possible combinations of the nucleotides are read off along a strand of DNA as required to produce the desired amino acids, which are the building blocks of proteins. Khorana added details about which serial combinations of nucleotides form which specific amino acids. He also proved that the nucleotide code is always transmitted to the cell in groups of three, called codons. Khorana also determined that some of the codons prompt the cell to start or stop the manufacture of proteins. Khorana made another contribution to genetics in 1970, when he and his research team were able to synthesize the first artificial copy of a yeast gene. His later research explored the molecular mechanisms underlying the cell signaling pathways of vision in vertebrates. His studies were concerned primarily with the structure and function of rhodopsin, a light-sensitive protein found in the retina of the vertebrate eye. Khorana also investigated mutations in rhodopsin that are associated with retinitis pigmentosa, which causes night blindness.

Nobel Prize winners pose after the award ceremony in Stockholm, Sweden, in December 1968. Among them are Har Gobind Khorana (left), *Robert W. Holley* (second from left), *and Marshall W. Nirenberg* (fourth from left). Central Press/Hulton Archive/Getty Images

One of the crowning achievements of molecular biology was the elucidation during the 1960s of the genetic code. Principals in this effort were Har G. Khorana and Marshall Warren Nirenberg, who shared a Nobel Prize in 1968. Khorana and Nirenberg used artificial templates and protein synthesizing systems in the test tube to determine the coding potential of all 64 possible triplet codons. The key feature of the genetic code is that the 20 amino acids are encoded by 61 codons. Thus, there is degeneracy in the code such that one amino acid is often specified by more than one codon. In the case of serine and leucine, six codons can be used for each. Among organisms that have been examined in detail, the code appears to be almost universal, from bacteria through archaea to eukaryotes. The known exceptions are found in the mitochondria of humans and many other organisms, as well as in some species of bacteria. The structure within the genetic code whereby many amino acids are uniquely coded by the first two bases of the codon strongly suggests that the code has itself evolved from a more primitive code involving 16 dinucleotides. How the individual amino acids became associated with the different codons remains a matter of speculation.

CHAPTER 2

Amino acids are organic molecules that consist of a basic amino group (-NH$_2$), an acidic carboxyl group (-COOH), and an organic R group (or side chain) that is unique to each amino acid. The term *amino acid* is short for "α-amino [alpha-amino] carboxylic acid." Each molecule contains a central carbon (C) atom, termed the α-carbon, to which both an amino and a carboxyl group are attached. The remaining two bonds of the α-carbon atom are generally satisfied by a hydrogen (H) atom and the R group. The formula of a general amino acid is:

$$R - \underset{\underset{H}{|}}{\overset{\overset{NH_2}{|}}{C}} - COOH$$

The amino acids differ from each other in the particular chemical structure of their R group. Of over 100 natural amino acids, each with a different R group, only 20 make up the proteins of all living organisms. Humans can synthesize 10 of them (by interconversions, or mutual conversions) from each other or from other molecules of intermediary metabolism, but the other 10 (essential amino acids: arginine, histidine, isoleucine, leucine, lysine, methionine, phenylalanine, threonine, tryptophan, and valine) must be consumed in the diet.

BUILDING BLOCKS OF PROTEINS

Proteins are of primary importance to the continuing functioning of life on Earth. Proteins catalyze the vast majority of chemical reactions that occur in the cell. They provide many of the structural elements of a cell, and they help to bind cells together into tissues. Some proteins act as contractile elements to make movement possible. Others are responsible for the transport of vital materials from the outside of the cell ("extracellular") to its inside ("intracellular"). Proteins, in the form of antibodies, protect animals from disease and, in the form of interferon, mount an intracellular attack against viruses that have eluded destruction by the antibodies and other immune system defenses. Many hormones are proteins. Last but certainly not least, proteins control the activity of genes ("gene expression").

This plethora of vital tasks is reflected in the incredible spectrum of known proteins that vary markedly in their overall size, shape, and charge. By the end of the 19th century, scientists appreciated that, although there exist many different kinds of proteins in nature, all proteins upon their hydrolysis yield a class of simpler compounds, the building blocks of proteins, called amino acids. The simplest amino acid is called glycine, and it was one of the first amino acids to be identified, having been isolated from the protein gelatin in 1820. In the mid-1950s scientists involved in elucidating the relationship between proteins and genes agreed that 20 amino acids (called standard or common amino acids) were to be considered the essential building blocks of all proteins. The last of these to be discovered, threonine, had been identified in 1935.

CHIRALITY

All the amino acids but glycine are chiral molecules. That is, they exist in two optically active, asymmetric forms (called enantiomers) that are the mirror images of each other. (This property is conceptually similar to the spatial relationship of the left hand to the right hand.) One enantiomer is designated D and the other L. It is important to note that the amino acids found in proteins almost always possess only the L-configuration. This reflects the fact that the enzymes responsible for protein synthesis have evolved to utilize only the L-enantiomers. Reflecting this near universality, the prefix L is usually omitted. Some D-amino acids are found in microorganisms, particularly in the cell walls of bacteria and in several of the antibiotics. However, these are not synthesized in the ribosome.

ACID-BASE PROPERTIES

Another important feature of free amino acids is the existence of both a basic and an acidic group at the central α-carbon.

Compounds such as amino acids that can act as either an acid or a base are called amphoteric. The basic amino group typically has a pK_a (a measurement of the strength of acid in solution) between 9 and 10, while the acidic α-carboxyl group has a pK_a that is usually close to 2 (a very low value for carboxyls). The pK_a of a group is the pH value at which the concentration of the group that has acquired an extra proton equals that of the unprotonated group. Thus, at physiological pH (about 7–7.4), the free amino acids exist largely as dipolar ions or "zwitterions" (German for "hybrid ions"; a zwitterion carries an equal number of positively and negatively charged groups). Any free amino acid and likewise any protein will, at some specific pH, exist in the form of a zwitterion. That is, all amino acids and all proteins, when subjected to changes in pH, pass through a state at which there are an equal number of positive and negative charges on the molecule. The pH at which this occurs is known as the isoelectric point (or isoelectric pH) and is denoted as pI. When dissolved in water, all amino acids and all proteins are present predominantly in their isoelectric form. Stated another way, there is a pH (the isoelectric point) at which the molecule has a net zero charge (equal number of positive and negative charges), but there is no pH at which the molecule has an absolute zero charge (complete absence of positive and negative charges). That is, amino acids and proteins are always in the form of ions; they always carry charged groups. This fact is vitally important in considering further the bio-chemistry of amino acids and proteins.

STANDARD AMINO ACIDS

One of the most useful manners by which to classify the standard amino acids is based on the polarity (i.e., the distribution of electric charge) of the R group (e.g., side chain). Using this approach, the 20 standard amino acids — those that are essential for generating proteins — can be divided into four distinct groups: nonpolar amino acids; polar, uncharged amino acids; acidic amino acids;and basic amino acids.

GROUP I: NONPOLAR AMINO ACIDS

Group I amino acids are alanine, valine, leucine, isoleucine, proline, phenylalanine, methionine, and tryptophan. The R groups of these amino acids have either aliphatic or aromatic groups. This makes them hydrophobic ("water-fearing"). In aqueous solutions, globular proteins will fold into a three-dimensional shape to bury these hydrophobic side chains in the protein interior. The chemical structures of Group I amino acids are

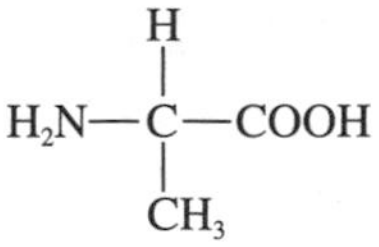

alanine
(Ala, A)

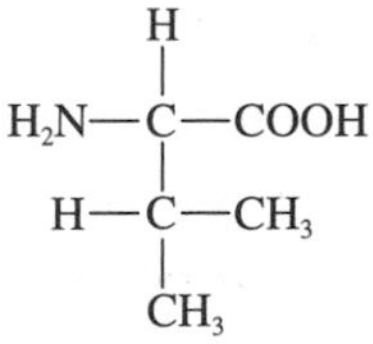

valine
(Val, V)

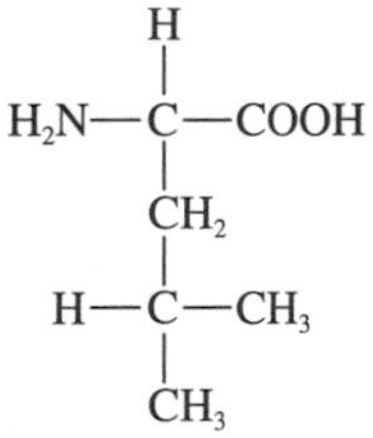

leucine
(Leu, L)

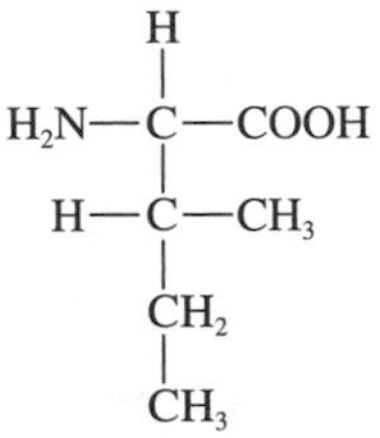

isoleucine
(Ile, I)

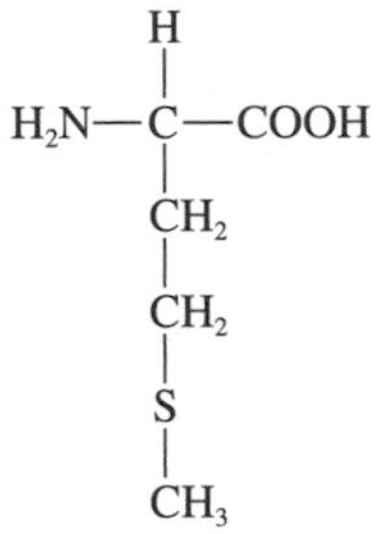

methionine
(Met, M)

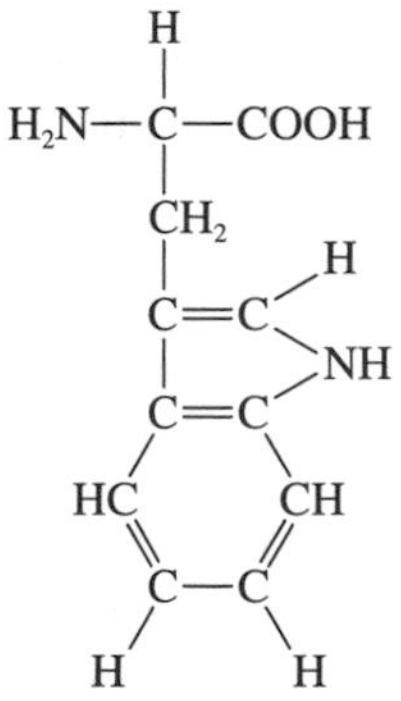

tryptophan
(Try or Trp, W)

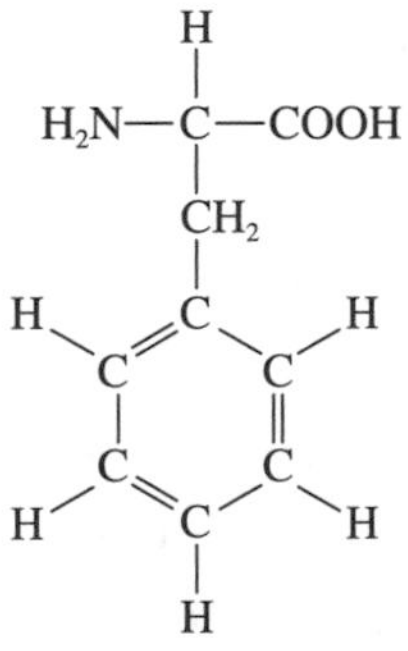

phenylalanine
(Phe, F)

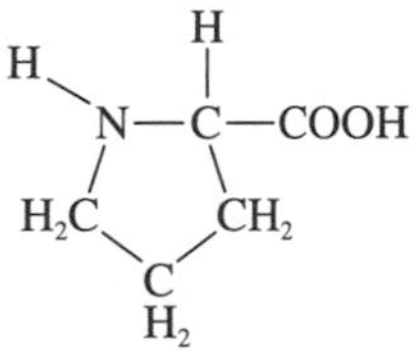

proline
(Pro, P)
an imino acid

Alanine is either of two amino acids, one of which, L-alanine, or alpha-alanine (α-alanine), is a constituent of proteins. An especially rich source of L-alanine is silk fibroin, from which the amino acid was first isolated in 1879. Alanine is one of several so-called nonessential amino acids for birds and mammals, meaning that they can synthesize it from pyruvic acid (formed in the breakdown of carbohydrates) and do not require dietary sources.

D-alanine, or beta-alanine (β-alanine), is not found in proteins but occurs naturally in two peptides, carnosine and anserine, found in mammalian muscle. It is an important constituent of the vitamin pantothenic acid.

Valine is obtained by hydrolysis of proteins and was first isolated by the German chemist Emil Fischer (1901) from casein (a protein formed from milk). It is one of several essential amino acids for birds and mammals (i.e., they cannot synthesize it and require dietary sources). It is synthesized in plants and microorganisms from pyruvic acid.

Leucine is obtainable by the hydrolysis of most common proteins. Among the first of the amino acids to be discovered (1819), in muscle fibre and wool, it is present in large proportions (about 15 percent) in hemoglobin (the oxygen-carrying pigment of red blood cells) and is one of the essential amino acids for rats, birds, and humans. In plants and microorganisms it is synthesized from pyruvic acid.

Isoleucine is an isomer of leucine, and it contains two chiral carbon atoms. It is present in most common proteins, sometimes comprising 2 to 10 percent by weight. First isolated in 1904 from fibrin, a protein involved in blood-clot formation, isoleucine is an essential amino acid for birds, rats, and other higher animals, including humans. In microorganisms and plants, isoleucine is synthesized from the amino acid threonine.

Proline is unique among the standard amino acids in that it does not have both free α-amino and free α-carboxyl groups. Instead, its side chain forms a cyclic structure as the nitrogen atom of proline is linked to two carbon atoms. (Strictly speaking, this means that proline is not an amino acid but rather an α-imino acid.) Unlike other amino acids, proline, first isolated from casein (1901), is readily soluble in alcohol. Collagen, the principal protein of connective tissue, yields about 15 percent proline. Proline is one of the nonessential amino acids—animals can synthesize it from glutamic acid and thus do not require dietary sources.

Phenylalanine, as the name implies, consists of a phenyl group attached to alanine. Human hemoglobin is one of the richest sources of phenylalanine, yielding 9.6 percent by weight. First isolated in 1881 from lupine seedlings, phenylalanine is an essential amino acid for birds and mammals. Microorganisms synthesize it from glucose and pyruvic acid.

First isolated from casein (1922), methionine accounts for about 5 percent of the weight of egg albumin. Other proteins contain much smaller amounts of methionine. Methionine is one of two amino acids that possess a sulfur atom, and it is an essential amino acid for mammals and birds. Methionine plays a central role in protein biosynthesis (translation) as it is almost always the initiating amino acid. It is important in methylation (the process by which methyl, or -CH$_3$, groups are added to compounds) and is also a precursor of two other amino acids, cystine and cysteine. Microorganisms are capable of synthesizing methionine from cysteine and aspartic acid.

Tryptophan, a nutritionally important amino acid, contains an indole ring attached to the alanyl side chain.

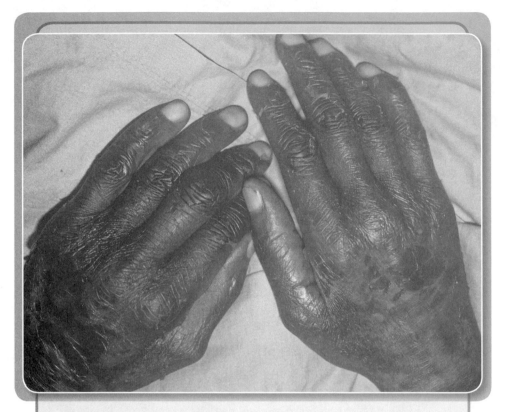

Pellagra symptoms on human hands. Pellagra is a disease caused by niacin deficiency in the diet. Dr. Kenneth Greer/Visuals Unlimited/Getty Images

It is an essential amino acid, and thus humans and certain other animals must obtain it from their diets. Infants require greater amounts of tryptophan than adults to ensure normal growth and development. Tryptophan is used by the body to manufacture several important substances, including the neurotransmitter serotonin and the vitamin niacin. Diets poor in tryptophan can lead to pellagra, a disease resulting from niacin deficiency that is now relatively rare in developed countries. In 1901 the British biochemist Sir Frederick Gowland Hopkins isolated tryptophan from casein.

Sir Frederick Gowland Hopkins

(b. June 20, 1861, Eastbourne, East Sussex, Eng.—d. May 16, 1947, Cambridge)

British biochemist Sir Frederick Gowland Hopkins contributed to the discovery of essential nutrient factors—now known as vitamins—needed in animal diets to maintain health. He received (with Christiaan Eijkman) the 1929 Nobel Prize for Physiology or Medicine for his work.

In 1901 Hopkins discovered the amino acid tryptophan, isolated it from protein, and eventually (1906–07) showed that it and certain other amino acids (known as essential amino acids) cannot be manufactured by certain animals from other nutrients and must be supplied in the diet. Noticing that rats failed to grow on a diet of artificial milk but grew rapidly when a small quantity of cow's milk was added to their daily ration, Hopkins realized that no animal can live on a mixture of pure protein, fat, and carbohydrate, even when mineral salts are added, and termed the missing factors—later called vitamins—"accessory substances."

In 1907 Hopkins and Sir Walter Fletcher laid the foundations for a modern understanding of the chemistry of muscular contraction when they demonstrated that working muscle accumulates lactic acid. Fifteen years later, Hopkins isolated from living tissue the tripeptide (three amino acids linked in sequence) glutathione and showed that it is vital to the utilization of oxygen by the cell.

Hopkins spent most of his career at Cambridge University (1898–1943). He was knighted in 1925 and received many other honours, including the presidency of the Royal Society (1930) and the Order of Merit (1935).

GROUP II: POLAR, UNCHARGED AMINO ACIDS

Group II amino acids are glycine, serine, cysteine, threonine, tyrosine, asparagine, and glutamine. The side chains in this group possess a spectrum of functional groups.

However, most have at least one atom (nitrogen, oxygen, or sulfur) with electron pairs available for hydrogen bonding to water and other molecules. The chemical structures of Group II amino acids are

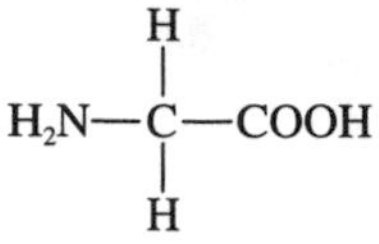

$$H_2N-\overset{\overset{\displaystyle H}{|}}{\underset{\underset{\displaystyle H}{|}}{C}}-COOH$$

glycine
(Gly, G)

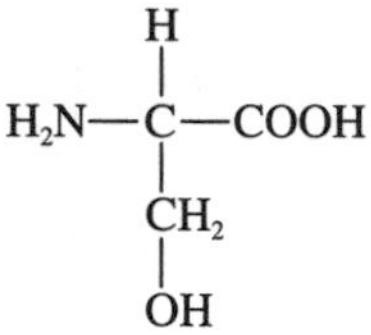

$$H_2N-\overset{\overset{\displaystyle H}{|}}{\underset{\underset{\underset{\displaystyle OH}{|}}{\underset{\displaystyle CH_2}{|}}}{C}}-COOH$$

serine
(Ser, S)

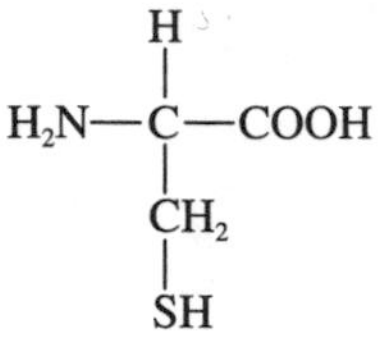

$$H_2N-\overset{\overset{\displaystyle H}{|}}{\underset{\underset{\underset{\displaystyle SH}{|}}{\underset{\displaystyle CH_2}{|}}}{C}}-COOH$$

cysteine
(CysH, C)

$$H_2N-\overset{\overset{\displaystyle H}{|}}{\underset{\underset{\displaystyle CH_2}{|}}{C}}-COOH$$

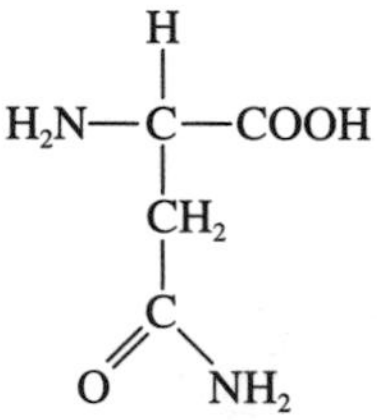

asparagine
(AspNH₂ or Asn, N; Asx or B)

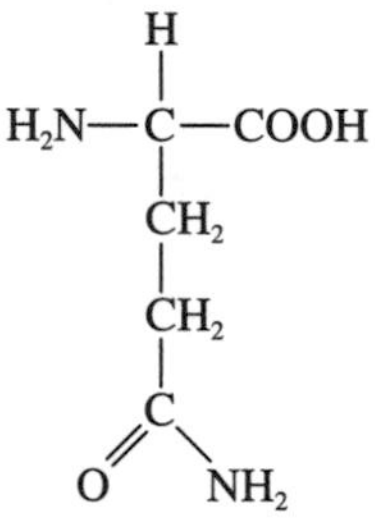

$$H_2N-\overset{\overset{\displaystyle H}{|}}{\underset{\underset{\displaystyle CH_2}{|}}{C}}-COOH$$

glutamine
(GluNH₂, GluN,
or Gln, Q; Glx or Z)

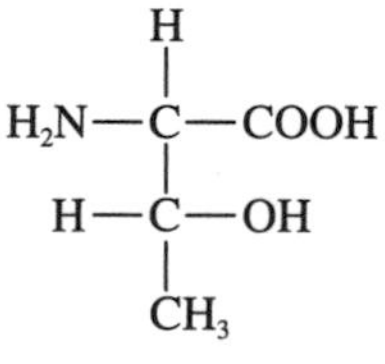

$$H_2N-\overset{\overset{\displaystyle H}{|}}{\underset{\underset{\underset{\displaystyle CH_3}{|}}{\underset{\displaystyle H-C-OH}{|}}}{C}}-COOH$$

threonine
(Thr, T)

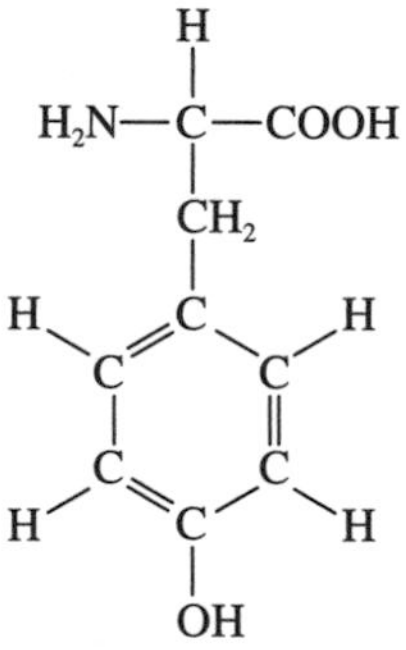

tyrosine
(Tyr, Y)

Glycine is the simplest amino acid and is obtainable by hydrolysis of proteins. Glycine, named for its sweet taste (*glyco*: "sugar"), was among the earliest amino acids to be isolated from gelatin (1820). Especially rich sources include gelatin and silk fibroin. Glycine is the only amino acid that does not have an asymmetric (chiral) carbon atom. It is a nonessential amino acid for mammals (mammals can synthesize it from the amino acids serine and threonine and from other sources).

Serine and threonine are distinguished by the fact that they contain aliphatic hydroxyl groups (-OH). Serine is obtainable by hydrolysis of most common proteins, sometimes constituting 5 to 10 percent by weight of the total product. It was first isolated in 1865 from sericin, a silk protein, and is a nonessential amino acid for mammals (mammals can synthesize it from glucose). Serine and some of its derivatives (e.g., ethanolamine) are also important components of a class of lipids (phospholipids) found in biological membranes. Threonine is obtainable from many proteins. It was one of the last amino acids to be isolated (1935) and is one of the essential amino acids. Threonine is synthesized in microorganisms from the amino acid aspartic acid.

Cysteine, similar to methionine, contains a sulfur atom. Unlike methionine's sulfur atom, however, cysteine's sulfur is very chemically reactive. In peptides and proteins, the sulfur atoms of two cysteine molecules are bonded to each other to make cystine, another amino acid. The bonded sulfur atoms form a disulfide bridge, a principal factor in the shape and function of skeletal and connective tissue proteins and in the great stability of structural proteins such as keratin.

Tyrosine possesses a hydroxyl group in the aromatic ring, making it a phenol derivative. Tyrosine comprises about 1 to 6 percent by weight of the mixture obtained by hydrolysis of most proteins. First isolated from casein in 1846 by German chemist Justus, baron von Liebig, tyrosine is particularly abundant in insulin (a hormone) and papain (an enzyme found in fruit of the papaya), which contain 13 percent by weight. Tyrosine is an essential amino acid for certain animals. Other species can, however, convert phenylalanine, also an essential amino acid for birds and mammals, to tyrosine whenever necessary for protein synthesis.

Asparagine and glutamine both contain amide R groups. The carbonyl group can function as a hydrogen bond acceptor, and the amino group (NH_2) can function as a hydrogen bond donor. Asparagine is closely related to aspartic acid and was first isolated in 1932 from asparagus, from which its name is derived. Asparagine is widely distributed in plant proteins and is a nonessential amino acid in warm-blooded animals.

Glutamine is the monoamide of glutamic acid. It was first isolated from gliadin, a protein present in wheat (1932). Glutamine is widely distributed in plants, with examples of its sources being beets, carrots, and radishes. Important in cellular metabolism in animals, glutamine is the only amino acid capable of readily crossing the barrier between blood and brain and, with glutamic acid, is thought to account for about 80 percent of the amino nitrogen ($-NH_2$) of brain tissue. It is a nonessential amino acid.

GROUP III: ACIDIC AMINO ACIDS

The two amino acids in this group are aspartic acid and glutamic acid. Each has a carboxylic acid on its side chain that gives it acidic (proton-donating) properties. In an aqueous solution at physiological pH, all three functional groups on these amino acids will ionize, thus giving an overall charge of -1. In the ionic forms, the amino acids are called aspartate and glutamate. The chemical structures of Group III amino acids are

$$H_2N—\overset{\displaystyle H}{\underset{\displaystyle \underset{\displaystyle \underset{O \quad OH}{C}}{CH_2}}{C}}—COOH$$

aspartic acid
(Asp, D; Asx or B)

$$H_2N—\overset{\displaystyle H}{\underset{\displaystyle \underset{\displaystyle \underset{\displaystyle \underset{O \quad OH}{C}}{CH_2}}{CH_2}}{C}}—COOH$$

glutamic acid
(Glu, E; Glx or Z)

The side chains of aspartate and glutamate can form ionic bonds ("salt bridges"), and they can also function as hydrogen bond acceptors. Many proteins that bind metal ions ("metalloproteins") for structural or functional purposes possess metal-binding sites containing aspartate or glutamate side chains, or both.

Certain plant proteins (e.g., gliadin) yield as much as 45 percent of their weight as glutamate, whereas other proteins yield 10 to 20 percent. Much of this content may result from the presence of a related substance, glutamine, in proteins. Glutamine is converted to glutamate when a protein is hydrolyzed. Free glutamate and glutamine play a central role in amino acid metabolism. Glutamate is the most abundant excitatory neurotransmitter in the central nervous system.

Glutamate was first isolated in 1865 and is a nonessential amino acid (animals can synthesize it from oxoglutaric acid). Monosodium glutamate (MSG), a salt of glutamate, is sometimes used as a condiment for flavouring foods. Aspartate was first isolated in 1868 from legumin in plant seeds and also is a nonessential amino acid (mammals can synthesize it from oxaloacetic acid).

GROUP IV: BASIC AMINO ACIDS

The three amino acids in this group are arginine, histidine, and lysine. Each side chain is basic (i.e., can accept a proton). Lysine and arginine both exist with an overall charge of +1 at physiological pH. The guanidino group in arginine's side chain is the most basic of all R groups (a fact reflected in its pK_a value of 12.5). The side chains of arginine and lysine also form ionic bonds. The chemical structures of Group IV amino acids are

Arginine is obtainable by hydrolysis of many common proteins but is particularly abundant in protamines and histones, proteins associated with nucleic acids. Arginine, which was first isolated from animal horn (1895), plays an important role in mammals in the synthesis of urea, the principal form in which these species excrete nitrogen. Arginine is a nonessential amino acid for adult mammals (mammals can synthesize it from glutamic acid).

Histidine is obtainable by hydrolysis of many proteins, with a particularly rich source being hemoglobin, which yields about 8.5 percent by weight of histidine. Histidine was first isolated in 1896 from various proteins. It is an essential amino acid for humans. In microorganisms histidine is synthesized from the sugar ribose and the nucleotide adenosine triphosphate (ATP). Histamine, a compound involved in the physiological processes associated with allergic reactions, is formed in the human body by decarboxylation of histidine.

The imidazole side chain of histidine allows it to function in both acid and base catalysis near physiological pH values. None of the other standard amino acids possesses this important chemical property. Therefore, histidine is an amino acid that most often makes up the active sites of protein enzymes.

Lysine is released in the hydrolysis of many common proteins, but it is present in small amounts or is lacking in certain plant proteins, such as gliadin from wheat and zein from corn (maize). Lysine was first isolated from casein (1889) and is an essential amino acid for warm-blooded animals. (It is formed in plants, algae, and fungi by two distinct biosynthetic pathways.) Human populations dependent on grains as a sole source of dietary protein suffer from lysine deficiency.

The majority of amino acids in Groups II, III, and IV are hydrophilic ("water-loving"). As a result, they are often found clustered on the surface of globular proteins in aqueous solutions.

AMINO ACID REACTIONS

Amino acids via their various chemical functionalities (carboxyls, amino, and R groups) can undergo numerous chemical reactions. However, two reactions (peptide bond and cysteine oxidation) are of particular importance because of their effect on protein structure.

PEPTIDE BOND

Amino acids can be linked by a condensation reaction in which an -OH is lost from the carboxyl group of one

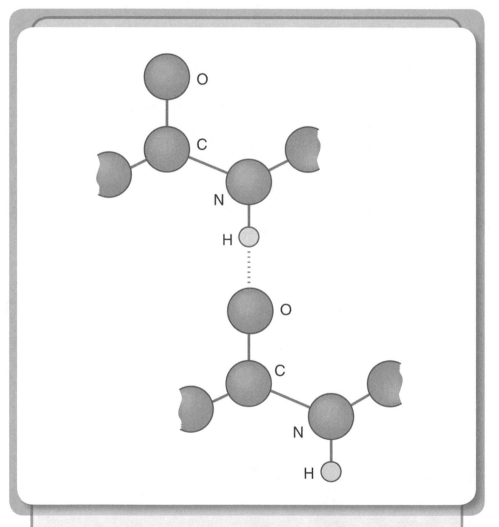

The linking of atoms in a peptide bond. Copyright Encyclopædia Britannica; rendering for this edition by Rosen Educational Services

amino acid along with a hydrogen from the amino group of a second, forming a molecule of water and leaving the two amino acids linked via an organic compound called an amide—in this case, a peptide bond. At the turn of the 20th century, German chemist Emil Fischer first proposed this linking together of amino acids. Note that when individual amino acids are combined to form proteins, their carboxyl and amino groups are no longer able to act as acids or bases, since they have reacted to form the peptide bond. Therefore, the acid-base properties of proteins are dependent upon the overall ionization characteristics of the individual R groups of the component amino acids.

Amino acids joined by a series of peptide bonds are said to constitute a peptide. After they are incorporated into a peptide, the individual amino acids are referred to as amino acid residues. Small polymers of amino acids (fewer than 50) are termed oligopeptides, while larger ones (more than 50) are referred to as polypeptides. Hence, a protein molecule is a polypeptide chain composed of many amino acid residues, with each residue joined to the next by a peptide bond. The lengths for different proteins range from a few dozen to thousands of amino acids, and each protein contains different relative proportions of the 20 standard amino acids.

Emil Fischer

(b. Oct. 9, 1852, Euskirchen, Prussia [Ger.]—d. July 15, 1919, Berlin, Ger.)

Emil Fischer was known for his investigations of the sugar and purine groups of substances. He was awarded the 1902 Nobel Prize for Chemistry in recognition of his work.

Fischer studied chemistry at the University of Bonn, where he attended the lectures of August Kekule. In 1872 he transferred to the University of Strasbourg, where Adolph von Baeyer had recently been appointed as director of the chemical institute. Fischer earned a doctorate under Baeyer in 1874, and Baeyer chose Fischer to be a private assistant in his research laboratory. Baeyer retained Fischer as an assistant when he moved to the University of Munich in 1875 and soon recommended Fischer for the position of associate professor in charge of the analytical division. While at Strasbourg and Munich, Fischer quickly earned a reputation as an excellent organic chemist. He discovered the compound phenylhydrazine in 1875, and with his cousin Otto Fischer he established the structure of the rosaniline dyes discovered earlier by the German chemist August Wilhelm von Hofmann. On the basis of his work in organic chemistry, Fischer was appointed director of the chemical institutes at the provincial Bavarian universities of Erlangen (1882) and Würzburg (1885).

After leaving Baeyer's laboratory, Fischer applied the classical chemical methods of organic chemistry to establish the structure of biological compounds such as sugars, purines, and proteins. Fischer began research on the purines in 1882, and during the next 17 years he showed that uric acid, xanthine, caffeine, and other natural compounds were all related to a nitrogen-containing base with a bicyclic structure that he named purine.

In 1884 Fischer began a long study to establish the chemical structure and configuration of the known isomeric sugars—glucose, galactose, fructose, and sorbose—with the goal of ascertaining the source of their isomerism. The key to this study was the reaction of the sugars with phenylhydrazine. The sugars themselves had been difficult to purify and characterize, but they reacted with phenylhydrazine (an organic compound commonly used in the synthesis of indole) to give osazones that were highly crystalline, easily purified compounds. Fischer soon realized that these sugars were spatial isomers and could be differentiated by applying the theory of the tetrahedral carbon atom, first proposed in 1874 by the Dutch chemist Jacobus Henricus van 't Hoff. Fischer recognized that the known isomers of glucose represented only 4 out of the 16 possible spatial isomers predicted by van 't Hoff's theory. Using the osazone derivatives and synthetic techniques for the sugars developed by the German chemists Bernhard Tollens and Heinrich Kiliani, Fischer was able not only to differentiate the known isomers but to synthesize nine of the predicted isomers.

In 1892, largely on the basis of his extensive study of sugars and purines, Fischer was chosen to succeed Hofmann as professor of chemistry at the University of Berlin, at the time the largest and most prestigious chemical institute in Germany. In Berlin, Fischer's research moved to the study of enzymes and proteins. Fischer's extensive study of the sugars included an investigation of their digestion by yeast, and he found that of the known stereoisomers of glucose, only a few were capable of being digested by the enzymes in yeast. Because these isomers differed only in their spatial properties, Fischer concluded that the enzyme in yeast must also have a specific spatial orientation to receive the sugar molecule and react with it.

Thus, Fischer also became involved in establishing the chemical structure of enzymes and proteins. Proteins were known to be composed of amino acids, but Fischer specifically proposed that the amino acids in proteins were linked together by amide bonds, called peptide bonds by Fischer, who established the presence of this class of molecules in proteins by developing synthetic methods for creating long chains of amino acids held together by peptide bonds to make proteinlike substances. In 1907 he created a polypeptide with 18 amino acids and showed that it could be broken down by enzymes in the same way as a natural protein.

CYSTEINE OXIDATION

The thiol (sulfur-containing) group of cysteine is highly reactive. The most common reaction of this group is a reversible oxidation that forms a disulfide. Oxidation of two molecules of cysteine forms cystine, a molecule that contains a disulfide bond. When two cysteine residues in a protein form such a bond, it is referred to as a disulfide bridge. Disulfide bridges are a common mechanism used in nature to stabilize many proteins. Such disulfide bridges are often found among extracellular proteins that are secreted from cells. In eukaryotic organisms, formation of disulfide bridges occurs within the organelle called the endoplasmic reticulum.

In extracellular fluids (such as blood), the sulfhydryl groups of cysteine are rapidly oxidized to form cystine. In a genetic disorder known as cystinuria, there is a defect that results in excessive excretion of cystine into the urine. Because cystine is the least soluble of the amino acids, crystallization of the excreted cystine results in formation of calculi—more commonly known as "stones"—in the kidney, ureter, or urinary bladder. The stones may cause intense pain, infection, and blood in the urine. Medical intervention often involves the administration of D-penicillamine. Penicillamine works by forming a complex with cystine. This complex is 50 times more water-soluble than cystine alone.

In summary, it is the sequence of amino acids that determines the shape and biological function of a protein, as well as its physical and chemical properties. Thus, the functional diversity of proteins arises because proteins are polymers of 20 different kinds of amino acids. For example, a "simple" protein is the hormone insulin, which has 51 amino acids. With 20 different amino acids to chose from at each of these 51 positions, a total of 20^{51}, or about 10^{66}, different proteins could theoretically be made.

OTHER FUNCTIONS OF AMINO ACIDS

Amino acids are precursors of a variety of complex nitrogen-containing molecules. Prominent among these are the nitrogenous base components of nucleotides and the nucleic acids (DNA and RNA). Furthermore, there are complex amino-acid–derived cofactors such as heme and chlorophyll. Heme is the iron-containing organic group required for the biological activity of vitally important proteins such as the oxygen-carrying hemoglobin and the electron-transporting cytochrome *c*. Chlorophyll is a pigment required for photosynthesis.

Several α-amino acids (or their derivatives) act as chemical messengers. For example, γ-aminobutyric acid (gamma-aminobutyric acid, or GABA; a derivative of glutamic acid), serotonin and melatonin (derivatives of tryptophan), and histamine (synthesized from histidine) are neurotransmitters. Thyroxine (a tyrosine derivative produced in the thyroid gland of animals) and indole acetic acid (a tryptophan derivative found in plants) are two examples of hormones.

Several standard and nonstandard amino acids often are vital metabolic intermediates. Important examples of this are the amino acids arginine, citrulline, and ornithine, which are all components of the urea cycle. The synthesis of urea is the principal mechanism for the removal of nitrogenous waste.

NONSTANDARD AMINO ACIDS

Nonstandard amino acids refer to those amino acids that have been chemically modified after they have been incorporated into a protein (termed a "posttranslational modification") and those amino acids that occur in living organisms but are not found in proteins. Among these modified amino acids is γ-carboxyglutamic acid, a calcium-binding amino acid residue found in the blood-clotting protein prothrombin (as well as in other proteins that bind calcium as part of their biological function).

The most abundant protein by mass in vertebrates is collagen. Significant proportions of the amino acids in collagen are modified forms of proline and lysine: 4-hydroxyproline and 5-hydroxylysine.

Arguably, the most important posttranslational modification of amino acids in eukaryotic organisms (including humans) is the reversible addition of a phosphate molecule to the hydroxyl portion of the *R* groups of serine, threonine, and tyrosine. This event is known as phosphorylation and is used to regulate the activity of proteins in their minute-to-minute functioning in the cell. Serine is the most commonly phosphorylated residue in proteins, threonine is second, and tyrosine is third.

Proteins with carbohydrates (sugars) covalently attached to them are called glycoproteins. Glycoproteins are widely distributed in nature and provide the spectrum of functions already discussed for unmodified proteins. The sugar groups in glycoproteins are attached to amino acids through either oxygen (O-linked sugars) or nitrogen atoms (N-linked sugars) in the amino acid residues. The O-linked sugars are attached to proteins through the oxygen atoms in serine, threonine, hydroxylysine, or hydroxylproline residues. The N-linked sugars are attached to proteins through the nitrogen atom in asparagine.

Finally, there is the case of selenocysteine. Although it is part of only a few known proteins, there is a sound scientific reason to consider this the 21st amino acid because it is in fact introduced during protein biosynthesis rather than created by a posttranslational modification. Selenocysteine is actually derived from the amino acid serine (in a very complicated fashion), and it contains selenium instead of the sulfur of cysteine.

ANALYSIS OF AMINO ACID MIXTURES

The modern biochemist has a wide array of methods available for the separation and analysis of amino acids and proteins. These methods exploit the chemical differences of amino acids and in particular their ionization and solubility behaviour.

A typical determination of the amino acid composition of proteins involves three basic steps:

1. Hydrolysis of the protein to its constituent amino acids.
2. Separation of the amino acids in the mixture.
3. Quantification of the individual amino acids.

Hydrolysis is accomplished by treatment of a purified protein with a concentrated acid solution (6N HCl) at a very high temperature (usually 110 °C [230 °F]) for up to 70 hours. These conditions cleave the peptide bond between each and every amino acid residue.

The hydrolyzed protein sample is then separated into its constituent amino acids. Methods important for amino acid separations include ion exchange chromatography, gas chromatography, high-performance liquid chromatography, and most recently, capillary zone electrophoresis.

The sensitivity of the analysis of separated amino acids has been greatly improved by the use of fluorescent molecules that are attached to the amino acids, followed by their subsequent detection using fluorescence spectroscopy. For example, amino acids may be chemically "tagged" with a small fluorescent molecule (such as o-phthalaldehyde). These approaches routinely allow as little as a picomole (10^{-12} mole) of an amino acid to be detected. Most recently, this range of sensitivity has been extended to the attomole (10^{-18} mole) range.

SOME COMMON USES OF AMINO ACIDS

The industrial production of amino acids is an important worldwide business. The first report of the commercial production of an amino acid was in 1908. It was then that the flavouring agent monosodium glutamate (MSG) was prepared from a type of large seaweed. This led to the commercial production of MSG, which is now produced using a bacterial fermentation process with starch and molasses as carbon sources. Glycine, cysteine, and D, L-alanine are also used as food additives, and mixtures of amino acids serve as flavour enhancers in the food industry. The amino acid balance of soy or corn protein for animal feed is significantly enhanced upon the addition of the nutritionally limiting amino acids methionine and lysine.

Amino acids are used therapeutically for nutritional and pharmaceutical purposes. For example, patients are often infused with amino acids to supply these nutrients before and after surgical procedures. Treatments with single amino acids are part of the medical approach to control certain disease states. Examples include L-dihydroxyphenylalanine (L-dopa) for Parkinson disease; glutamine and histidine to treat peptic ulcers; and arginine, citrulline, and ornithine to treat liver diseases.

Certain derivations of amino acids, especially of glutamate, are used as surface-active agents in mild soaps and shampoos. D-phenylglycine and D-hydroxyphenylglycine are intermediates used for the chemical synthesis of β-lactam antibiotics (e.g., synthetic versions of penicillin). Aspartame is a sweetener prepared from the individual component amino acids aspartic acid and phenylalanine.

AMINO ACIDS AND THE ORIGIN OF LIFE ON EARTH

The question of why organisms on Earth consist of L-amino acids instead of D-amino acids is still an unresolved riddle. Some scientists have long suggested that a substantial fraction of the organic compounds that were the precursors to amino acids—and perhaps some amino acids themselves—on the early Earth may have been derived from comet and meteorite impacts. One such organic-rich meteorite impact occurred on Sept.

Murchison Meteorite

The Murchison meteorite fell as a shower of stones in Victoria, Australia, in 1969. More than 100 kg (220 pounds) of the meteorite were collected and distributed to museums all over the world. The Murchison meteorite is classified as a carbonaceous chondrite. It was pervasively altered by water, probably when it was part of its parent asteroid, and it consists mostly of hydrated clay minerals. Because of the availability of samples and its freedom from contamination with terrestrial material, the meteorite has been widely studied for the organic matter that it contains. Amino acids, alcohols, aldehydes, ketones, amines, kerogens, and other organic compounds have been detected and analyzed. The molecular structures of these organic compounds preclude their origin in biological life on Earth. Their unusual hydrogen isotopic compositions suggest that the compounds originally formed in interstellar space, although they have been modified in the early solar nebula and in asteroids.

28, 1969, over Murchison, Victoria, in Australia. This meteorite is suspected to be of cometary origin due to its high water content of 12 percent. More than 92 different amino acids have been identified within the Murchison meteorite. Nineteen of these are found on Earth. The remaining amino acids have no apparent terrestrial source. Most intriguing are the reports that amino acids in the Murchison meteorite exhibit an excess of L-amino acids. An extraterrestrial source for an L-amino acid excess in the solar system could predate the origin of life on Earth and thus explain the presence of a similar excess of L-amino acids on the prelife Earth.

CHAPTER 3

P roteins are highly complex substances that are present in all living organisms. They are of great nutritional value and are directly involved in the chemical processes essential for life. The importance of proteins was recognized by the chemists in the early 19th century who coined the name for these substances from the Greek *proteios*, meaning "holding first place." Proteins are species-specific. In other words, the proteins of one species differ from those of another species. They are also organ-specific. For instance, within a single organism, muscle proteins differ from those of the brain and liver.

A protein molecule is very large compared to molecules of sugar or salt and consists of many amino acids joined together to form long chains, much as beads are arranged on a string. There are about 20 different amino acids that occur naturally in proteins. Proteins of similar function have similar amino acid composition and sequence. Although it is not yet possible to explain all of the functions of a protein from its amino acid sequence, established correlations between structure and function can be attributed to the properties of the amino acids that compose proteins.

Plants can synthesize all of the amino acids, whereas animals cannot, even though all of them are essential for life. Plants can grow in a medium containing inorganic nutrients that provide nitrogen, potassium, and other substances essential for growth. They utilize the carbon dioxide in the air during the process of photosynthesis to form organic compounds such as carbohydrates. Animals, however, must obtain organic nutrients from outside sources. Because the protein content of most plants is low, very large amounts of plant material are required by animals, such as ruminants (e.g., cows), that eat only plant material to meet their amino acid requirements.

Ruminants, such as this dairy cow near St. Moritz, Switz., rely on vegetative foods like grass to meet their daily protein needs. Sean Gallup/Getty Images

Nonruminant animals, including humans, obtain proteins principally from animals and their products—e.g., meat, milk, and eggs. The seeds of legumes are increasingly being used to prepare inexpensive protein-rich food.

The protein content of animal organs is usually much higher than that of the blood plasma. Muscles, for example, contain about 30 percent protein, the liver 20 to 30 percent, and red blood cells 30 percent. Higher percentages of protein are found in hair, bones, and other organs and tissues with a low water content. The quantity of free amino acids and peptides in animals is much smaller than the amount of protein. Evidently, protein molecules are produced in cells by the stepwise alignment of amino acids and are released into the body fluids only after synthesis is complete.

The high protein content of some organs does not mean that the importance of proteins is related to their amount in an organism or tissue. On the contrary, some of the most important proteins, such as enzymes and hormones, occur in extremely small amounts. The importance of proteins is related principally to their function. All enzymes identified thus far are proteins. Enzymes, which are the catalysts of all metabolic reactions, enable an organism to build up the chemical substances necessary for life—proteins, nucleic acids, carbohydrates, and lipids—to convert them into other substances, and to degrade them. Life without enzymes is not possible.

Several protein hormones fulfill important regulatory functions. For example, in all vertebrates, the respiratory protein hemoglobin acts as oxygen carrier in the blood, transporting oxygen from the lung to body organs and tissues. Likewise, a large group of structural proteins maintains and protects the structure of the animal body.

LEVELS OF STRUCTURAL ORGANIZATION IN PROTEINS

Analytical and synthetic procedures reveal only the primary structure of the proteins—that is, the amino acid sequence of the peptide chains. They do not reveal information about the conformation (arrangement in space) of the peptide chain—whether the peptide chain is present as a long straight thread or is irregularly coiled and folded into a globule. The configuration, or conformation, of a protein is determined by mutual attraction or repulsion of polar or nonpolar groups in the side chains (R groups) of the amino acids. The former have positive or negative charges in their side chains, whereas the latter repel water but attract each other. Some parts of a peptide chain containing 100 to 200 amino acids may form a loop, or helix, whereas others may be straight or form irregular coils.

PRIMARY STRUCTURE

The terms *secondary*, *tertiary*, and *quaternary structure* are frequently applied to the configuration of the peptide chain of a protein. A nomenclature committee of the International Union of Biochemistry (IUB) has defined these terms as follows: The primary structure of a protein is determined by its amino acid sequence without any regard for the arrangement of the peptide chain in space. The secondary structure is determined by the spatial arrangement of the main peptide chain without any regard for the conformation of side chains or other segments of the main chain. The tertiary structure is determined by both the side chains and other adjacent segments of the main chain, without regard for neighbouring peptide chains. Finally, the term *quaternary structure* is used for the arrangement of identical or different subunits of a large protein in which each subunit is a separate peptide chain.

SECONDARY STRUCTURE

The nitrogen and carbon atoms of a peptide chain cannot lie on a straight line because of the magnitude of the bond angles between adjacent atoms of the chain; the bond angle is about 110°. Each of the nitrogen and carbon atoms can rotate to a certain extent, however, so that the chain has a limited flexibility. Because all of the amino acids, except glycine, are asymmetric L-amino acids, the peptide chain tends to assume an asymmetric helical shape. Some of the fibrous proteins consist of elongated helices around a straight screw axis. Such structural features result from properties common to all peptide chains. The product of their effects is the secondary structure of the protein.

TERTIARY STRUCTURE

The tertiary structure is the product of the interaction between the side chains (R) of the amino acids composing the protein. Some of them contain positively or negatively charged groups, others are polar, and still others are nonpolar. The number of carbon atoms in the side chain varies from zero in glycine to nine in tryptophan. Positively and negatively charged side chains have the tendency to attract each other, whereas side chains with identical charges repel each other. The bonds formed by the forces between the negatively charged side chains of aspartic or glutamic acid on the one hand, and the positively charged side chains of lysine or arginine on the other hand, are called salt bridges. Mutual attraction of adjacent peptide chains also results from the formation of numerous hydrogen bonds. Hydrogen bonds form as a result of the attraction between the nitrogen-bound hydrogen atom (the imide hydrogen) and the unshared pair of electrons of the oxygen atom in the double bonded carbon–oxygen group (the carbonyl group). The result is a slight displacement of the imide hydrogen toward the oxygen atom of the carbonyl group. Although the hydrogen bond is much weaker than a covalent bond (i.e., the type of bond between two atoms, which share the pair of bonding electrons between them), the large number of imide and carbonyl groups in peptide chains results in the formation of numerous hydrogen bonds. Another type of attraction is that between nonpolar side chains of valine, leucine, isoleucine, and phenylalanine. This attraction results in the displacement of water molecules and is called hydrophobic interaction.

In proteins rich in cystine, the conformation of the peptide chain is determined to a considerable extent by the disulfide bonds (-S-S-) of cystine. The halves of cystine may be located in different parts of the peptide chain and thus may form a loop closed by the disulfide bond. If the disulfide bond is reduced (i.e., hydrogen is added) to two sulfhydryl (-SH) groups, the tertiary structure of the protein undergoes a drastic change—closed loops are broken and adjacent disulfide-bonded peptide chains separate.

QUATERNARY STRUCTURE

The nature of the quaternary structure is demonstrated by the structure of hemoglobin. Each molecule of human hemoglobin consists of four peptide chains, two α-chains and two β-chains (i.e., it is a tetramer). The four subunits are linked to each other by hydrogen bonds and hydrophobic interaction. Because the four subunits are so closely linked, the hemoglobin tetramer is called a molecule, even though no covalent bonds occur between the peptide chains of the four subunits. In other proteins, the subunits are bound to each other by covalent bonds (disulfide bridges).

THE ISOLATION AND DETERMINATION OF PROTEINS

Animal material usually contains large amounts of protein and lipids and small amounts of carbohydrate. In plants, the bulk of the dry matter is usually carbohydrate. No general method exists for the isolation of proteins from organs or tissues. If it is necessary to determine the amount of protein in a mixture of animal foodstuffs, a sample is converted to ammonium salts by boiling with sulfuric acid and a suitable inorganic catalyst, such as copper sulfate (Kjeldahl method). The method is based on the assumption that proteins contain 16 percent nitrogen, and that nonprotein nitrogen is present in very small amounts. The assumption is justified for most tissues from higher animals but not for insects and crustaceans, in which a considerable portion of the body nitrogen is present in the form of chitin, a carbohydrate. Large amounts of nonprotein nitrogen are also found in the sap of many plants. In such cases, the precise quantitative analyses are made after the proteins have been separated from other biological compounds.

Proteins are sensitive to heat, acids, bases, organic solvents, and radiation exposure. For this reason, the chemical methods employed to purify organic compounds cannot be applied to proteins. Salts and molecules of small size are removed from protein solutions by dialysis. Dialysis entails placing the solution into a sac of semipermeable material, such as cellulose or acetylcellulose, which will allow small molecules to pass through but not large protein molecules, and immersing the sac in water or a salt solution. Small molecules can also be removed either by passing the protein solution through a column of resin that adsorbs only the protein or by gel filtration. In gel filtration, the large protein molecules pass through the column, and the small molecules are adsorbed to the gel.

Groups of proteins are separated from each other by salting out—the stepwise addition of sodium sulfate or ammonium sulfate to a protein solution. Some proteins, called globulins, become insoluble and precipitate when the solution is half-saturated with ammonium sulfate or when its sodium sulfate content exceeds about 12 percent. Other proteins, the albumins, can be precipitated from the supernatant solution (i.e., the solution remaining after a precipitation has taken place) by saturation with ammonium sulfate. Water-soluble proteins can be obtained in a dry state by freeze-drying (lyophilization), in which the protein solution is deep-frozen by lowering the temperature below -15 °C (5 °F) and removing the water. The protein is obtained as a dry powder.

Most proteins are insoluble in boiling water and are denatured by it—that is, irreversibly converted into an insoluble material. Heat denaturation cannot be used with connective tissue because the principal structural protein, collagen, is converted by boiling water into water-soluble gelatin.

Fractionation (separation into components) of a mixture of proteins of different molecular weight can be accomplished by gel filtration. The size of the proteins retained by the gel depends upon the properties of the gel. The proteins retained in the gel are removed from the column by solutions of a suitable concentration of salts and hydrogen ions.

Many proteins were originally obtained in crystalline form, but crystallinity is not proof of purity, since many crystalline protein preparations contain other substances. Various tests are used to determine whether a protein preparation contains only one protein. The purity of a protein solution can be determined by such techniques as chromatography and gel filtration. In addition, a solution of pure protein will yield one peak when spun in a centrifuge at very high speeds (ultracentrifugation) and will migrate as a single band in electrophoresis (migration of the protein in an electrical field). After these methods and others (such as amino acid analysis) indicate that the protein solution is pure, it can be considered so. Because chromatography, ultracentrifugation, and electrophoresis cannot be applied to insoluble proteins, little is known about them. They may be mixtures of many similar proteins.

Very small (microheterogeneous) differences in some of the apparently pure proteins are known to occur. They are differences in the amino acid composition of otherwise identical proteins and are transmitted from generation to generation, meaning that they are genetically determined. For example, some humans have two hemoglobins, hemoglobin A and hemoglobin S, which differ in one amino acid at a specific site in the molecule. In hemoglobin A the site is occupied by glutamic acid, and in hemoglobin S by valine. Refinement of the techniques of protein analysis has resulted in the discovery of other instances of "microheterogeneity."

The quantity of a pure protein can be determined by weighing or by measuring the ultraviolet absorbancy at 280 nm. The absorbency at 280 nm depends on the content of tyrosine and tryptophan in the protein. Sometimes the slightly less sensitive biuret reaction, a purple colour given by alkaline protein solutions upon the addition of copper sulfate, is used. Its intensity depends only on the number of peptide bonds per gram, which is similar in all proteins.

PHYSICOCHEMICAL PROPERTIES OF PROTEINS

The physical and chemical properties of a protein are determined by the analogous properties of the amino acids in it. Among the most important physicochemical properties of proteins are molecular weight, shape, and water content. In addition, the characteristics of the charged groups within a protein molecule influence its electrical behaviour, which in turn influences its physical and chemical behaviour. Because proteins are macromolecular polypeptides—very large molecules composed of many peptide-bonded amino acids—their physicochemical properties can be extraordinarily complex.

THE MOLECULAR WEIGHT OF PROTEINS

Many proteins contain more than 100 amino acids linked to each other in a long peptide chain. The average molecular weight (based on the weight of a hydrogen atom as 1) of each amino acid is approximately 100 to 125. The weights of some of the most common proteins are usually in the range of 10,000 to 100,000 daltons (one dalton is the weight of one hydrogen atom).

The molecular weight of proteins cannot be determined by the methods of classical chemistry (e.g., freezing-point depression) because they require solutions of a higher concentration of protein than can be prepared. If a protein contains only one molecule of one of the amino acids or one atom of iron, copper, or another element, the minimum molecular weight of the protein or a subunit can be calculated. For example, the protein myoglobin contains 0.34 gram (0.01 oz) of iron in 100 grams (3.5 oz) of protein. The atomic weight of iron is 56. Thus, the minimum molecular weight of myoglobin is $(56 \times 100)/0.34$ = about 16,500 daltons. Direct measurements of the molecular weight of myoglobin yield the same value. The molecular weight of hemoglobin, however, which also contains 0.34 percent iron, has been found to be 66,000 or $4 \times 16,500$. Thus, hemoglobin contains four atoms of iron.

The method most frequently used to determine the molecular weight of proteins is ultracentrifugation (spinning in a centrifuge at velocities up to about 60,000 revolutions per minute). Centrifugal forces of more than 200,000 times the gravitational force on the surface of the Earth are achieved at such velocities. The first ultracentrifuges, built in 1920, were used to determine the molecular weight of proteins. The molecular weights of a large number of proteins have been determined. Most consist of several subunits, the molecular weight of which is usually less than 100,000 and frequently ranges from 20,000 to 30,000. Proteins of very high molecular weights are found among hemocyanins, the copper-containing respiratory proteins of invertebrates. Some proteins range as high as several million daltons. Although there is no definite lower limit for the molecular weight of proteins, short amino acid sequences are usually called peptides.

THE SHAPE OF PROTEIN MOLECULES

In the technique of X-ray diffraction the X rays are allowed to strike a protein crystal. The X rays, diffracted (bent) by the crystal, impinge on a photographic plate, forming a pattern of spots. This method reveals that peptide chains can assume very complicated, apparently irregular shapes. Two extremes in shape include the closely folded structure of the globular proteins and the elongated, unidimensional structure of the thread-like fibrous proteins. Both were recognized many years before the technique of X-ray diffraction was developed. Solutions of fibrous proteins are extremely viscous (i.e., sticky), whereas those of the globular proteins have low viscosity (i.e., they flow easily). A 5 percent solution of a globular protein—ovalbumin, for example—easily flows through a narrow glass tube. In contrast, a 5 percent solution of gelatin, a fibrous protein, does not flow

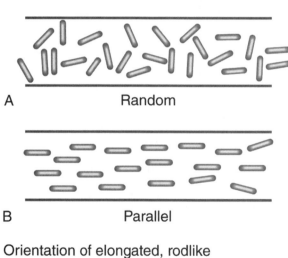

A   Random

B   Parallel

Orientation of elongated, rodlike maromolecules (A) in resting solution, or (B) during flow through a horizontal tube.

Flow birefringence. Copyright Encyclopædia Britannica; rendering for this edition by Rosen Educational Services

through the tube because it is liquid only at high temperatures and solidifies at room temperature. Even solutions containing only 1 or 2 percent of gelatin are highly viscous and flow through a narrow tube either very slowly or only under pressure. The elongated peptide chains of the fibrous proteins can be imagined to become entangled not only mechanically but also by mutual attraction of their side chains. In this way they incorporate large amounts of water. Most of the hydrophilic (water-attracting) groups of the globular proteins, however, lie on the surface of the molecules. As a result, globular proteins incorporate only a few water molecules. If a solution of a fibrous protein flows through a narrow tube, the elongated molecules become oriented parallel to the direction of the flow, and the solution thus becomes birefringent like a crystal (it splits a light ray into two components that travel at different velocities and are polarized at right angles to each other). Globular proteins do not show this phenomenon, which is called flow birefringence. Solutions of myosin, the contractile protein of muscles, show very high flow birefringence. Other proteins with very high flow birefringence include solutions of fibrinogen, the clotting material of blood plasma, and solutions of tobacco mosaic virus. The gamma-globulins of the blood plasma show low flow birefringence, and none can be observed in solutions of serum albumin and ovalbumin.

HYDRATION OF PROTEINS

When dry proteins are exposed to air of high water content, they rapidly bind water up to a maximum quantity, which differs for different proteins. In general, water content makes up 10 to 20 percent of the weight of the protein. The hydrophilic groups of a protein are chiefly the positively charged groups in the side chains of lysine and arginine, and the negatively charged groups of aspartic and glutamic acid. Hydration (i.e., the binding of water) may also occur at the hydroxyl (-OH) groups of serine and threonine or at the amide (-CONH$_2$) groups of asparagine and glutamine.

The binding of water molecules to either charged or polar (partly charged) groups is explained by the dipolar structure of the water molecule, in which the two positively charged hydrogen atoms form an angle of about 105°, with the negatively charged oxygen atom at the apex. The centre of the positive charges is located between the two hydrogen atoms, while the centre of the negative charge of the oxygen atom is at the apex of the angle. The negative pole of the dipolar water molecule binds to positively charged groups, and the positive pole binds negatively charged ones. The negative pole of the water molecule also binds to the hydroxyl and amino groups of the protein.

The water of hydration is essential to the structure of protein crystals. When they are completely dehydrated, the crystalline structure disintegrates. In some proteins this process is accompanied by denaturation and loss of the biological function.

In aqueous solutions, proteins bind some of the water molecules very firmly, whereas others are either very loosely bound or form islands of water molecules between loops of folded peptide chains. Because the water molecules in such an island are thought to be oriented as in ice, which is crystalline water, the islands of water in proteins are called icebergs. Water molecules may also form bridges between the carbonyl groups of adjacent peptide chains, resulting in structures similar to those of the pleated sheet but with a water molecule in the position of the hydrogen bonds of that configuration. The extent of hydration of protein molecules in aqueous solutions is important, because some of the methods used to determine the molecular weight of proteins yield the molecular weight of the hydrated protein. The amount of water bound to 1 gram of a globular protein in solution varies from 0.2 to 0.5 gram. Much larger amounts of water are mechanically immobilized between the elongated peptide chains of fibrous proteins. For example, 1 gram of gelatin can immobilize at room temperature 25 to 30 grams of water.

Hydration of proteins is necessary for their solubility in water. If the water of hydration of a protein dissolved in water is reduced by the addition of a salt such as ammonium sulfate, the protein is no longer soluble and is salted out, or precipitated. The salting-out process is reversible because the protein is not denatured (i.e., irreversibly converted to an insoluble material) by the addition of salts such as sodium chloride, sodium sulfate, or ammonium sulfate. Some globulins, called euglobulins, are insoluble in water in the absence of salts. Their insolubility is attributed to the mutual interaction of polar groups on the surface of adjacent molecules, a process that results in the formation of large aggregates of molecules. Addition of small amounts of salt causes the euglobulins to become soluble. This process, called salting in, results from a combination between anions (negatively charged ions) and cations (positively charged ions) of the salt and positively and negatively charged side chains of the euglobulins. The combination prevents the aggregation of euglobulin molecules by preventing the formation of salt bridges between them. The addition of more sodium or ammonium sulfate causes the euglobulins to salt out again and to precipitate.

ELECTROCHEMISTRY OF PROTEINS

Because the α-amino group and α-carboxyl group of amino acids are converted into peptide bonds in the protein molecule, there is only one α-amino group (at the N terminus) and one α-carboxyl group (at the C terminus) in a given protein molecule. The electrochemical character of a protein is affected very little by these two groups. Of importance, however, are the numerous positively charged ammonium groups ($-NH_3^+$) of lysine and arginine, and the negatively charged carboxyl groups ($-COO^-$) of aspartic acid and glutamic acid. In most proteins, the number of positively and negatively charged groups varies from 10 to 20 per 100 amino acids.

ELECTROMETRIC TITRATION

When measured volumes of hydrochloric acid are added to a solution of protein in salt-free water, the pH decreases in proportion to the amount of hydrogen ions added until it is about 4. Further addition of acid causes much less decrease in pH because the protein acts as a buffer at pH values of 3 to 4. The reaction that takes place in this pH range is the protonation of the carboxyl group—that is, the conversion of $-COO^-$ into $-COOH$. Electrometric titration of an isoelectric protein with potassium hydroxide causes a very slow increase in pH and a weak buffering action of the protein at pH 7. In contrast, a very strong buffering action occurs in the pH range from 9 to 10. The buffering action at pH 7, which is caused by loss of protons (positively charged hydrogen) from the imidazolium groups (i.e., the five-member ring structure in the side chain) of histidine, is weak because the histidine content of proteins is usually low. The much stronger buffering action at pH values from 9 to 10 is caused by the loss of

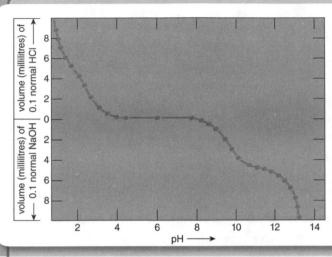

Addition of measured quantities of known-concentration hydrochloric acid (HCl) to glycine is shown in the upper half of the diagram; sodium hydroxide (NaOH) in the lower half. The dots indicate the experimental results. The addition of a trace of acid or base to pure glycine, the isoelectric point of which is close to pH 6.1, causes a strong change in pH. Glycine acts as a buffer, however, in the acidic pH range below 3 and in the alkaline pH range above 8.

Electrometric titration of glycine. Copyright Encyclopædia Britannica; rendering for this edition by Rosen Educational Services

protons from the hydroxyl group of tyrosine and from the ammonium groups of lysine. Finally, protons are lost from the guanidinium groups (i.e., the nitrogen-containing terminal portion of the arginine side chains) of arginine at pH 12. Electrometric titration makes possible the determination of the approximate number of carboxyl groups, ammonium groups, histidines, and tyrosines per molecule of protein.

ELECTROPHORESIS

The positively and negatively charged side chains of proteins cause them to behave like amino acids in an electrical field—that is, they migrate during electrophoresis at low pH values to the cathode (negative terminal) and at high pH values to the anode (positive terminal). The isoelectric point, the pH value at which the protein molecule does not migrate, is in the range of pH 5 to 7 for many proteins. Proteins such as lysozyme, cytochrome *c*, histone, and others rich in lysine and arginine, however, have isoelectric points in the pH range between 8 and 10. The isoelectric point of pepsin, which contains very few basic amino acids, is close to 1.

Free-boundary electrophoresis, the original method of determining electrophoretic migration, has been replaced in many instances by zone electrophoresis, in which the protein is placed in either a gel of starch, agar, or polyacrylamide, or in a porous medium such as paper or cellulose acetate. The migration of hemoglobin and other coloured proteins can be followed visually. Colourless proteins are made visible after the completion of electrophoresis by staining them with a suitable dye.

CONFORMATION OF GLOBULAR PROTEINS

Proteins may be composed of twisted chains of amino acids or of amino acid sheets. In globular proteins, the folding of amino acid chains and the various other arrangements they adopt are meant to place polar groups at the protein surface, thereby increasing the molecule's water solubility. The overall result of the folding process also gives rise to the protein's generally spherical, or globelike, shape.

The sheets and chains of amino acids within proteins are held in their folded positions by complex intermolecular and intramolecular forces. Elucidating the conformation of and the molecular interactions within proteins forms a large area of chemical and biochemical research. Several techniques have been developed to determine protein structure, among the most powerful of which is X-ray diffraction.

X-RAY DIFFRACTION AND STRUCTURE DETERMINATION

Most knowledge concerning secondary and tertiary structure of globular proteins has been obtained by the examination of their crystals using X-ray diffraction. In this technique X rays are allowed to strike the crystal.

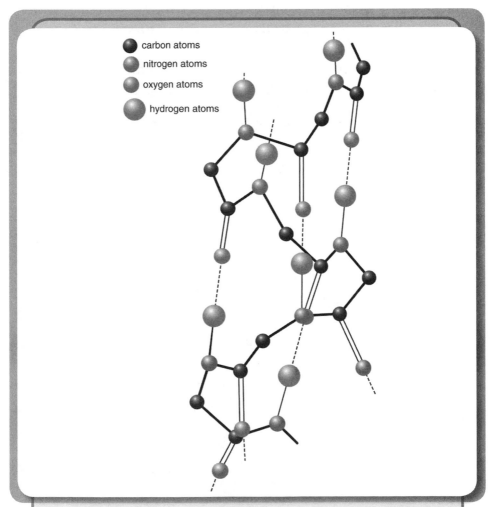

carbon atoms
nitrogen atoms
oxygen atoms
hydrogen atoms

The α-helix. Copyright Encyclopædia Britannica; rendering for this edition by Rosen Educational Services

The X rays are diffracted by the crystal and impinge on a photographic plate, forming a pattern of spots. The measured intensity of the diffraction pattern, as recorded on a photographic film, depends particularly on the electron density of the atoms in the protein crystal. This density is lowest in hydrogen atoms, and they do not give a visible diffraction pattern. Although carbon, oxygen, and nitrogen atoms yield visible diffraction patterns, they are present in such great number—about 700 or 800 per 100 amino acids—that the resolution of the structure of a protein containing more than 100 amino acids is almost impossible. Resolution is considerably improved

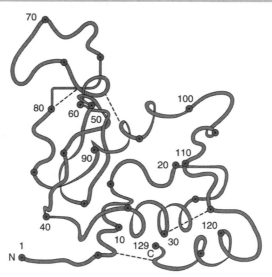

The simplified structure of lysozyme from hen's egg white has a single peptide chain of 129 amino acids. The amino acid residues are numbered from the terminal Q amino group (N) to the terminal carboxyl group (C). Circles indicate every fifth residue; every tenth residue is numbered. Broken lines indicate the four disulfide bridges. alpha-helices are visible in the ranges 25 to 35, 90 to 100, and 120 to 125.

Conformation of lysozyme. Copyright Encyclopædia Britannica; rendering for this edition by Rosen Educational Services

by substituting into the side chains of certain amino acids very heavy atoms, particularly those of heavy metals. Mercury ions, for example, bind to the sulfhydryl (-SH) groups of cysteine. Platinum chloride has been used in other proteins. In the iron-containing proteins, the iron atom already in the molecule is adequate.

Although the X-ray diffraction technique cannot resolve the complete three-dimensional conformation (the secondary and tertiary structure of the peptide chain), complete resolution has been obtained by combination of the results of X-ray diffraction with those of amino acid sequence analysis. In this way the complete conformation of such proteins as myoglobin, chymotrypsinogen, lysozyme, and ribonuclease has been resolved.

Max Ferdinand Perutz

(b. May 19, 1914, Vienna, Austria—d. Feb. 6, 2002, Cambridge, Cambridgeshire, England)

Austrian-born British biochemist Max Ferdinand Perutz was known for his X-ray diffraction analysis of the structure of hemoglobin, the protein that transports oxygen from the lungs to the tissues via blood cells. He shared the 1962 Nobel Prize for Chemistry with British biochemist John Cowdery Kendrew.

Perutz was educated at the University of Vienna and at the University of Cambridge, where he received a Ph.D. in 1940. While at Cambridge he began research at the Cavendish Laboratory (1937), taking the first X-ray diffraction pictures of hemoglobin crystals and working with the most powerful tool for examining the structure of hemoglobin—X-ray crystallography.

In 1947, along with Kendrew, Perutz founded the Medical Research Council Unit for Molecular Biology at Cambridge. There the two men continued their investigation of hemoproteins, with

Kendrew trying to determine the molecular structure of myoglobin (muscular hemoglobin) and Perutz concentrating on the hemoglobin molecule itself. By 1959 Perutz had shown that the hemoglobin molecule is composed of four separate polypeptide chains that form a tetrameric structure, with four heme groups near the molecule's surface. Perutz subsequently showed that in oxygenated hemoglobin the four chains are rearranged, a discovery that led to the full determination of the molecular mechanism of oxygen transport and release by hemoglobin. Perutz was director of the Unit for Molecular Biology from its inception until 1962. From 1962 until his retirement in 1979, he was chairman of the Medical Research Council molecular biology laboratory (at the School of Clinical Medicine, Cambridge).

Perutz also investigated the flow of glaciers, making a crystallographic study of the transformation of snow into glacial ice (1938). Measuring for the first time the velocity distribution of a glacier, he proved that the fastest flow occurs at the surface and the slowest near the bed of the glacier. Perutz wrote several books, including the essay collections *Is Science Necessary?* (1989) and *I Wish I'd Made You Angry Earlier* (1998). He was appointed a Commander of the British Empire in 1963 and received the Order of Merit in 1989.

The X-ray diffraction method has revealed regular structural arrangements in proteins. One is an extended form of antiparallel peptide chains that are linked to each other by hydrogen bonds between the carbonyl groups. This conformation, called the pleated sheet, or β-structure, is found in some fibrous proteins. Short strands of the β-structure have also been detected in some globular proteins.

A second important structural arrangement is the α-helix. This conformation is formed by a sequence of amino acids wound around a straight axis in either a right-handed or a left-handed spiral. Each turn of the helix corresponds to a distance of 5.4 angstroms (=0.54 nm) in the direction of the screw axis and contains 3.7 amino acids. Hence, the length of the α-helix per amino acid residue is 5.4 divided by 3.7, or 1.5 angstroms (1 angstrom = 0.1 nm). The stability of the α-helix is maintained by hydrogen bonds between the carbonyl and imino groups of neighbouring turns of the helix. It was once thought, based on data from analyses of the myoglobin molecule, more than half of which consists of α-helices, that the α-helix is the predominant structural element of the globular proteins. It is now known, however, that myoglobin

Sir John Cowdery Kendrew

(b. March 24, 1917, Oxford, Oxfordshire, Eng.—d. Aug. 23, 1997, Cambridge, Cambridgeshire)

British biochemist Sir John Cowdery Kendrew determined the three-dimensional structure of the muscle protein myoglobin, which stores oxygen in muscle cells. For his achievement he shared the Nobel Prize for Chemistry with Max Ferdinand Perutz in 1962.

Kendrew was educated at Trinity College, Cambridge, receiving his Ph.D. there in 1949. In 1946–47 he and Perutz founded the Medical Research Council Unit for Molecular Biology at Cambridge. They used the technique of X-ray crystallography to study the structures of proteins, with Perutz studying hemoglobin and Kendrew trying to determine the structure of the somewhat simpler molecule of myoglobin. By 1960, with the use of special diffraction techniques and the help of computers to analyze the X-ray data, Kendrew was able to devise a three-dimensional model of the arrangement of the amino acid units in the myoglobin molecule, which was the first time this had been accomplished for any protein.

A fellow of Peterhouse College, Cambridge, from 1947 to 1975, Kendrew was also deputy chairman of the Medical Research Council Unit and, from 1971, chairman of the Defence Scientific Advisory Council. He was knighted in 1974 and became president of St. John's College, Oxford, in 1981.

is exceptional in this respect. The other globular proteins for which the structures have been resolved by X-ray diffraction contain only small regions of α-helix. In most of them the peptide chains are folded in an apparently random fashion, for which the term random coil has been used. The term is misleading, however, because the folding is not random. Rather, it is dictated by the primary structure and modified by the secondary and tertiary structures.

The first proteins for which the internal structures were completely resolved are the iron-containing proteins myoglobin and hemoglobin. The investigation of the hydrated crystals of these proteins at Cambridge by Max Ferdinand Perutz and John Cowdery Kendrew, who won a Nobel Prize for their work, revealed that the folding of the peptide chains is so tight that most of the water is displaced from the centre of the globular molecules. The amino acids that carry the ammonium ($-NH_3^+$) and carboxyl ($-COO^-$) groups were found to be shifted to the surface of the globular molecules, and the nonpolar amino acids were found to be concentrated in the interior.

OTHER APPROACHES TO THE DETERMINATION OF PROTEIN STRUCTURE

None of the several other physical methods that have been used to obtain information on the secondary and tertiary structure of proteins provides as much direct information as the X-ray diffraction technique. Most of the techniques, however, are much more simple than X-ray diffraction, which requires, for the resolution of the structure of one protein, many years of work and equipment such as electronic computers. Some of the simpler techniques are based on the optical properties of proteins—refractivity, absorption of light of different wavelengths, rotation of the plane polarized light at different wavelengths, and luminescence.

SPECTROPHOTOMETRIC BEHAVIOUR

Spectrophotometry of protein solutions (the measurement of the degree of absorbance of light by a protein within a specified wavelength) is useful within the range of visible light only with proteins that contain coloured prosthetic groups (the nonprotein components). Examples of such proteins include the red heme proteins of the blood, the purple pigments of the retina of the eye, green and yellow proteins that contain bile pigments, blue copper-containing proteins, and dark brown proteins called melanins. Peptide bonds, because of their carbonyl groups, absorb light energy at very short wavelengths (185–200 nanometres). The aromatic rings of phenylalanine, tyrosine, and tryptophan, however, absorb ultraviolet light between wavelengths of 280 and 290 nanometres. The absorbance of ultraviolet light by tryptophan is greatest, that of tyrosine is less, and that of phenylalanine is least. If the tyrosine or tryptophan content of the protein is known, therefore, the concentration of the protein solution can be determined by measuring its absorbance between 280 and 290 nanometres.

OPTICAL ACTIVITY

Amino acids, with the exception of glycine, exhibit optical activity (rotation of the plane of polarized light). It is not surprising, therefore, that proteins also are optically active. They are usually levorotatory (i.e., they rotate the plane of polarization to the left) when polarized light of wavelengths in the visible range is used. Although the specific rotation (a function of the concentration of a protein solution and the distance the light travels in it) of most

L-amino acids varies from -30° to +30°, the amino acid cystine has a specific rotation of approximately -300°. Although the optical rotation of a protein depends on all of the amino acids of which it is composed, the most important ones are cystine and the aromatic amino acids phenylalanine, tyrosine, and tryptophan. The contribution of the other amino acids to the optical activity of a protein is negligibly small.

CHEMICAL REACTIVITY OF PROTEINS

Information on the internal structure of proteins can be obtained with chemical methods that reveal whether certain groups are present on the surface of the protein molecule and thus able to react or whether they are buried inside the closely folded peptide chains and thus are unable to react. The chemical reagents used in such investigations must be mild ones that do not affect the structure of the protein.

The reactivity of tyrosine is of special interest. It has been found, for example, that only three of the six tyrosines found in the naturally occurring enzyme ribonuclease can be iodinated (i.e., reacted to accept an iodine atom). Enzyme-catalyzed breakdown of iodinated ribonuclease is used to identify the peptides in which the iodinated tyrosines are present. The three tyrosines that can be iodinated lie on the surface of ribonuclease. The others, assumed to be inaccessible, are said to be buried in the molecule. Tyrosine can also be identified by using other techniques, such as by treatment with diazonium compounds or tetranitromethane. Because the compounds formed are coloured, they can easily be detected when the protein is broken down with enzymes.

Cysteine can be detected by coupling with compounds such as iodoacetic acid or iodoacetamide. These reactions result in the formation of carboxymethylcysteine or carbamidomethylcysteine, which can be detected by amino acid determination of the peptides containing them. The imidazole groups of certain histidines can also be located by coupling with the same reagents under different conditions. Unfortunately, few other amino acids can be labelled without changes in the secondary and tertiary structure of the protein.

Association of Protein Subunits

Many proteins with molecular weights of more than 50,000 occur in aqueous solutions as complexes: dimers, tetramers, and higher polymers — that is, as chains of two, four, or more repeating basic structural units. The subunits, which are called monomers or protomers, usually are present as an even number. Less than 10 percent of the polymers have been found to have an odd number of monomers. The arrangement of the subunits is thought to be regular and may be cyclic, cubic, or tetrahedral. Some of the small proteins also contain subunits. Insulin, for example, with a molecular weight of about 6,000, consists of two peptide chains linked to each other by disulfide bridges (-S-S-). Similar interchain disulfide bonds have been found in the immunoglobulins. In other proteins, hydrogen bonds and hydrophobic bonds (resulting from the interaction between the amino acid side chains of valine, leucine, isoleucine, and phenylalanine) cause the formation of aggregates of the subunits. The subunits of some proteins are identical, whereas those of others differ. Hemoglobin is a tetramer consisting of two α-chains and two β-chains.

Protein Denaturation

When a solution of a protein is boiled, the protein frequently becomes insoluble — that is, it is denatured — and remains insoluble even when the solution is cooled. The denaturation of the proteins of egg white by heat—as when boiling an egg—is an example of irreversible denaturation. The denatured protein has the same primary structure as the original, or native, protein. However, the weak forces between charged groups and the weaker forces of mutual attraction of nonpolar groups are disrupted at elevated temperatures. As a result, the tertiary structure of the protein is lost. In some instances the original structure of the protein can be regenerated, a process is called renaturation.

Denaturation can be brought about in various ways. Proteins are denatured by treatment with alkaline or acid, oxidizing or reducing agents, and certain organic solvents. Interesting among denaturing agents are those that affect the secondary and tertiary structure without affecting the primary structure. The agents most frequently used for this purpose are urea and guanidinium chloride. These molecules, because of their high affinity for peptide bonds, break the hydrogen bonds and the salt bridges between positive and negative side chains, thereby abolishing the tertiary structure of the peptide chain. When denaturing agents are removed from a protein solution, the native protein re-forms in many cases. Denaturation can also be accomplished by reduction of the disulfide bonds of cystine—that is, conversion of the disulfide bond (-S-S-) to two sulfhydryl groups (-SH). This, of course, results in the formation of two cysteines. Reoxidation of the cysteines by exposure to air sometimes regenerates the native protein. In other cases, however, the wrong cysteines become bound to each other, resulting in a different protein. Finally, denaturation can also be accomplished by exposing proteins to organic solvents such as ethanol or acetone. It is believed that the organic solvents interfere with the mutual attraction of nonpolar groups.

Some of the smaller proteins, however, are extremely stable, even against heat. For example, solutions of ribonuclease can be exposed for short periods of time to temperatures of 90 °C (194 °F) without undergoing significant denaturation. Denaturation does not involve identical changes in protein molecules. A common property of denatured proteins, however, is the loss of biological activity—for example, the ability to act as enzymes or hormones.

Although denaturation had long been considered an all-or-none reaction, it is now thought that many intermediary states exist between native and denatured protein. In some instances, however, the breaking of a key bond could be followed by the complete breakdown of the conformation of the native protein.

Although many native proteins are resistant to the action of the enzyme trypsin, which breaks down proteins during digestion, they are hydrolyzed by the same enzyme after denaturation. Evidently, the peptide bonds that can be split by trypsin are inaccessible in the native proteins but become accessible during denaturation. Similarly, denatured proteins give more intense colour reactions for tyrosine, histidine, and arginine than do the same proteins in the native state. The increased accessibility of reactive groups of denatured proteins is attributed to an unfolding of the peptide chains.

If denaturation can be brought about easily and if renaturation is difficult, how is the native conformation of globular proteins maintained in living organisms, in which they are produced stepwise, by incorporation of one amino acid at a time? Experiments on the biosynthesis of proteins from amino acids containing radioactive carbon or heavy hydrogen reveal that the protein molecule grows stepwise from the N terminus to the C terminus. In each step a single amino acid residue is incorporated. As soon as the growing peptide chain contains six or seven amino acid residues, the side chains interact with each other and thus cause deviations from the straight or β-chain configuration. Depending on the nature of the side chains, this may result in the formation of an α-helix or of loops closed by hydrogen bonds or disulfide bridges. The final conformation is probably frozen when the peptide chain attains a length of 50 or more amino acid residues.

Conformation of Proteins in Interfaces

Like many other substances with both hydrophilic and hydrophobic groups, soluble proteins tend to migrate into the interface between air and water or oil and water (the term *oil* here means a hydrophobic liquid such as benzene or xylene). Within the interface, proteins spread, forming thin films. Measurements of the surface tension, or interfacial tension, of such films indicate that tension is reduced by the protein film. Proteins, when forming an interfacial film, are present as a monomolecular layer (a layer one molecule in height). Although it was once thought that globular protein molecules unfold completely in the interface, it has now been established that many proteins can be recovered from films in the native state. The application of lateral pressure on a protein film causes it to increase in thickness and finally to form a layer with a height corresponding to the diameter of the native protein molecule. Protein molecules in an interface, because of Brownian motions (molecular vibrations), occupy much more space than do those in the film after the application of pressure. The Brownian motion of compressed molecules is limited to the two dimensions of the interface, since the protein molecules cannot move upward or downward.

The motion of protein molecules at the air–water interface has been used to determine the molecular weight of proteins. The technique involves measuring the force exerted by the protein layer on a barrier. When a protein solution is vigorously shaken in air, it forms a foam, because the soluble proteins migrate into the air–water interface and persist there, preventing or slowing the reconversion of the foam into a homogeneous solution. Some of the unstable, easily modified proteins are denatured when spread in the air–water interface. The formation of a permanent foam when egg white is vigorously stirred is an example of irreversible denaturation by spreading in a surface.

CHAPTER 4

The identification of common physicochemical features among the many different types of proteins has enabled scientists to develop general systems for their classification. Historically, large groups of proteins were distinguished from one another on the basis of solubility in different chemical solvents. Today, scientists often distinguish between the many different types of proteins based on their biological activities. This approach is particularly valuable for recognizing and understanding the biological significance of proteins. However, it is complicated by the fact that some proteins are multifunctional and that the cellular functions of certain other proteins are unknown. As a result, many scientists also consider structural characteristics in protein classification, though this approach is made difficult due to the absence of structure information for many substances. Thus, the ongoing discovery and characterization of the different structures and functions of proteins is fundamental in forming a coherent system of protein classification.

CLASSIFICATION OF PROTEINS

After German chemists Emil Fischer and Franz Hofmeister independently stated in 1902 that proteins are essentially polypeptides consisting of many amino acids, an attempt was made to classify proteins according to their chemical and physical properties, because the biological function of proteins had not yet been established. (The protein character of enzymes was not proved until the 1920s.) Proteins were classified primarily according to their solubility in a number of solvents. This classification is no longer satisfactory, however, because proteins of quite different structure and function sometimes have similar solubilities. Conversely, proteins of the same function and similar structure sometimes have different solubilities. The terms associated with the old classification, however, are still widely used. They are defined below.

Albumins are proteins that are soluble in water and in water half-saturated with ammonium sulfate. On the other hand, globulins are salted out (i.e., precipitated) by half-saturation with ammonium sulfate. Globulins that are soluble in salt-free water are called pseudoglobulins, and those insoluble in salt-free water are euglobulins. Both prolamins and glutelins, which are plant proteins, are insoluble in water. Rather, the prolamins dissolve in 50 to 80 percent ethanol, and the glutelins in acidified or alkaline solution. The term *protamine* is used for a number of proteins in fish sperm that consist of approximately 80 percent arginine and therefore are strongly alkaline. Histones, which are less alkaline, apparently occur only in cell nuclei, where they are bound to nucleic acids. The term *scleroproteins* has been used for the insoluble proteins of animal organs. They include keratin, the insoluble protein of certain epithelial tissues such as the skin or hair, and collagen, the protein of the connective tissue. A large group of proteins has been called conjugated proteins, because they are complex molecules of protein consisting of protein and nonprotein moieties. The nonprotein portion is called the prosthetic group. Conjugated proteins can be subdivided into mucoproteins, which, in addition to protein, contain carbohydrate; lipoproteins, which contain lipids; phosphoproteins, which are rich in phosphate; chromoproteins, which contain pigments such as iron-porphyrins, carotenoids, bile pigments, and melanin; and finally, nucleoproteins, which contain nucleic acid.

The weakness of classification by solubility lies in the fact that many, if not all, globulins contain small amounts of carbohydrate. Thus, there is no sharp borderline between globulins and mucoproteins. Moreover, the phosphoproteins do not have a prosthetic group that can be isolated. They are merely proteins in which some of the hydroxyl groups of serine are phosphorylated (i.e., contain phosphate). Finally, the globulins include proteins with quite different roles—enzymes, antibodies, fibrous proteins, and contractile proteins.

In view of the unsatisfactory state of the old classification, it is preferable to classify the proteins according to their biological function. Such a classification is far from ideal, however, because one protein can have more than one function. The contractile protein myosin, for example, also acts as an ATPase (adenosine triphosphatase), an enzyme that hydrolyzes adenosine triphosphate (removes a phosphate group from ATP by introducing a water molecule). Another problem with functional classification is that the definite function of a protein frequently is not known. A protein cannot be called an enzyme as long as its substrate (the specific compound upon which it acts) is not known. It cannot even be tested for its enzymatic action when its substrate is not known.

SPECIAL STRUCTURE AND FUNCTION OF PROTEINS

Despite its weaknesses, a functional classification is used here in order to demonstrate, whenever possible, the correlation between the structure and function of a protein. The structural, fibrous proteins are presented first, because their structure is simpler than that of the globular proteins and more clearly related to their function, which is the maintenance of either a rigid or a flexible structure.

STRUCTURAL PROTEINS

Collagen is the structural protein of bones, tendons, ligaments, and skin. For many years collagen was considered to be insoluble in water. Part of the collagen of calf skin, however, can be extracted with citrate buffer at pH 3.7. A precursor of collagen called procollagen is converted in the body into collagen. Procollagen has a molecular weight of 120,000 daltons. Cleavage of one or a few peptide bonds of procollagen yields collagen, which has three subunits, each with a molecular weight of 95,000. Therefore, the molecular weight of collagen is 285,000 (3 × 95,000). The three subunits are wound as spirals around an elongated straight axis. The length of each subunit is 2,900 angstroms, and its diameter is approximately 15 angstroms. The three chains are staggered, so that the trimer has no definite terminal limits.

Collagen differs from all other proteins in its high content of proline and hydroxyproline. Hydroxyproline does not occur in significant amounts in any other protein except elastin. Most of the proline in collagen is present in the sequence glycine–proline-X, in which X is frequently alanine or hydroxyproline. Collagen does not contain cystine or tryptophan and therefore cannot substitute for other proteins in the diet. The presence of proline causes kinks in the peptide chain and thus reduces the length of the amino acid unit from 3.7 angstroms in the extended chain of the β-structure to 2.86 angstroms in the collagen chain. In the intertwined triple helix, the glycines are inside, close to the axis, and the prolines are outside.

Native collagen resists the action of trypsin but is hydrolyzed by the bacterial enzyme collagenase. When collagen is boiled with water, the triple helix is destroyed, and the subunits are partially hydrolyzed. The product

In Fez, Morocco, dyers tan and dye leather in large, round clay dye pits, as they have for centuries. Travel Ink/Gallo Images/Getty Images

of this process is gelatin. The unfolded peptide chains of gelatin trap large amounts of water, resulting in a hydrated molecule.

When collagen is treated with tannic acid or with chromium salts, cross-links form between the collagen fibres, and it becomes insoluble. The conversion of hide into leather is based on this tanning process. The tanned material is insoluble in hot water and cannot be converted to gelatin. On exposure to water at 62 to 63 °C (144 to 145 °F), however, the cross links formed by the tanning agents collapse, and the leather contracts irreversibly to about one-third its original volume.

Collagen seems to undergo an aging process in living organisms that may be caused by the formation of cross-links between collagen fibres. They are formed by the conversion of some lysine side chains to aldehydes (compounds with the general structure RCHO), and the combination of the aldehydes with the ε-amino groups of intact lysine side chains. The protein elastin, which occurs in the elastic fibres of connective tissue, contains similar cross-links and may result from the combination of collagen fibres with other proteins. When cross-linked collagen or elastin is degraded, products of the cross-linked lysine fragments, called desmosins and isodesmosins, are formed.

Keratin, the structural protein of epithelial cells in the outermost layers of the skin, has been isolated from hair, nails, hoofs, and feathers. Keratin is completely insoluble in cold or hot water. It is not attacked by proteolytic enzymes (i.e., enzymes that break apart, or lyse, protein molecules), and therefore it cannot replace proteins in the diet. The great stability of keratin results from the numerous disulfide bonds of cystine. The amino acid composition of keratin differs from that of collagen. Cystine may account for 24 percent of the total amino acids. The peptide chains of keratin are arranged in approximately equal amounts of antiparallel and parallel pleated sheets, in which the peptide chains are linked to each other by hydrogen bonds between the carbonyl groups.

Reduction of the disulfide bonds to sulfhydryl groups results in dissociation of the peptide chains, the molecular weight of which is 25,000 to 28,000 each. The formation of permanent waves in the beauty treatment of hair is based on partial reduction of the disulfide bonds of hair keratin by thioglycol, or some other mild reducing agent, and subsequent oxidation of the sulfhydryl groups (-SH) in the reoriented hair to disulfide bonds (-S-S-) by exposure to the oxygen of the air. The length of keratin fibres depends on their water content. They can bind approximately 16 percent of water. This hydration is accompanied by an increase in the length of the fibres of 10 to 12 percent.

The most thoroughly investigated keratin is hair keratin, particularly that of wool. It consists of a mixture of peptides with high and low cystine content. When wool is heated in water to about 90 °C (190 °F), it shrinks irreversibly. This is attributed to the breakage of hydrogen bonds and other noncovalent bonds. The disulfide bonds do not seem to be affected.

The most thoroughly investigated scleroprotein has been fibroin, the insoluble material of silk. The raw silk comprising the cocoon of the silkworm consists of two proteins. One, sericin, is soluble in hot water, whereas the other, fibroin, is not. The amino acid composition of the latter differs from that of all other proteins. It contains large amounts of glycine, alanine, tyrosine, and serine; small amounts of the other amino acids; and no sulfur-containing ones. The peptide chains are arranged in antiparallel β-structures. Fibroin is partly soluble in concentrated solutions of lithium thiocyanate or in mixtures of cupric salts and ethylene diamine. Such solutions contain a protein of molecular weight 170,000, which is a dimer of two subunits.

Little is known about either the scleroproteins of the marine sponges or the insoluble proteins of the cellular membranes of animal cells. Some of the membranes are soluble in detergents; the membrane of the red blood cells contains an insoluble membrane protein that consists of a single peptide chain of molecular weight 200,000.

MUSCLE PROTEINS

The total amount of muscle proteins in mammals, including humans, exceeds that of any other protein. About

40 percent of the body weight of a healthy human adult weighing about 70 kg (150 pounds) is muscle, which is composed of about 20 percent muscle protein. Thus, the human body contains about 5 to 6 kg (11 to 13 pounds) of muscle protein. An albumin-like fraction of these proteins, originally called myogen, contains various enzymes—phosphorylase, aldolase, glyceraldehyde phosphate dehydrogenase, and others. It does not seem to be involved in contraction. The globulin fraction contains myosin, the contractile protein, which also occurs in blood platelets, small bodies found in blood. Similar contractile substances occur in other contractile structures, such as in the cilia or flagella (whiplike organs of locomotion) of bacteria and protozoans. In contrast to the scleroproteins, the contractile proteins are soluble in salt solutions and susceptible to enzymatic digestion.

The energy required for muscle contraction is provided by the oxidation of carbohydrates or lipids. The term *mechanochemical reaction* has been used for this conversion of chemical into mechanical energy. Although the molecular process underlying the reaction is not yet completely understood, it is known to involve the fibrous muscle proteins, the peptide chains of which undergo a change in conformation during contraction.

Myosin, which can be removed from fresh muscle by adding it to a chilled solution of dilute potassium chloride and sodium bicarbonate, is insoluble in water. Myosin, solutions of which are highly viscous, consists of an elongated—probably double-stranded—peptide chain, which is coiled at both ends in such a way that a terminal globule is formed. The length of the molecule is approximately 160 nm and its average diameter 2.6 nm. The equivalent weight of each of the two terminal globules is approximately 30,000. The molecular weight of myosin is close to 500,000. Trypsin splits myosin into large fragments called meromyosin. Myosin contains many amino acids with positively and negatively charged side chains; they form 18 and 16 percent, respectively, of the total number of amino acids. Myosin catalyzes the hydrolytic cleavage of ATP (adenosine triphosphate). A smaller protein with properties similar to those of myosin is tropomyosin. It has a molecular weight of 70,000 and dimensions of 45 by 2 nm. More than 90 percent of its peptide chains are present in the α-helix form.

Myosin combines easily with another muscle protein called actin, the molecular weight of which is about 50,000. Actin forms about 12 to 15 percent of the muscle proteins. It can exist in two forms—one, G-actin, is globular, while the other, F-actin, is fibrous. Actomyosin is a complex molecule formed by one molecule of myosin and one or two molecules of actin. In muscle, actin and myosin filaments are oriented parallel to each other and to the long axis of the muscle. The actin filaments are linked to each other lengthwise by fine threads called S filaments. During contraction the S filaments shorten, so that the actin filaments slide toward each other, past the myosin filaments, thus causing a shortening of the muscle.

FIBRINOGEN AND FIBRIN

Fibrinogen, the protein of the blood plasma, is converted into the insoluble protein fibrin during the clotting process. The fibrinogen-free fluid obtained after removal of the clot, called blood serum, is blood plasma minus fibrinogen. The fibrinogen content of the blood plasma is 0.2 to 0.4 percent.

Fibrinogen can be precipitated from the blood plasma by half-saturation with sodium chloride. Fibrinogen solutions are highly viscous and show strong flow birefringence. In electron micrographs the molecules appear as rods with a length of 47.5 nm and a diameter of 1.5 nm; in addition, two terminal and a central nodule are visible. The molecular weight is 340,000. An unusually high percentage, about 36 percent, of the amino acid side chains are positively or negatively charged.

The clotting process is initiated by the enzyme thrombin, which catalyzes the breakage of a few peptide bonds of fibrinogen. As a result, two small fibrinopeptides with molecular weights of 1,900 and 2,400 are released. The remainder of the fibrinogen molecule, a monomer, is soluble and stable at pH values less than 6 (i.e., in acid solutions). In neutral solution (pH 7) the monomer is converted into a larger molecule, insoluble fibrin, which results from the formation of new peptide bonds. The newly formed peptide bonds form intermolecular and intramolecular cross links, thus giving rise to a large clot, in which all molecules are linked to each other. Clotting, which takes place only in the presence of calcium ions, can be prevented by compounds such as oxalate or citrate, which have a high affinity for calcium ions.

SOLUBLE PROTEINS

The blood plasma, the lymph, and other animal fluids usually contain 1 to 7 grams of protein (0.04 to 0.25 oz) per 100 ml of fluid (3.4 oz), which includes small amounts of hundreds of enzymes and a large number of protein hormones. Human blood serum contains about 7 percent protein, two-thirds of which is in the albumin fraction. The other third is in the globulin fraction. Electrophoresis of serum reveals a large albumin peak and three smaller globulin peaks, the alpha-, beta-, and gamma-globulins. The amounts of alpha-, beta-, and gamma-globulin in normal human serum are approximately 1.5, 1.9, and 1.1 percent, respectively. Each globulin fraction is a mixture of many different proteins, as has been demonstrated by immunoelectrophoresis. In this method, the serum of a rabbit injected with human serum is allowed to diffuse into the four protein bands—albumin, alpha-, beta-, and gamma-globulin—obtained from the electrophoresis of human serum. Because the rabbit has previously been injected with human serum, its blood contains antibodies (substances formed in response to a foreign substance introduced into the body) against each of the human serum proteins. Thus, each antibody combines with the serum protein (antigen) that caused its formation in the rabbit. The result is the formation of about 20 regions of insoluble antigen-antibody precipitate, which appear as white arcs in the transparent gel of the electrophoresis medium. Each region corresponds to a different human serum protein.

Serum albumin is much less heterogeneous (i.e., contains fewer distinct proteins) than are the globulins. In fact, it is one of the few serum proteins that can be obtained in a crystalline form. Serum albumin combines easily with many acidic dyes (e.g., Congo red and methyl orange); with bilirubin, the yellow bile pigment; and with fatty acids. It seems to act, in living organisms, as a carrier for certain biological substances. Present in blood serum in relatively high concentration, serum albumin also acts as a protective colloid, a protein that stabilizes other proteins. Albumin (molecular weight of 68,000) has a single free sulfhydryl (-SH) group, which on oxidation forms a disulfide bond with the sulfhydryl group of another serum albumin molecule, thus forming a dimer. The isoelectric point of serum albumin is pH 4.7.

The alpha-globulin fraction of blood serum is a mixture of several conjugated proteins. The best known are an α-lipoprotein (combination of lipid and protein) and two mucoproteins (combinations of carbohydrate and protein). One mucoprotein is called orosomucoid, or α_1-acid glycoprotein. The other is called haptoglobin because it combines specifically with globin, the protein component of hemoglobin. Haptoglobin contains about 20 percent carbohydrate. The beta-globulin fraction of serum contains, in addition to lipoproteins and mucoproteins, two metal-binding proteins, transferrin and ceruloplasmin, which bind iron and copper, respectively. They are the principal iron and copper carriers of the blood.

The gamma-globulins are the most heterogeneous globulins. Although most have a molecular weight of approximately 150,000, that of some, called macroglobulins, is as high as 800,000. Because typical antibodies are of the same size and exhibit the same electrophoretic behaviour as γ-globulins, they are called immunoglobulins. The designation IgM or gamma M (γM) is used for the macroglobulins, and the designation IgG or gamma G (γG) is used for γ-globulins of molecular weight 150,000.

Milk contains the following: an albumin, α-lactalbumin; a globulin, beta-lactoglobulin; and a phosphoprotein, casein. If acid is added to milk, casein precipitates. The remaining watery liquid (the supernatant solution), or whey, contains lactalbumin and lactoglobulin. Both have been obtained in crystalline form, and their molecular weights are 16,000 and 18,500, respectively. Lactoglobulin also occurs as a dimer of molecular weight 37,000. Genetic variations can produce small variations in the amino acid composition of lactoglobulin. The amino acid composition and the tertiary structure of lactalbumin resemble that of lysozyme, an egg protein.

Casein is precipitated not only by the addition of acid but also by the action of the enzyme rennin, which is found in gastric juice. Rennin from calf stomachs is used to precipitate casein, from which cheese is made. Milk fat precipitates with casein. Milk sugar, however, remains

Workers make a Beaufort cheese in the cellar of a French cheese-maker in Saint-François-Longchamp, central France. Jean-Pierre Clatot/AFP/ Getty Images

in the supernatant (whey). Casein is a mixture of several similar phosphoproteins, called α-, β-, γ-, and κ-casein, all of which contain some serine side chains combined with phosphoric acid. Approximately 75 percent of casein is α-casein. Cystine has been found only in κ-casein. In milk, casein seems to form polymeric globules (micelles) with radially arranged monomers, each with a molecular weight of 24,000. The acidic side chains occur predominantly on the surface of the micelle, rather than inside.

About 50 percent of the proteins of egg white are composed of ovalbumin, which is easily obtained in crystals. Its molecular weight is 46,000 and its amino acid composition differs from that of serum albumin. Other proteins of egg white are conalbumin, lysozyme, ovoglobulin, ovomucoid, and avidin. Lysozyme is an enzyme that hydrolyzes the carbohydrates found in the capsules certain bacteria secrete around themselves; it causes lysis (disintegration) of the bacteria. The molecular weight of lysozyme is 14,100. Its three-dimensional structure is similar to that of α-lactalbumin, which stimulates the formation of lactose by the enzyme lactose synthetase. Lysozyme has also been found in the urine of patients suffering from leukemia.

Avidin is a glycoprotein that combines specifically with biotin, a vitamin. In animals fed large amounts of raw egg white, the action of avidin results in "egg-white injury." The molecular weight of avidin, which forms a tetramer, is 68,000. Its amino acid sequence is known.

Egg-yolk proteins contain a mixture of lipoproteins and livetins. The latter are similar to serum albumin, α-globulin, and β-globulin. The yolk also contains a phosphoprotein, phosvitin. Phosvitin, which has also been found in fish sperm, has a molecular weight of 40,000 and an unusual amino acid composition. One third of its amino acids are phosphoserine.

Albrecht Kossel

(b. Sept. 16, 1853, Rostock, Mecklenburg [now Germany]—d. July 5, 1927, Heidelberg, Ger.)

German biochemist Albrecht Kossel was known for his contributions to understanding the chemistry of nucleic acids and proteins. He discovered the nucleic acids that are the bases in the DNA molecule. He was awarded the Nobel Prize for Physiology or Medicine in 1910 for his work.

After graduating in medicine (1878) from the German University (now the University of Strasbourg), Kossel did research there and at the Physiological Institute in Berlin. In 1895 he became professor of physiology and director of the Physiological Institute at Marburg, going in 1901 to a similar post at Heidelberg, where he eventually became director of the Heidelberg Institute for Protein Investigation.

In 1879 Kossel began studying the recently isolated substances known as "nucleins" (nucleoproteins), which he showed to consist of a protein portion and a nonprotein portion (nucleic acid). From 1885 to 1901 he and his students used hydrolysis and other techniques to chemically analyze the nucleic acids, thus discovering their component compounds: adenine, cytosine, guanine, thymine, and uracil. Kossel also discovered the amino acid histidine (1896), thymic acid, and agmatine (a product of L-arginine decarboxylation).

Albrecht Kossel. George Grantham Bain Collection/Library of Congress, Washington, D.C. (Digital File Number: LC-DIG-ggbain-05408)

Protamines are found in the sperm cells of fish. The most thoroughly investigated protamines are salmine from salmon sperm and clupeine from herring sperm. The protamines are bound to DNA, forming nucleoprotamines. The amino acid composition of the protamines is simple—they contain, in addition to large amounts of arginine, small amounts of five or six other amino acids. The composition of the salmine molecule, for example, is: Arg_{51}, Ala_4, Val_4, Ile_1, Pro_7, and Ser_6, in which the subscript numbers indicate the number of each amino acid in the molecule. Because of the high arginine content, the isoelectric points of the protamines are at pH values of 11 to 12 (i.e., the protamines are alkaline). The molecular weights of salmine and clupeine are close to 6,000. All of the protamines investigated thus far are mixtures of several similar proteins.

The histones are less basic than the protamines. They contain high amounts of either lysine or arginine and small amounts of aspartic acid and glutamic acid. Histones occur in combination with DNA as nucleohistones in the nuclei of the body cells of animals and plants, but not in animal sperm. The molecular weights of histones vary from 10,000 to 22,000. In contrast to the protamines, the histones contain most of the 20 amino acids, with the exception of tryptophan and the sulfur-containing ones. Like the protamines, histone preparations are heterogeneous mixtures. The amino acid sequence of some of the histones has been determined.

Plant Proteins

Plant proteins, mostly globulins, have been obtained chiefly from the protein-rich seeds of cereals and legumes. Small amounts of albumins are found in seeds. The best known globulins, insoluble in water, can be extracted from seeds by treatment with 2 to 10 percent solutions of sodium chloride. Many plant globulins have been obtained in crystalline form, including edestin from hemp, molecular weight 310,000; amandin from almonds, 330,000; concanavalin A (42,000) and B (96,000); and canavalin (113,000) from jack beans. They are polymers of smaller subunits. Edestin, for example, is a hexamer of a subunit with a molecular weight of 50,000, and concanavalin B a trimer of a subunit with a molecular weight of 30,000. After extraction of lipids from cereal seeds by ether and alcohol, further extraction with water containing 50 to 80 percent of alcohol yields proteins that are insoluble in water but soluble in water–ethanol mixtures and have been called prolamins. Their solubility in aqueous ethanol may result from their high proline and glutamine content. Gliadin, the prolamin from wheat, contains 14 grams (0.05 oz) of proline and 46 grams (1.6 oz) of glutamic acid in 100 grams (3.5 oz) of protein. Most of the glutamic acid is in the form of glutamine. The total amounts of the basic amino acids (arginine, lysine, and histidine) in gliadin are only 5 percent of the weight of gliadin. Because the glysine content is either low or nonexistent, human populations dependent on grain as a sole protein source suffer from lysine deficiency.

PROTEINS AND PROSTHETIC GROUPS

The link between a protein molecule and its prosthetic group is a covalent (electron-sharing) bond in the glycoproteins, the biliproteins, and some of the heme proteins. In lipoproteins, nucleoproteins, and some heme proteins, the two components are linked by noncovalent bonds. The bonding results from the same forces that are responsible for the tertiary structure of proteins: hydrogen bonds, salt bridges between positively and negatively charged groups, disulfide bonds, and mutual interaction of hydrophobic groups. In the metalloproteins (proteins with a metal element as a prosthetic group), the metal ion usually forms a centre to which various groups are bound.

MUCOPROTEINS AND GLYCOPROTEINS

The prosthetic groups in mucoproteins and glycoproteins are oligosaccharides (carbohydrates consisting of a small number of simple sugar molecules) usually containing from four to 12 sugar molecules. The most common sugars are galactose, mannose, glucosamine, and galactosamine. Xylose, fucose, glucuronic acid, sialic acid, and other simple sugars sometimes also occur. Some mucoproteins contain 20 percent or more of carbohydrate, usually in several oligosaccharides attached to different parts of the peptide chain. The designation mucoprotein is used for proteins with more than 3 to 4 percent carbohydrate. If the carbohydrate content is less than 3 percent, the protein is sometimes called a glycoprotein or simply a protein.

Mucoproteins, highly viscous proteins originally called mucins, are found in saliva, in gastric juice, and in other animal secretions. Mucoproteins occur in large amounts in cartilage, synovial fluid (the lubricating fluid of joints and tendons), and egg white. The mucoprotein of cartilage is formed by the combination of collagen with chondroitinsulfuric acid, which is a polymer of either glucuronic or iduronic acid and acetylhexosamine or acetylgalactosamine. It is not yet clear whether chondroitinsulfate is bound to collagen by covalent bonds.

LIPOPROTEINS AND PROTEOLIPIDS

The bond between the protein and the lipid portion of lipoproteins and proteolipids is a noncovalent one. It is believed that some of the lipid is enclosed in a meshlike arrangement of peptide chains and becomes accessible for reaction only after the unfolding of the chains by denaturing agents. Although lipoproteins in the α- and β-globulin fraction of blood serum are soluble in water (but insoluble in organic solvents), some of the brain lipoproteins, because they have a high lipid content, are soluble in organic solvents. These substances are called proteolipids. The β-lipoprotein of human blood serum is a macroglobulin with a molecular weight of about 1,300,000 daltons, 70 percent of which is lipid. Of the lipid, about 30 percent is phospholipid and 40 percent cholesterol and compounds derived from it. Because of their lipid content, the lipoproteins have the lowest density (mass per unit volume) of all proteins and are usually classified as low- and high-density lipoproteins (LDL and HDL, respectively).

Coloured lipoproteins are formed by the combination of protein with carotenoids. Crustacyanin, the pigment of lobsters, crayfish, and other crustaceans, contains astaxanthin, which is a compound derived from carotene. Among the most interesting of the coloured lipoproteins are the pigments of the retina of the eye. They contain retinal, which is a compound derived from carotene and which is formed by the oxidation of vitamin A. In rhodopsin, the red pigment of the retina, the aldehyde group (-CHO) of retinal forms a covalent bond with an amino ($-NH_2$) group of opsin, the protein carrier. Colour vision is mediated by the presence of several visual pigments in the retina that differ from rhodopsin either in the structure of retinal or in that of the protein carrier.

METALLOPROTEINS

Proteins in which heavy metal ions are bound directly to some of the side chains of histidine, cysteine, or some other amino acid are called metalloproteins. Two metalloproteins, transferrin and ceruloplasmin, occur in the globulin fractions of blood serum, where they act as carriers of iron and copper, respectively. Transferrin has a molecular weight of 84,000 and consists of two identical subunits, each of which contains one ferric ion (Fe^{3+}) that seems to be bound to tyrosine. Several genetic variants of transferrin are known to occur in humans. Another iron protein, ferritin, which contains 20 to 22 percent iron, is the form in which iron is stored in animals. It has been obtained in crystalline form from liver and spleen. The ferritin molecule consists of 20 subunits, and its molecular weight is approximately 480,000. The iron can be removed by reduction from the ferric (Fe^{3+}) to the ferrous (Fe^{2+}) state. The iron-free protein, apoferritin, is synthesized in the body before the iron is incorporated.

Green plants and some photosynthetic and nitrogen-fixing bacteria (i.e., bacteria that convert atmospheric nitrogen, N_2, into amino acids and proteins in their own bodies) contain various ferredoxins. They are small proteins containing 50 to 100 amino acids and a chain of iron and disulfide units (FeS_2). Some of the sulfur atoms are contributed by cysteine, whereas others occur in the form of sulfide ions (S^{2-}). The number of FeS_2 units per ferredoxin molecule varies from five in the ferredoxin of spinach to 10 in the ferredoxin of certain bacteria. Ferredoxins act as electron carriers in photosynthesis and in nitrogen fixation.

Ceruloplasmin is a copper-containing globulin that has a molecular weight of 151,000. The molecule consists of eight subunits, each containing one copper ion. Ceruloplasmin is the principal carrier of copper in organisms, although copper can also be transported by the iron-containing globulin transferrin. Another copper-containing protein, erythrocuprein (molecular weight 64,000), has been isolated from red blood cells. It has also been found in the liver and in the brain. The molecule, which consists of four subunits with a molecular weight of 16,000 each, contains four copper ions and four zinc ions. Because of their copper content, ceruloplasmin and erythrocuprein may have some catalytic activity in oxidation-reduction reactions. Another copper-containing protein is hemocyanin.

Many animal enzymes contain zinc ions, which are usually bound to the sulfur of cysteine. The protein metallothionein, which was discovered in horse kidneys in the 1950s, is rich in cysteines and therefore has a high affinity for heavy metals, such as zinc and cadmium. A vanadium-protein complex (homovanadin) has been found in surprisingly high amounts in yellowish green cells (vanadocytes) of tunicates, which are marine invertebrates.

HEME PROTEINS AND OTHER CHROMOPROTEINS

Although the heme proteins contain iron, they are usually not classified as metalloproteins, because their prosthetic group is an iron-porphyrin complex in which the iron is bound very firmly. The intense red or brown colour of the heme proteins is not caused by iron but by porphyrin, a complex cyclic structure. All porphyrin compounds absorb light intensely at or close to 410 nm. Porphyrin consists of four pyrrole rings (five-membered closed structures containing one nitrogen and four carbon atoms) linked to each other by methine groups (-CH=). The iron atom is kept in the centre of the porphyrin ring by interaction with the four nitrogen atoms. The iron atom can combine with two other substituents. In oxyhemoglobin, one substituent is a histidine of the protein carrier, and the other is an oxygen molecule. In some heme proteins, the protein is also bound covalently to the side chains of porphyrin.

Little is known about the structure of the chromoprotein melanin, a pigment found in dark skin, dark hair, and melanotic tumours. It is probably formed by the oxidation of tyrosine, which results in the formation of red, brown, or dark-coloured derivatives.

Green chromoproteins called biliproteins are found in many insects, such as grasshoppers, and also in the eggshells of many birds. The biliproteins are derived from the bile pigment biliverdin, which in turn is formed from porphyrin. Biliverdin contains four pyrrole rings and three of the four methine groups of porphyrin. Large amounts of biliproteins, the molecular weights of which are about 270,000, have been found in red algae and in blue-green algae. The red protein is called phycoerythrin, and the blue one is called phycocyanobilin. Phycocyanobilin consists of eight subunits with a molecular weight of 28,000 each. About 89 percent of the molecule is protein with a large amount of carbohydrate.

A green respiratory protein, chlorocruorin, has been found in the blood of the marine worm *Spirographis*. It has the same high molecular weight as erythrocruorin, but differs from hemoglobin in its prosthetic group. A red metalloprotein, hemerythrin, acts as a respiratory protein in marine worms of the phylum Sipuncula. The molecule consists of eight subunits with a molecular weight of 13,500 each. Hemerythrin contains no porphyrins and therefore is not a heme protein.

A metalloprotein containing copper is the respiratory protein of crustaceans (shrimps, crabs, etc.) and of some gastropods (snails). The protein, called hemocyanin, is pale yellow when not combined with oxygen, and blue when combined with oxygen. The molecular weights of hemocyanins vary from 300,000 to 9,000,000. Each animal investigated thus far apparently has a species-specific hemocyanin.

PROTEIN HORMONES

Some hormones that are products of endocrine glands are proteins or peptides, whereas others are steroids. None of the hormones has any enzymatic activity. Each has a target organ in which it elicits some biological action, such as the secretion of gastric or pancreatic juice, the production of milk, or the production of steroid hormones. The mechanism by which the hormones exert their effects is not fully understood. Cyclic adenosine monophosphate is involved in the transmittance of the hormonal stimulus to the cells whose activity is specifically increased by the hormone.

Hormones of the Thyroid Gland

Thyroglobulin, the active groups of which are two molecules of the iodine-containing compound thyroxine, has a molecular weight of 670,000. Thyroglobulin contains the thyroid hormones thyroxine, with four iodine atoms, and triiodothyronine, with three iodine atoms. Injection of the hormone causes an increase in metabolism, whereas a lack of it results in a decrease in metabolic rate.

Another hormone, calcitonin, which lowers the calcium level of the blood, occurs in the thyroid gland. The amino acid sequences of calcitonin from pig, beef, and salmon differ from human calcitonin in some amino acids. All of them, however, have the half-cystines and the prolinamide in the same position. Porcine calcitonin has been synthesized in the laboratory.

The parathyroid hormone (parathormone), produced in small glands that are embedded in or lie behind the thyroid gland, is essential for maintaining the calcium level of the blood. Its lack results in the disease hypocalcemia. Bovine parathormone has a molecular weight of 8,500. It does not contain cystine or cysteine, but it is rich in aspartic acid, glutamic acid, or their amides.

Hormones of the Pancreas

Although the structure of insulin has been known since 1949, repeated attempts to synthesize it gave very poor yields because of the failure of the two peptide chains to combine forming the correct disulfide bridge. The ease of the biosynthesis of insulin is explained by the discovery in the pancreas of proinsulin, from which insulin is formed. The single peptide chain of proinsulin loses a peptide consisting of 33 amino acids and called the connecting peptide, or C peptide, during its conversion to insulin.

In aqueous solutions insulin exists predominantly as a complex of six subunits, each of which contains an *A*- and a *B*-chain. The insulins of several species have been isolated and analyzed. Their amino acid sequences have been found to differ somewhat, but all apparently contain the same disulfide bridges between the two chains.

Although the injection of insulin lowers the level of sugar in the blood, administration of glucagon, another pancreas hormone, raises the blood sugar level. Glucagon consists of a straight peptide chain of 29 amino acids. Its structure is free of cystine and isoleucine. It has been synthesized, and the synthetic product has the full biological activity of natural glucagon.

The pituitary gland has an anterior lobe, a posterior lobe, and an intermediate portion. These parts differ in cellular structure and in the structure and action of the hormones they form. The posterior lobe produces two similar hormones, oxytocin and vasopressin. The former causes contraction of the pregnant uterus, and the latter raises blood pressure. Both are octapeptides formed by a ring of five amino acids (the two cystine halves count as one amino acid) and a side chain of three amino acids. The two cystine halves are linked to each other by a disulfide bond, and the C-terminal amino acid is glycinamide. The structure has been established and confirmed. Human vasopressin differs from oxytocin in that isoleucine is replaced by phenylalanine and leucine by arginine. Porcine vasopressin contains lysine instead of arginine.

The intermediate part of the pituitary gland produces the melanocyte-stimulating hormone (MSH), which causes expansion of the pigmented melanophores (cells) in the skin of frogs and other batrachians. Two hormones, called α-MSH and β-MSH, have been prepared from hog pituitary glands. α-MSH consists of 13 amino acids). Its N-terminal serine is acetylated (i.e., the acetyl group, CH_3CO, of acetic acid is attached), and its C-terminal valine residue is present as valinamide. β-MSH contains in its 18 amino acids many of those occurring in α-MSH.

The anterior pituitary lobe produces several protein hormones—thyroid-stimulating hormone, molecular weight 28,000; prolactin (a lactogenic hormone), molecular weight 22,500; growth hormone, molecular weight 21,500; luteinizing hormone, molecular weight 30,000; and follicle-stimulating hormone, molecular weight 29,000. Thyroid-stimulating hormone (thyrotropin) consists of α and β subunits with a composition similar to the subunits of luteinizing hormone. When separated, neither of the two subunits has hormonal activity. When combined, however, they regain about 50 percent of the original activity. Prolactin from sheep pituitary glands contains 190 amino acids. Their sequence has been elucidated. A similar peptide chain of 188 amino acids that has been synthesized not only has 10 percent of the biological activity of the natural hormone but also some activity of growth hormone. The amino acid sequence of growth hormone (somatotropic hormone) is also known. It seems to stimulate the synthesis of RNA and in this way to accelerate growth. Luteinizing hormone consists of two subunits, each with a molecular weight of approximately 15,000. When separated, the subunits recombine spontaneously. Luteinizing hormone is a mucoprotein containing about 12 percent carbohydrate.

The urine of pregnant women contains human chorionic gonadotropin, the presence of which makes possible early diagnosis of pregnancy. The amino acid sequence is known. The sequence of 160 of its 190 amino acids is identical with those of the growth hormone, and 100 of these also occur in the same sequence as in prolactin. The different pituitary hormones and human chorionic gonadotropin thus may have been derived from a common substance that, during evolution, underwent differentiation.

Peptides with Hormonelike Activity

Small peptides have been discovered that, like hormones, act on certain target organs. One peptide, angiotensin (angiotonin or hypertensin), is formed in the blood from angiotensinogen by the action of renin, an enzyme of the kidney. It is an octapeptide and increases blood pressure. Similar peptides include bradykinin, which stimulates smooth muscles; gastrin, which stimulates secretion of hydrochloric acid and pepsin in the stomach; secretin, which stimulates the flow of pancreatic juice; and kallikrein, the activity of which is similar to bradykinin.

Antibodies

Antibodies, proteins that combat foreign substances in the body, are associated with the globulin fraction of the immune serum. When the serum globulins are separated into α-, β-, and γ- fractions, antibodies are associated with the γ-globulins. Antibodies can be purified by precipitation with the antigen (i.e., the foreign substance) that caused their formation, followed by separation of the antigen–antibody complex. Antibodies prepared in this way consist of a mixture of many similar antibody molecules, which differ in molecular weight, amino acid composition, and other properties. The same differences are found in the γ-globulins of normal blood serums.

It is believed that the γ-globulin of normal blood serum is a mixture of thousands of different γ-globulins, each of which occurs in amounts too small for isolation. Because the physical and chemical properties of normal γ-globulins are the same as those of antibodies, the γ-globulins are frequently called immunoglobulins. They may be considered to be antibodies against unknown antigens. If solutions of γ-globulin are resolved by gel filtration through dextran, the first fraction has a molecular weight of 800,000. This fraction is called IgM or γM (Ig is an abbreviation for immunoglobulin and M for macroglobulin). The next two fractions are IgA (γA) and IgG (γG), with molecular weights of about 300,000 and 150,000 respectively. Two other immunoglobulins, known as IgD and IgE, have also been detected in much smaller amounts in some immune sera.

The bulk of the immunoglobulins is found in the IgG fraction, which also contains most of the antibodies. The IgM molecules are apparently pentamers—aggregates of five of the IgG molecules. Electron microscopy shows their five subunits to be linked to each other by disulfide bonds in the form of a pentagon. The IgA molecules are found principally in milk and in secretions of the intestinal mucosa. Some of them contain, in addition to a dimer of IgG, a "secretory piece" that enables the passage of IgA molecules between tissue and fluid. The IgM and IgA immunoglobulins and antibodies contain 10 to 15 percent carbohydrate. The carbohydrate content of the IgG molecules is 2 to 3 percent.

IgG molecules treated with the enzyme papain split into three fragments of almost identical molecular weight of 50,000. Two of these, called Fab fragments, are identical. The third fragment is abbreviated Fc. Reduction to sulfhydryl groups of some of the disulfide bonds of IgG results in the formation of two heavy, or *H*, chains (molecular weight 55,000) and two light, or *L*, chains (molecular weight 22,000). They are linked by disulfide bonds in the order *L-H-H-L*. Each *H* chain contains four intrachain disulfide bonds, each *L* chain contains two.

Antibody preparations of the IgG type, even after removal of IgM and IgA antibodies, are heterogeneous. The *H* and *L* chains consist of a large number of different *L* chains and a variety of *H* chains. Pure IgG, IgM, and IgA immunoglobulins, however, occur in the blood serum of patients suffering from myelomas, which are malignant tumours of the bone marrow. The tumours produce either an IgG, an IgM, or an IgA protein, but rarely more than one class. A protein called the Bence-Jones protein, which is found in the urine of patients suffering from myeloma tumours, is identical with the *L* chains of the myeloma protein. Each patient has a different Bence-Jones protein—no two of the more than 100 Bence-Jones proteins that have been analyzed thus far are identical. It is thought that one lymphoid cell among hundreds of thousands becomes malignant and multiplies rapidly, forming the mass of a myeloma tumour that produces one γ-globulin.

Analyses of the Bence-Jones proteins have revealed that the *L* chains of humans and other mammals are of two quite different types, kappa (κ) and lambda (λ). Both consist of approximately 220 amino acids. The N-terminal halves of κ- and λ-chains are variable, differing in each Bence-Jones protein. The C-terminal halves of these same *L* chains have a constant amino acid sequence of either the κ- or the λ-type. The fact that one half of a peptide chain is variable and the other half invariant is contradictory to the view that the amino acid sequence of each peptide chain is determined by one gene. Evidently, two genes, one of them variable, the

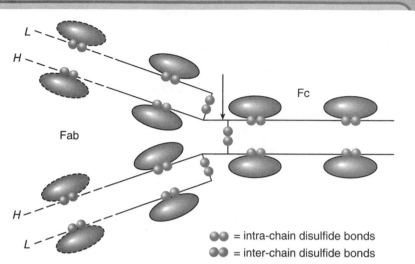

L

H

Fc

Fab

H

L

●● = intra-chain disulfide bonds
●● = inter-chain disulfide bonds

Two heavy chains (H) and two light chains (L) are linked to each other by inter-chain disulfide bonds. Intra-chain disulfide bonds cause loops to form in the 12 peptide portions, each of which contains about 110 amino acid residues. The 12 peptide regions have cystine residues at similar positions and other similarities in their amino acid sequences. The broken lines represent variable portions and the solid lines represent constant portions of the chains. Specific sites that bind antigens are formed by the variable portions. The vertical arrow indicates cleavage of the IgG molecule into two Fab fragments and one Fc fragment by the action of the enzyme papain.

Diagram of an IgG immunoglobulin. Copyright Encyclopædia Britannica; rendering for this edition by Rosen Educational Services

other invariant, fuse to form the gene for the single peptide chain of the *L* chains. Whereas the normal human *L* chains are always mixtures of the κ- and λ-types, the *H* chains of IgG, IgM, and IgA are different. They have been designated as gamma (γ), mu (μ), and alpha (α) chains, respectively. The N-terminal quarter of the *H* chains has a variable amino acid sequence, whereas the C-terminal three-quarters of the *H* chains have a constant amino acid sequence.

Some of the amino acid sequences in the *L* and *H* chains are transmitted from generation to generation. As a result, the constant portion of the human *L* chains of the κ-type has in position 191 either valine or leucine.

They correspond to two alleles (character-determining portions) of a gene. The two types are called allotypes. The valine-containing genetic type has been designated as InV(a⁺), the leucine-containing type as InV(b⁺). Many more allotypes, called Gm allotypes, have been found in the gamma chains of the human IgG immunoglobulins. Certain combinations of Gm types occur. For example, the combination of Gm types 5, 6, and 11 has been found in Caucasians and African Americans but not in Asians. The combination of 1, 2, and 17 has not been found in African Americans, and the combination of 1, 4, and 17 has not been found in Caucasians. Allotypes have also been discovered to occur in a number of other animals, including rabbits and mice.

It is understandable from the occurrence of a large number of allotypes that antibodies, even if produced in response to a single antigen, are mixtures of different allotypes. The existence of several classes of antibodies, of different allotypes, and of adaptation of the variable portions of antibodies to different regions of an antigen molecule results in a multiplicity of antibody molecules even if only a single antigen is administered.

ENZYMES

Enzymes are substances that act as catalysts in living organisms, regulating the rate at which chemical reactions proceed without itself being altered in the process. The biological processes that occur within all living organisms are chemical reactions, and most are regulated by enzymes. Without enzymes, many of these reactions would not take place at a perceptible rate. Enzymes catalyze all aspects of cell metabolism. This includes the digestion of food, in which large nutrient molecules (such as proteins, carbohydrates, and fats) are broken down into smaller molecules; the conservation and transformation of chemical energy; and the construction of cellular macromolecules from smaller precursors. Many inherited human diseases, such as albinism, result from a deficiency of a particular enzyme.

Enzymes also have valuable industrial and medical applications. The fermenting of wine, leavening of bread,

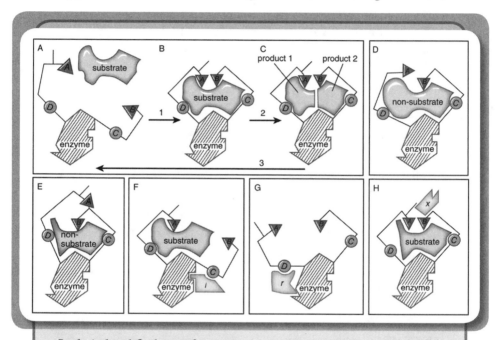

In the induced-fit theory of enzyme-substrate binding, a substrate approaches the surface of an enzyme (step 1 in box A, B, C) and causes a change in the enzyme shape that results in the correct alignment of the catalytic groups (triangles A and B; circles C and D represent substrate-binding groups on the enzyme that are essential for catalytic activity). The catalytic groups react with the substrate to form products (step 2). The products then separate from the enzyme, freeing it to repeat the sequence (step 3). Boxes D and E represent examples of molecules that are too large or too small for proper catalytic alignment. Boxes F and G demonstrate binding of an inhibitor molecule (I and I') to an allosteric site, thereby preventing interaction of the enzyme with the substrate. Box H illustrates binding of an allosteric activator (X), a nonsubstrate molecule capable of reacting with the enzyme. Copyright Encyclopædia Britannica; rendering for this edition by Rosen Educational Services

curdling of cheese, and brewing of beer have been practiced from earliest times, but not until the 19th century were these reactions understood to be the result of the catalytic activity of enzymes. Since then, enzymes have assumed an increasing importance in industrial processes that involve organic chemical reactions. The uses of enzymes in medicine include killing disease-causing microorganisms, promoting wound healing, and diagnosing certain diseases.

CHEMICAL NATURE

All enzymes were once thought to be proteins, but since the 1980s the catalytic ability of the nucleic acids known as messenger RNAs has been demonstrated, thereby refuting this axiom. However, little is yet known about the enzymatic functioning of RNA, and hence much of what is known about enzymes comes from studies of protein enzymes. A large protein enzyme molecule, similar to noncatalytic proteins, is composed of one or more amino acid chains, resulting in the formation of polypeptide chains. The amino acid sequence determines the characteristic folding patterns of the protein's structure, which is essential to enzyme specificity. If the enzyme is subjected to changes, such as fluctuations in temperature or pH, the protein structure may lose its integrity (denature) and its enzymatic ability. Denaturation is sometimes, but not always, reversible.

Bound to some enzymes is an additional chemical component called a cofactor, which is a direct participant in the catalytic event and thus is required for enzymatic activity. A cofactor may be either a coenzyme—an organic molecule, such as a vitamin—or an inorganic metal ion. Some enzymes require both types of cofactor. A cofactor may be either tightly or loosely bound to the enzyme. If tightly connected, the cofactor is referred to as a prosthetic group.

NOMENCLATURE

An enzyme will interact with only one type of substance or group of substances, called the substrate, to catalyze a certain kind of reaction. Because of this specificity, enzymes often have been named by adding the suffix "-ase" to the substrate's name (as in urease, which catalyzes the breakdown of urea). Not all enzymes have been named in this manner, however, and to ease the confusion surrounding enzyme nomenclature, a classification system has been developed based on the type of reaction the enzyme catalyzes. There are six principal categories and their reactions: (1) oxidoreductases, which are involved in electron transfer; (2) transferases, which transfer a chemical group from one substance to another; (3) hydrolases, which cleave the substrate by uptake of a water molecule (hydrolysis); (4) lyases, which form double bonds by adding or removing a chemical group; (5) isomerases, which transfer a group within a molecule to form an isomer; and (6) ligases, or synthetases, which couple the formation of various chemical bonds to the breakdown of a pyrophosphate bond in ATP or a similar nucleotide.

MECHANISM OF ENZYME ACTION

In most chemical reactions, an energy barrier exists that must be overcome for the reaction to occur. This barrier prevents complex molecules such as proteins and nucleic acids from spontaneously degrading, and so is necessary for the preservation of life. When metabolic changes are required in a cell, however, certain of these complex molecules must be broken down, and this energy barrier must be surmounted. Heat could provide the additional needed energy (called activation energy), but the rise in temperature would kill the cell. The alternative is to lower the activation energy level through the use of a catalyst. This is the role that enzymes play. They react with the substrate to form an intermediate complex—a "transition state"—that requires less energy for the reaction to proceed. The unstable intermediate compound quickly breaks down to form reaction products, and the unchanged enzyme is free to react with other substrate molecules.

Only a certain region of the enzyme, called the active site, binds to the substrate. The active site is a groove or pocket formed by the folding pattern of the protein. This three-dimensional structure, together with the chemical and electrical properties of the amino acids and cofactors within the active site, permits only a particular substrate to bind to the site, thus determining the enzyme's specificity.

Enzyme synthesis and activity also are influenced by genetic control and distribution in a cell. Some enzymes are not produced by certain cells, and others are formed only when required. Enzymes are not always found uniformly within a cell. Often they are compartmentalized in the nucleus, on the cell membrane, or in subcellular structures. The rates of enzyme synthesis and activity are further influenced by hormones, neurosecretions, and other chemicals that affect the cell's internal environment.

FACTORS AFFECTING ENZYME ACTIVITY

Because enzymes are not consumed in the reactions they catalyze and can be used over and over again, only a very small quantity of an enzyme is needed to catalyze a reaction. A typical enzyme molecule can convert 1,000 substrate molecules per second. The rate of an enzymatic reaction increases with increased substrate concentration, reaching maximum velocity when all active sites of the enzyme molecules are engaged. The enzyme is then said to be saturated, the rate of the reaction being determined by the speed at which the active sites can convert substrate to product.

Enzyme activity can be inhibited in various ways. Competitive inhibition occurs when molecules very similar to the substrate molecules bind to the active site and prevent binding of the actual substrate. Penicillin is a competitive inhibitor that blocks the active site of an enzyme that many bacteria use to construct their cell walls.

Noncompetitive inhibition occurs when an inhibitor binds to the enzyme at a location other than the active site. In some cases of noncompetitive inhibition, the inhibitor is thought to bind to the enzyme in such a way as to physically block the normal active site. In other instances, the binding of the inhibitor is believed to change the shape of the enzyme molecule, thereby deforming its active site and preventing it from reacting with its substrate. This latter type of noncompetitive inhibition is called allosteric inhibition. The place where the inhibitor binds to the enzyme is called the allosteric site. Frequently, an end-product of a metabolic pathway serves as an allosteric inhibitor on an earlier enzyme of the pathway. This inhibition of an enzyme by a product of its pathway is a form of negative feedback.

Allosteric control can involve stimulation of enzyme action as well as inhibition. An activator molecule can be bound to an allosteric site and induce a reaction at the active site by changing its shape to fit a substrate that could not induce the change by itself. Common activators include hormones and the products of earlier enzymatic reactions. Allosteric stimulation and inhibition allow production of energy and materials by the cell when they are needed and inhibit production when the supply is adequate.

CHAPTER 5

Lipids are a diverse group of organic compounds that includes fats, oils, hormones, and certain components of membranes. These substances are grouped together because they do not interact appreciably with water. One type of lipid, the triglycerides, is sequestered as fat in adipose cells, which serve as the energy-storage depot for organisms and also provide thermal insulation. Some lipids such as steroid hormones serve as chemical messengers between cells, tissues, and organs, and others communicate signals between biochemical systems within a single cell. The membranes of cells and organelles (structures within cells) are microscopically thin structures formed from two layers of phospholipid molecules. Membranes function to separate individual cells from their environments and to compartmentalize the cell interior into structures that carry out special functions. Because of their fundamental role in sustaining the survival of living cells, membranes and the lipids that form them are believed to have been essential to the origin of life on Earth.

Water is the biological milieu—the substance that makes life possible—and almost all the molecular components of living cells, whether they be found in animals, plants, or microorganisms, are soluble in water. Molecules such as proteins, nucleic acids, and carbohydrates have an affinity for water and are called hydrophilic ("water-loving"). Lipids, however, are not hydrophilic but hydrophobic ("water-fearing"). Some lipids are amphipathic—part of their structure is hydrophilic and another part, usually a larger section, is hydrophobic. Amphipathic lipids exhibit a unique behaviour in water: They spontaneously form ordered molecular aggregates, with their hydrophilic ends on the outside, in contact with the water, and their hydrophobic parts on the inside, shielded from the water. This property makes them the basis for the cellular and organelle membranes.

Although biological lipids are not large macro-molecular polymers like proteins, nucleic acids, and polysaccharides, many are formed by the chemical link-ing of several small constituent molecules. Many of these molecular building blocks are similar, or homologous, in structure. The homologies allow lipids to be classified into a few major groups: fatty acids, fatty acid derivatives, cho-lesterol and its derivatives, and lipoproteins.

FATTY ACIDS

Fatty acids rarely occur as free molecules in nature but are usually found as components of many complex lipid molecules such as fats (energy-storage compounds) and phospholipids (the primary lipid components of cellular membranes). They are distinguished from other lipids by their unique physical and chemical properties. Fatty acids also are important nutritional components of the diets of living organisms, and they can be produced within organ-isms through the metabolic breakdown of stored fats.

STRUCTURE OF FATTY ACIDS

Biological fatty acids, members of the class of compounds known as carboxylic acids, are composed of a hydrocarbon chain with one terminal carboxyl group (COOH). The fragment of a carboxylic acid not including the hydroxyl (OH) group is called an acyl group. Under physiological conditions in water, this acidic group usually has lost a hydrogen ion (H^+) to form a negatively charged carboxyl-ate group (COO^-). Most biological fatty acids contain an even number of carbon atoms because the biosynthetic pathway common to all organisms involves chemically

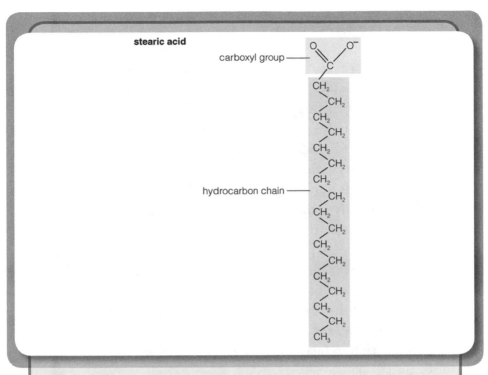

Structural formula of stearic acid. Copyright Encyclopædia Britannica; rendering for this edition by Rosen Educational Services

linking two-carbon units together (although relatively small amounts of odd-number fatty acids do occur in some organisms).

In stearic acid (C_{18}, indicating a hydrocarbon chain with 18 carbon atoms), the molecule as a whole is water-insoluble by virtue of its hydrophobic hydrocarbon chain. The negatively charged carboxylate, however, is hydrophilic. This common form for biological lipids—one that contains well-separated hydrophobic and hydrophilic parts—is called amphipathic. In addition to straight-chain hydrocarbons, fatty acids may also contain pairs of carbons linked by one or more double bonds, methyl branches, or a three-carbon cyclopropane ring near the centre of the carbon chain.

SATURATED FATTY ACIDS

The simplest fatty acids are unbranched, linear chains of CH_2 groups linked by carbon-carbon single bonds with one terminal carboxylic acid group. The term *saturated* indicates that the maximum possible number of hydrogen atoms are bonded to each carbon in the molecule. Many saturated fatty acids have a trivial or common name as well as a chemically descriptive systematic name. The systematic names are based on numbering the carbon atoms, beginning with the acidic carbon. Although the chains are usually between 12 and 24 carbons long, several shorter-chain fatty acids are biochemically important. For instance, butyric acid (C_4) and caproic acid (C_6) are lipids found in milk. Palm kernel oil, an important dietary source of fat in certain areas of the world, is rich in fatty acids that contain 8 and 10 carbons (C_8 and C_{10}).

UNSATURATED FATTY ACIDS

Unsaturated fatty acids have one or more carbon-carbon double bonds. The term *unsaturated* indicates that fewer than the maximum possible number of hydrogen atoms are bonded to each carbon in the molecule. The number of double bonds is indicated by the generic name—*monounsaturated* for molecules with one double bond or *polyunsaturated* for molecules with two or more double bonds. Oleic acid is an example of a monounsaturated fatty acid. The prefix *cis-9* in the systematic name of palmitoleic acid denotes that the position of the double bond is between carbons 9 and 10. Two possible conformations, *cis* and *trans*, can be taken by the two CH_2 groups immediately adjacent to the double-bonded carbons. In the *cis* configuration, the one occurring in all biological unsaturated fatty acids, the two adjacent carbons lie on the same side of the double-bonded carbons. In the *trans* configuration, the two adjacent carbons lie on opposite sides of the double-bonded carbons.

Fatty acids containing more than one carbon-carbon double bond (polyunsaturated fatty acids) are found in relatively minor amounts. The multiple double bonds are almost always separated by a CH_2 group ($-CH_2-CH=CH-CH_2-CH=CH-CH_2-$), a regular spacing motif that is the result of the biosynthetic mechanism by which the double bonds are introduced into the hydrocarbon chain. Arachidonic acid (C_{20}) is of particular interest as the precursor of a family of molecules, known as eicosanoids (from Greek *eikosi*, "twenty"), that includes

Structural formula of oleic acid. Copyright Encyclopædia Britannica; rendering for this edition by Rosen Educational Services

prostaglandins, thromboxanes, and leukotrienes. These compounds, produced by cells under certain conditions, have potent physiological properties. Animals cannot synthesize two important fatty acids, linoleate and linolenate, that are the precursors of the eicosanoids and so must obtain them in the diet from plant sources. For this reason, these precursors are called essential fatty acids.

Trans polyunsaturated fatty acids, although not produced biosynthetically by mammals, are produced by microorganisms in the gut of ruminant animals such as cows and goats, and they are also produced synthetically by partial hydrogenation of fats and oils in the manufacture of margarine. There is evidence that ingestion of these *trans* acids can have deleterious metabolic effects.

SUBSTITUENT GROUPS

In addition to the very common fatty acids with straight saturated or unsaturated acyl chains, many fatty acids are chemically modified by substituents on the hydrocarbon chain. For example, the preening gland of ducks secretes a fatty acid 10 carbons long with methyl (CH_3) groups substituted for one of the hydrogens on carbons 2, 4, 6, and 8. Some bacteria produce fatty acids that have a methyl group on the carbon atom farthest from the acidic group or on the penultimate carbon. Other bacteria incorporate a cyclopropane ring near the centre of the acyl chain. The bacterium that causes tuberculosis (*Mycobacterium tuberculosis*) synthesizes a whole family of cyclopropane-containing fatty acids called α-mycolic acids. Similar fatty acids are found in related bacteria. A third common constituent is a hydroxyl group (OH). Monohydroxyl acids are found in both plants and animals in relatively small amounts, but they are more prevalent in bacteria.

PHYSICAL PROPERTIES

Pure fatty acids form crystals that consist of stacked layers of molecules, with each layer the thickness of two extended molecules. The molecules in a layer are arranged so that the hydrophobic hydrocarbon chains form the interior of the layer and the hydrophilic carboxylic acid groups form the two faces. For a specific fatty acid the details of the molecular packing may vary, giving rise to different crystal forms termed polymorphs.

The melting temperatures of saturated fatty acids of biological interest are above 27 °C (81 °F) and rise with increasing length of the hydrocarbon chain. Monounsaturated and polyunsaturated molecules melt at

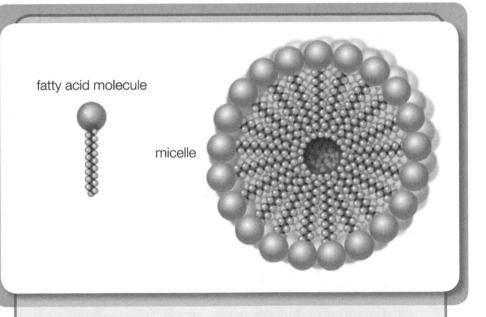

fatty acid molecule

micelle

When a soap is dissolved in water, fatty acids in the soap form spherical structures called micelles, in which the hydrophilic "heads" of the fatty acid molecules are turned toward the water and the hydrophobic "tails" are sheltered in the interior. Encyclopædia Britannica, Inc.

substantially lower temperatures than do their saturated analogs, with the lowest melting temperatures occurring when the carbon-carbon double bonds are located near the centre of the hydrocarbon chain, as they are in most biological molecules. As a result, these molecules form viscous liquids at room temperature.

The hydrophobic character of the hydrocarbon chain of most biological fatty acids exceeds the hydrophilic nature of the carboxylic acid group, making the water solubility of these molecules very low. For example, at 25 °C (77 °F) the solubility in grams of fatty acid per gram of solution is 3×10^{-6}. Water solubility decreases exponentially with the addition of each carbon atom to the hydrocarbon chain. This relationship reflects the energy required to transfer the molecule from a pure hydrocarbon solvent to water. With each CH_2 group, for instance, more energy is required to order water molecules around the hydrocarbon chain of the fatty acid, which results in the hydrophobic effect.

In pure water the carboxylate group can dissociate a positively charged hydrogen ion to only a very small degree, thus: $R\text{-}COOH \rightarrow RCOO^- + H^+$.

Here R represents the hydrocarbon chain. The carboxylate ion, bearing a negative charge, is more polar than the undissociated acid. RCOOH can be converted completely to the ion $RCOO^-$ by adding an equal number of molecules of a base such as sodium hydroxide (NaOH). This effectively replaces the H^+ with Na^+ to give the salt of the fatty acid, which is a soap. The very useful detergent property of soaps stems from the fact that the $RCOO^-$ anions in water spontaneously form stable, spherical aggregates called micelles. The interior of these structures, formed by the hydrocarbon chains, is an excellent solvent in which grease and hydrophobic dirt of all sorts can be sequestered. The diameter of each micelle is roughly twice the length of the extended fatty acid. Dispersions of micelles in water can be made quite concentrated and exhibit great cleansing power. These dispersions are stable and generally look very much like pure water. Bubbles and foams on the surface of soap dispersions are the result of the spontaneous adsorption of RCOO⁻ ions at the interface between the aqueous dispersion and air, with the result that the air–water interfaces are energetically stabilized and can therefore be mechanically expanded.

CHEMICAL PROPERTIES

The most chemically reactive portion of fatty acids is the acidic carboxyl group (COOH). It reacts with alcohols (R'OH) to form products known as esters (RCOOR') and releases water in the process. This ester bond is the principal covalent bond linking fatty acid moieties to other groups in more complex lipids. A second chemical bond, occurring much less frequently in biological lipids involving fatty acids, is the ether bond (R'-O-R). Ether bonds are chemically more stable than ester bonds.

The hydrocarbon part of a fatty acid molecule is quite resistant to chemical attack unless carbon-carbon double bonds are present. A number of different kinds of molecules react with such a double bond. For example, when a catalyst such as platinum is present, hydrogen gas adds to the double bond to give a saturated fatty acid. Halogens (chlorine, bromine, and iodine) and their derivatives such as hydroiodic acid (HI) also react with the double bond to form saturated fatty acids, but in these cases one or two atoms of the halogen replace one or two of the hydrogens normally found in the saturated acyl chain. Carbon-carbon double bonds can also react with oxygen in either nonenzymatic processes or enzymatically catalyzed oxidation reactions. This process generates a variety of products, some of which contribute to the rancid smell in spoiled meat and vegetable products. In general, the more highly unsaturated the fatty acid, the more easily it is oxidized.

BIOLOGICAL SOURCES

Fatty acids are found in biological systems either as free molecules or as components of more complex lipids. They are derived from dietary sources or produced by metabolism.

DIGESTION

The main source of fatty acids in the diet is triglycerides, generically called fats. In humans, fat constitutes an important part of the diet, and in the more developed countries it can contribute as much as 45 percent of energy intake. Triglycerides consist of three fatty acid molecules, each linked by an ester bond to one of the three OH groups of a glycerol molecule. After ingested triglycerides pass through the stomach and into the small intestine, detergents called bile salts are secreted by the liver via the gallbladder and disperse the fat as micelles. Pancreatic enzymes called lipases then hydrolyze the dispersed fats to give monoglycerides and free fatty acids. These products are absorbed into the cells lining the small intestine, where they are resynthesized into triglycerides. The triglycerides, together with other types of lipids, are then secreted by these cells in lipoproteins, large molecular complexes that are transported in the lymph and blood to recipient organs. In detail, the process of triglyceride or fat absorption from dietary sources is quite complex and differs somewhat depending upon the animal species.

STORAGE

After transport through the circulation, triglycerides are hydrolyzed yet again to fatty acids in the adipose tissue. There they are transported into adipose cells, where once again they are resynthesized into triglycerides and stored as droplets. Fat or adipose tissue essentially consists of cells the interior of which is largely occupied by a fat droplet. The triglyceride in these droplets is available to the body on demand as communicated to adipose tissue by hormone messengers.

Various animals store triglycerides in different ways. In sharks, for example, fat is stored in the liver, but in bony fish it is deposited in and around muscle fibres. Insects store fat in a special organ called the fat body. The development of true adipose tissue is found only in higher animals.

BIOSYNTHESIS

In mammals, fatty acids are synthesized in adipose and liver cells from glucose via a fairly complex pathway. In essence, the six carbons of a glucose molecule are oxidized to a pair of two-carbon carboxylic acid fragments called acetate. The starting point for biosynthesis is an acetate group chemically linked to a molecule of CoA (coenzyme A). The process of building up the acyl chain of a fatty acid then begins, basically through the sequential chemical addition of two-carbon fragments from CoA-acetate to generate, for example, the 16-carbon saturated fatty acid palmitate. This process is catalyzed by a complex enzyme known as fatty acid synthase. Elongation of the palmitate carbon chain and the introduction of carbon-carbon double bonds are carried out subsequently by other enzyme systems.

The overall process is basically the same in organisms ranging from bacteria to humans. The required energy is supplied by oxidation of part of the carbon in a glucose molecule to carbon dioxide (CO_2) as follows: 4½ molecules of glucose plus 4 molecules of oxygen yield 1 molecule of palmitic acid plus 11 molecules of CO_2 plus a small surplus of available energy as 5 molecules of ATP, the chemical energy currency of the cell.

FATTY ACID DERIVATIVES

Fatty acid derivatives may be divided into several major groups based on their structural organization and chemical properties. Among the best characterized of the fatty acid derivatives are the triglycerides, plant and animal waxes, and derivatives occurring in biological membranes.

TRIGLYCERIDES

Triglycerides (chemical name triacylglycerol), the principal means of storing fatty acids in biological systems, are a class of compounds that consist of glycerol (a three-carbon trihydroxy alcohol) with a fatty acid linked to each of the three OH groups by an ester bond. Because this molecule contains only one type of fatty acid, it is referred to as a simple triglyceride. Almost all naturally occurring triglyceride molecules, however, contain more than one type of fatty acid. When two or more in a given molecule are different, it is called a mixed triglyceride. For any specific combination of three fatty acids, three different molecules are possible, depending upon which of the three fatty acids is bonded to the central carbon of glycerol. Considering the numbers of common

tristearin (tristearic acid)

glycerol

stearic acid
(fatty acid) chains

Structural formula of tristearin (tristearic acid). Copyright Encyclopædia Britannica; rendering for this edition by Rosen Educational Services

saturated, monounsaturated, and polyunsaturated fatty acids, it is evident that there are a great many different triglycerides.

Triglycerides are hydrophobic substances that are soluble only in some organic solvents. Unlike many other types of complex lipids, they possess no electric charges and are therefore referred to as neutral lipids. The molecular structure of a few triglycerides that have been studied in crystals indicates that the acyl chains on the 1 and 2 carbons of glycerol, together with the 1 and 2 carbons of glycerol itself, form a straight line. Carbon 3 projects at right angles to this line, but the acyl chain on its glycerol folds over at the carboxyl carbon to lie alongside the acyl chain on carbon 1. Triglyceride molecules look much like a tuning fork and, when packed together, produce layered crystals.

The melting temperatures of mixed triglycerides are roughly an average of the melting temperatures of their constituent fatty acids. In simple triglycerides, melting temperatures rise with increasing acyl chain length but drop with increasing number of double bonds. Melted triglycerides are generally quite viscous oils. From the physiological standpoint, it is important that most stored triglycerides be fluid at body temperature in order to permit their rapid mobilization as an energy source. Liquidity is also important since subcutaneous stored fats perform an insulating function that must not interfere with the mobility of the organism and its parts.

WAXES

A second group of neutral lipids that are of physiological importance, though they are a minor component of biological systems, are waxes. Essentially, waxes consist of a long-chain fatty acid linked through an ester oxygen to a long-chain alcohol. These molecules are completely water-insoluble and generally solid at biological temperatures. Their strongly hydrophobic nature allows them to function as water repellents on the leaves of some plants, on feathers, and on the cuticles of certain insects. Waxes also serve as energy-storage substances in plankton (microscopic aquatic plants and animals) and in higher members of the aquatic food chain. Plankton apparently use the biosynthesis of waxes to adjust their buoyant density and thus their depth in the ocean. It has been suggested that a major source of petroleum found in deep-sea sediments originates from the deposition of wax-rich dead plankton over vast periods of time. Whales and many fishes also store large quantities of waxes.

BIOLOGICAL MEMBRANE LIPIDS

The three principal classes of lipids that form the bilayer matrix of biological membranes are

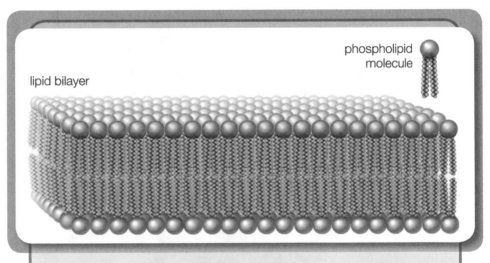

Phospholipid molecules, like molecules of many lipids, are composed of a hydrophilic "head" and one or more hydrophobic "tails." In a water medium, the molecules form a lipid bilayer, or two-layered sheet, in which the heads are turned toward the watery medium and the tails are sheltered inside, away from the water. This bilayer is the basis of the membranes of living cells. Encyclopædia Britannica, Inc.

glycerophospholipids, sphingolipids, and sterols (principally cholesterol). The most important characteristic of molecules in the first two groups is their amphipathic structure—well-separated hydrophilic (polar) and hydrophobic (nonpolar) regions. Generally, their shape is elongated, with a hydrophilic end or head attached to a hydrophobic moiety by a short intervening region of intermediate polarity. Because of the segregation of polarity and nonpolarity, amphipathic molecules in any solvent will spontaneously form aggregates that

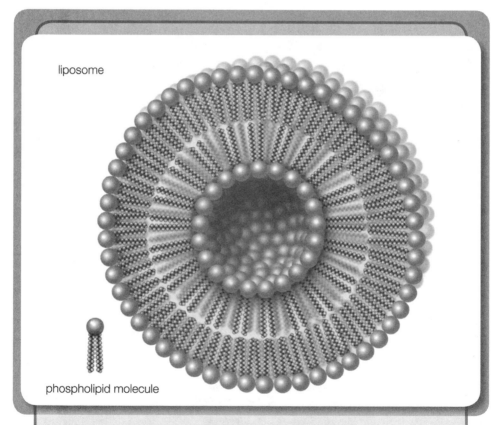

liposome

phospholipid molecule

Phospholipids can be used to form artificial structures called liposomes, which are double-walled, hollow spheres useful for encapsulating other molecules such as pharmaceutical drugs. Encyclopædia Britannica, Inc.

minimize energetically unfavourable contacts (by keeping unlike regions of molecules apart) and maximize favourable contacts with the solvent (by keeping similar regions of molecules together). The molecular arrangement of the aggregate depends upon the solvent and the details of the amphipathic structure of the lipid.

In water, micelles formed by soaps (the sodium or potassium salts of fatty acids) are one such aggregate. The polar or hydrophilic portion of the soap molecules forms the surface of the micelle, while the hydrocarbon chains form its interior and are thus completely protected from the energetically unfavourable contact with water. Biological membrane lipids, however, do not form spherical micelles in water but instead form topologically closed lamellar (layered) structures. The polar heads of the component molecules form the two faces of the lamella, while the hydrophobic moieties form its interior. Each lamella is thus two molecules in thickness, with the long axis of the component molecules perpendicular to the plane of the bilayer.

Other types of aggregates are also formed in water by certain amphipathic lipids. For example, liposomes are artificial collections of lipids arranged in a bilayer, having an inside and an outside surface. The lipid bilayers form a sphere that can trap a molecule inside. The liposome structure can be useful for protecting sensitive molecules that are to be delivered orally.

GLYCEROPHOSPHOLIPIDS

Lipids of this class are the most abundant in biological membranes. In glycerophospholipids, fatty acids (often referred to generically as R1 and R2) are linked through an ester oxygen to carbons 1 and 2 of glycerol, the backbone of the molecule. Phosphate is ester-linked to carbon 3, while any one of several possible sub-stituents (R3) is also linked to the phosphate moiety. Glycerophospholipids are amphipathic—glycerol and phosphate form the polar end of the molecule, while hydrocarbon chains form the nonpolar end. Although the fatty acids can be any of those common in biological systems, usually those attached to carbon 1 are satu-rated and those attached to carbon 2 are unsaturated. The various combinations of two fatty acids give rise to many different molecules bearing the same R3 sub-stituent group. Since this is true for each head group, there are altogether about a thousand possible types of glycerophospholipids. The great majority are found in biological membranes.

From the standpoint of physical properties, the greatest difference among various molecules lies in the particular R3 substituent. This is due in part to the different sizes of the various types of R3 and in part to differences in their electric charges. The phos-phatidylcholines and phosphatidylethanolamines are zwitterionic, meaning they have one negative and one positive charge on R3. Phosphatidic acid, phosphati-dylserine, and phosphatidylinositol have a net negative charge. Differences in fatty acid composition also con-tribute to differences in physical properties of a series of molecules with the same R3. In the presence of an excess of water, the molecules form aggregates with a variety of geometries, the most common of which is the bilayer.

In bilayers many glycerophospholipids as well as sphingomyelin can be in either one of two states, gel or liquid-crystalline. In the solidlike gel state, the lipid molecules in each half of the bilayer are arranged in a two-dimensional lattice, with their two acyl chains in the extended form. With the application of heat, the

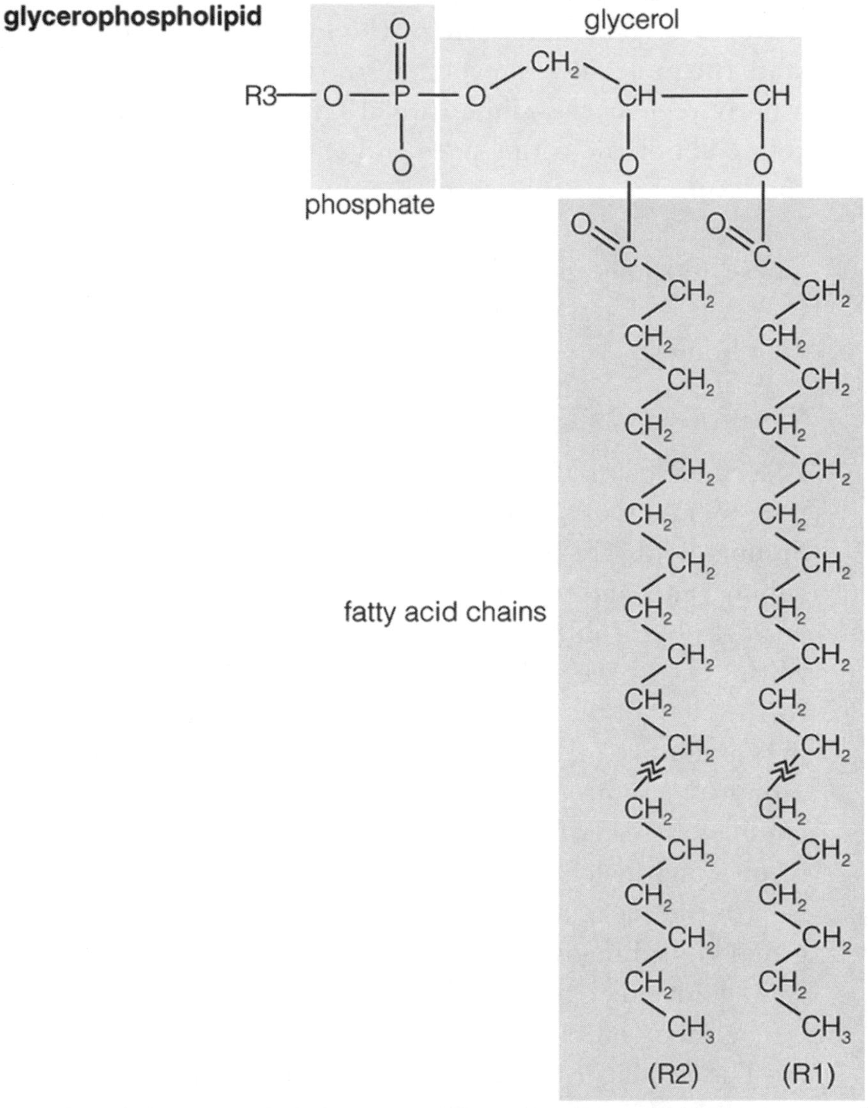

glycerophospholipid

glycerol

phosphate

fatty acid chains

(R2) (R1)

General structural formula of a glycerophospholipid. The composition of the specific molecule depends on the chemical group (designated R3 in the diagram) linked to the phosphate and glycerol "head" and also on the lengths of the fatty acid "tails" (R1 and R2). Copyright Encyclopædia Britannica; rendering for this edition by Rosen Educational Services

gel converts into the liquid-crystalline state at some temperature characteristic of the lipid mixture. In this state the molecules in each half of the bilayer remain in a fairly regular two-dimensional lattice but are free to rotate about their long axes and slide laterally through the layer. Their acyl chains now undergo considerable motion, leading to transiently kinked conformations. These motions give the bilayer a quasi-liquid behaviour that is characteristic of the bilayers in all biological membranes.

Sphingolipids

A second major class of lipids usually associated with the membranes surrounding cells is sphingolipids. Sphingolipids are based on an 18-carbon amine alcohol, sphingosine, and to a much lesser extent on a 20-carbon analog, phytosphingosine. All but one generic member of this class have a simple or complex sugar (R2) linked to the alcohol on carbon 1. The single deviant member is sphingomyelin, a molecule with a phosphorylcholine group (the same polar head group as in phosphatidylcholine) instead of the sugar moiety, making it an analog of phosphatidylcholine. All sphingolipids have, in addition to the sugar, a fatty acid (R1) attached to the amino group of sphingosine. Among the sphingolipids, only sphingomyelin, a phospholipid, is a major component of biological membranes.

The principal factor determining the physical properties of sphingolipids is the substituent group attached to carbon 1 of sphingosine. Minor variations in properties depend upon the particular fatty acid component. The glycosphingolipids, all containing a sugar attached to carbon 1 of sphingosine, have physical properties that depend primarily on the complexity and composition of

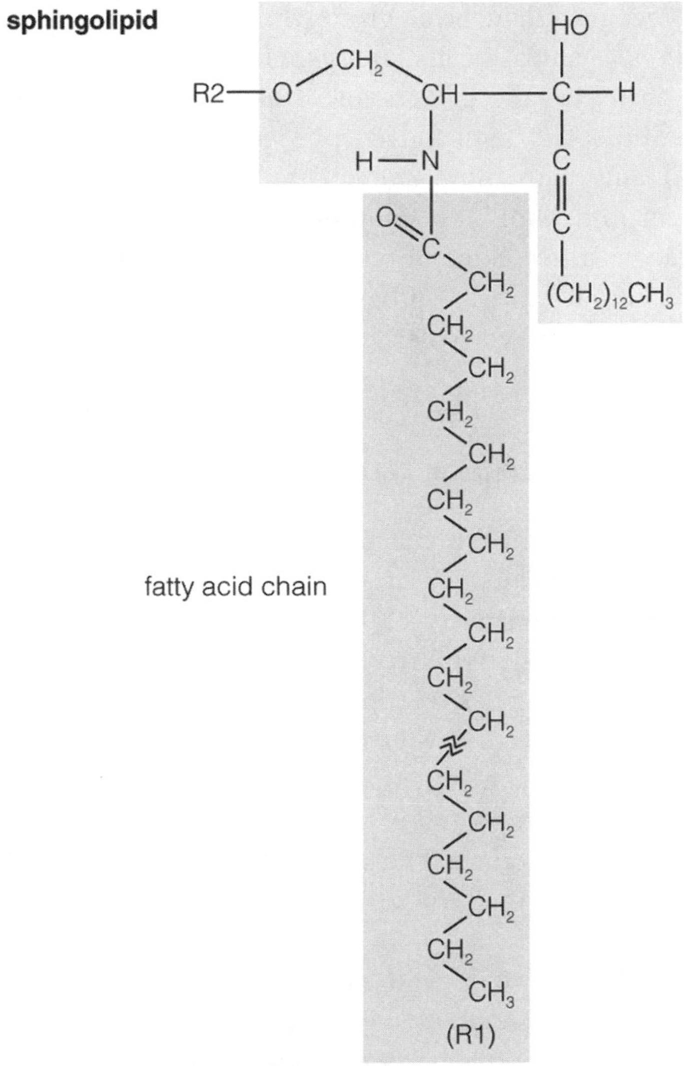
sphingolipid
R2—O
CH2
CH
HO
C—H
H—N
C
C
O
C
CH2
(CH2)12CH3
fatty acid chain
CH3
(R1)

General structural formula of a sphingolipid. The composition of the specific molecule depends on the chemical group (designated R2 in the diagram) linked to the alcohol "head" and also on the length of the fatty acid "tail" (R1). Copyright Encyclopædia Britannica; rendering for this edition by Rosen Educational Services

this substituent. Two generic types of glycosphingolipids are recognized: neutral glycosphingolipids, which contain only neutral sugars, and gangliosides, which contain one or more sialic acid residues linked to the sugar. Many hundreds of different glycosphingolipids have been isolated, and many more unidentified types probably exist. Glycosphingolipids are found exclusively on the external surface of the cell membrane, where their sugar moieties often act as antigens and as receptors for hormones and other signaling molecules.

CHOLESTEROL AND ITS DERIVATIVES

Cholesterol may be the most intensely studied small molecule of biological origin. Not only are its complex biosynthetic pathway and the physiologically important products derived from it of scientific interest, but also the strong correlation in humans between high blood cholesterol levels and the incidence of heart attack and stroke (diseases that are the leading causes of death in Europe and North America) is of paramount medical importance. The study of this molecule and its biological origin have resulted in more than a dozen Nobel prizes.

Cholesterol is a prominent member of a large class of lipids called isoprenoids that are widely distributed in nature. The class name derives from the fact that these molecules are formed by chemical condensation of a simple five-carbon molecule, isoprene. Isoprenoids encompass diverse biological molecules such as steroid hormones, sterols (cholesterol, ergosterol, and sitosterol), bile acids, the lipid-soluble vitamins (A, D, E, and K), phytol (a lipid component of the photosynthetic pigment chlorophyll),

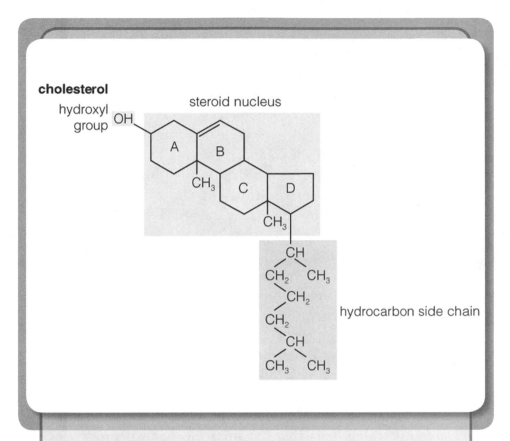

cholesterol

hydroxyl group

steroid nucleus

OH

A B

CH₃ C D

CH₃

CH

CH₂ CH₃

CH₂

CH₂

CH

CH₃ CH₃

hydrocarbon side chain

Structural formula of cholesterol. Copyright Encyclopædia Britannica; rendering for this edition by Rosen Educational Services

the insect juvenile hormones, plant hormones (gibberellins), and polyisoprene (the major component of natural rubber). Many other biologically important isoprenoids play more-subtle roles in biology.

STRUCTURE AND PROPERTIES

The sterols are major components of biological membranes in eukaryotes (organisms whose cells have a nucleus) but are rare in prokaryotes (cells without a nucleus, such as bacteria). Cholesterol is the principal sterol of animals, whereas the major sterol in fungi is ergosterol and that in plants is sitosterol. The characteristic feature of each of these three important molecules is a steroid nucleus composed of four rigidly fused carbon rings (for simplicity, referred to as A, B, C, and D) with a hydroxyl (OH) group attached to ring A. One molecule is distinguished from another by the positions of the carbon-carbon double bonds and by the structure of the hydrocarbon side chain on ring D.

Cholesterol and its relatives are hydrophobic molecules with exceedingly low water solubility. The overall hydrophobicity is negligibly affected by the hydrophilic OH group. The structure of cholesterol is such that it does not form aggregates in water, although it does shoehorn between the molecules of biological membranes, with its OH group located at the water-membrane interface. The stiff fused ring structure of cholesterol adds rigidity to liquid-crystalline phospholipid bilayers and strengthens them against mechanical rupture. Cholesterol is thus an important component of the membrane surrounding a cell, where its concentration may rise as high as 50 percent by weight.

BIOSYNTHESIS

Cholesterol biosynthesis can be divided into four stages. The first stage generates a six-carbon compound called mevalonic acid from three two-carbon acetate units (derived from the oxidation of fuel molecules—e.g., glucose) in the form of acetyl-CoA. In the second stage mevalonate is converted to a five-carbon molecule of isopentenyl pyrophosphate in a series of four reactions. The conversion of this product to a 30-carbon compound, squalene, in the third stage requires the condensation of six molecules of isopentenyl pyrophosphate. In the fourth stage the linear squalene molecule is formed into rings in a complex reaction sequence to give the 27-carbon cholesterol.

BIOSYNTHETIC DERIVATIVES

Two classes of important molecules, bile acids and steroid hormones, are derived from cholesterol in vertebrates. Bile acids are the primary components of bile, the greenish yellow secretion that is produced in the liver and aids in the digestion of fats in the duodenum, a region of the small intestine. Steroid hormones are secreted by three "steroid glands"—the adrenal cortex, testes, and ovaries—and are transported through the bloodstream to the cells of various target organs where they carry out the regulation of a wide range of physiological functions.

BILE ACIDS

The bile acids and their salts are detergents that emulsify fats in the gut during digestion. They are synthesized from cholesterol in the liver by a series of reactions that introduce a hydroxyl group into ring B and ring C and shorten the acyl side chain of ring D to seven carbons with the terminal carbon changed to a carboxyl group. The resulting molecule, cholic acid—as well as chenodeoxycholic acid (a close relative lacking the OH on ring C)—are usually found in the form of their salts, in which the amino acids taurine and glycine are chemically linked to the side-chain carboxyl group. These detergents are secreted from the liver into the gallbladder, where they are stored before being released through the bile duct into the small intestine. After performing an emulsifying action that is essential in fat digestion, they are reabsorbed in the lower small intestine, returned through the blood to the liver, and reused. This cyclic process, called the enterohepatic circulation, handles 20 to 30 grams (0.7 to 1.1 oz) of bile acids per day in humans. The small fraction that escapes this circulation is lost in the feces. This is the major excretory route for cholesterol (though a smaller fraction is lost through the normal sloughing of dead skin cells).

STEROID HORMONES

The steroid hormones consume a very small fraction of the total cholesterol available in the organism, but they are very important physiologically. There are five principal classes, all derived from cholesterol: progestins (active during pregnancy), the glucocorticoids (promoting the synthesis of glucose and suppressing inflammatory reactions), the mineralocorticoids (regulating ion balances), estrogens (promoting female sex characteristics), and androgens (promoting male sex characteristics). With the exception of progesterone, all of these closely related biologically active molecules have in common a shortened side chain in ring D and, in some cases, an oxidized OH group on ring A. The individual molecules are synthesized on demand by the placenta in pregnant women, by the adrenal cortex, and by the gonads.

REGULATION OF CHOLESTEROL METABOLISM

High blood levels of cholesterol have been recognized as a primary risk factor for heart disease. For this reason, much research has been focused on the control of cholesterol's biosynthesis, on its transport in the blood, and on its storage in the body. The overall level of cholesterol in the body is the result of a balance between dietary intake and cellular biosynthesis on the one hand and, on the other hand, elimination of cholesterol from the body (principally as its metabolic products, bile acids). As the dietary intake of cholesterol increases in normal persons, there is a corresponding decrease in absorption from the intestines and an increase in the synthesis and excretion of bile acids—which normally accounts for about 70 percent of the cholesterol lost from the body.

Regulation of cholesterol biosynthesis in the liver and other cells of the body is well characterized. The initial enzyme that forms mevalonate in the first stage of biosynthesis is controlled by two processes. One is inhibition of the synthesis of this enzyme by cholesterol itself or a derivative of it. The other is regulation of the catalytic activity of the enzyme by phosphorylation/dephosphorylation in response to intracellular signals. Several pharmacological agents also inhibit the enzyme, with the result that unhealthy levels of cholesterol can be lowered over a period of time.

TRANSPORT AND STORAGE

The normal human body contains about 100 grams (3.5 oz) of cholesterol, although this amount can vary considerably among healthy people. Approximately 60 grams (2.1 oz) of this total are moving dynamically through the organism. Because cholesterol is insoluble in water, the basis of the bodily fluids, it is carried through the circulatory system by transport particles in the blood called lipoproteins. These microscopic complexes contain both lipids and proteins that can accommodate cholesterol and still remain soluble in blood.

Cholesterol is absorbed into the cells of the intestinal lining, where it is incorporated into lipoprotein complexes called chylomicrons and then secreted into the lymphatic circulation. The lymph ultimately enters the bloodstream, and the lipoproteins are carried to the liver. Cholesterol, whether derived from the diet or newly synthesized by the liver, is transported in the blood in lipoproteins (very low-density [VLDL] and low-density lipoproteins [LDL]) to the tissues and organs of the body. There the cholesterol is incorporated into biological membranes or stored as cholesteryl esters—molecules formed by the reaction of a fatty acid (most commonly oleate) with the hydroxyl group of cholesterol. Esters of cholesterol are even more hydrophobic than cholesterol itself, and in cells they coalesce into droplets analogous to the fat droplets in adipose cells. Cholesterol is lost from cells in peripheral tissues by transfer to another type of circulating lipoprotein (high-density lipoprotein [HDL]) in the blood and is then returned to the liver, where it is metabolized to bile acids and salts.

LIPOPROTEINS

Lipoproteins are lipid–protein complexes that allow all lipids derived from food or synthesized in specific organs to be transported throughout the body by the circulatory system. The basic structure of these aggregates is that of an oil droplet made up of triglycerides and cholesteryl esters surrounded by a layer of proteins and amphipathic lipids—very similar to that of a micelle, a spherical structure. If the concentration of one or another lipoprotein becomes too high, then a fraction of the complex becomes insoluble and is deposited on the walls of arteries and capillaries. This buildup of deposits is called atherosclerosis and ultimately results in blockage of critical arteries to cause a heart attack or stroke. Because of the gravity of this condition, much research is focused on lipoproteins and their functions.

CLASSIFICATION AND FORMATION

There are four major classes of circulating lipoproteins, each with its own characteristic protein and lipid composition. They are chylomicrons, VLDLs, LDLs, and HDLs. Within all these classes of complexes, the various molecular components are not chemically linked to each other but are simply associated in such a way as to minimize hydrophobic contacts with water. The most distinguishing feature of each class is the relative amounts of lipid and protein. Because the lipid and protein composition is reflected in the density of each lipoprotein (lipid molecules being less dense than proteins), density, an easily measured attribute, forms the operational basis of defining the lipoprotein classes. Measuring density also provides the basis of separating and purifying lipoproteins from plasma for study and diagnosis.

The principal lipid components are triglycerides, cholesterol, cholesteryl esters, and phospholipids. The hydrophobic core of the particle is formed by the triglycerides and cholesteryl esters. The fatty acyl chains of these components are unsaturated, and so the core structure is liquid at body temperature. With the exception of LDL, which contains only one type of apoprotein, all classes have multiple apoprotein components. All the apoproteins, like phospholipids, are amphipathic and interact favourably with both lipids and water.

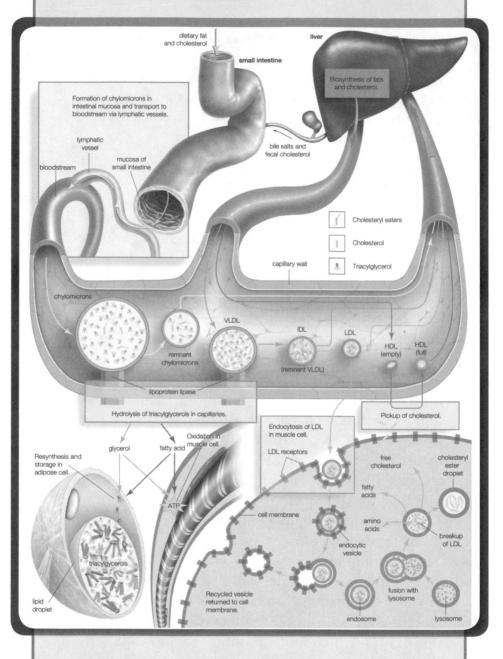

Synthesis of lipoprotein complexes in the small intestine, liver, and blood plasma, and their delivery to peripheral tissues of the body. Encyclopædia Britannica, Inc.

CHYLOMICRONS

Chylomicrons are the largest lipoproteins, with diameters of 75 to 600 nm (1 nm = 10^{-9} metre). They have the lowest protein-to-lipid ratio and therefore the lowest density. Chylomicrons are synthesized by the absorptive cells of the intestinal lining and are secreted by these cells into the lymphatic system, which joins the blood circulation at the subclavian vein. The triglyceride, cholesteryl ester, and free cholesterol content of these particles is derived from the digestion of dietary fat. Their primary destinations in peripheral areas are heart muscle, skeletal muscle, adipose tissue, and lactating mammary tissue. The transfer of triglycerides and cholesteryl esters to the tissues depletes the lipid-protein aggregates of these substances and leaves remnant chylomicrons, which are eventually taken up by the liver. The lipid and protein remnants are used to form VLDL and LDL.

VERY LOW-DENSITY LIPOPROTEINS

VLDL is a lipoprotein class synthesized by the liver that is analogous to the chylomicrons secreted by the intestine. Its purpose is also to deliver triglycerides, cholesteryl esters, and cholesterol to peripheral tissues. VLDL is largely depleted of its triglyceride content in these tissues and gives rise to an intermediate-density lipoprotein (IDL) remnant, which is returned to the liver in the bloodstream. As might be expected, the same proteins are present in both VLDL and IDL.

LOW-DENSITY LIPOPROTEINS

LDLs are derived from VLDL and IDL in the plasma and contain a large amount of cholesterol and cholesteryl esters. Their principal role is to deliver these two forms

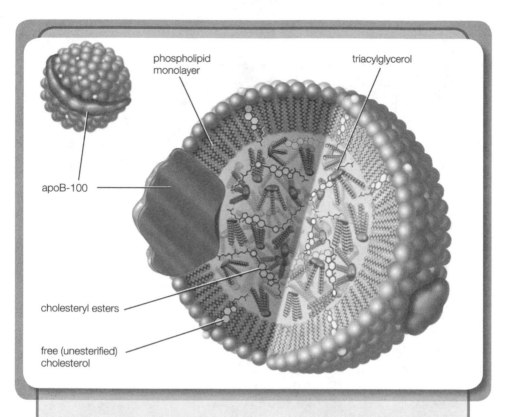

phospholipid monolayer

triacylglycerol

apoB-100

cholesteryl esters

free (unesterified) cholesterol

The low-density lipoprotein (LDL) complex is essentially a droplet of triacylglycerols and cholesteryl esters encased in a sphere made up of phospholipid, free cholesterol, and protein molecules known as apoprotein B-100 (apoB-100). The LDL complex is the principal vehicle for delivering cholesterol to body tissues through the blood. Encyclopædia Britannica, Inc.

of cholesterol to peripheral tissues. Almost two-thirds of the cholesterol and its esters found in plasma (blood free of red and white cells) is associated with LDL.

HIGH-DENSITY LIPOPROTEINS

Lipoproteins of this class are the smallest, with a diameter of 10.8 nm and the highest protein-to-lipid ratio. The resulting high density gives this class its name. HDL plays a primary role in the removal of excess cholesterol from cells and returning it to the liver, where it is metabolized to bile acids and salts that are eventually eliminated through the intestine. LDL and HDL together are the major factors in maintaining the cholesterol balance of the body. Because of the high correlation between blood cholesterol levels and atherosclerosis, high ratios of HDL to cholesterol (principally as found in LDL) correlate well with a lower incidence of this disease in humans.

FUNCTIONS, ORIGINS, AND RECYCLING OF APOLIPOPROTEINS

Chylomicrons are synthesized in the intestinal mucosa. The cells of this tissue, although able to make most apoproteins, are the principal source of apolippproteinB; (apoB; the B-48 form) and apoA-I. The apoC-II component of chylomicrons is an activator for a plasma enzyme that hydrolyzes the triglyceride of these complexes. This enzyme, called lipoprotein lipase, resides on the cell surface and makes the fatty acids of triglycerides available to the cell for energy metabolism. To some degree, the enzyme is also activated by apoC-II, present in minor amounts in chylomicrons.

VLDL, the lipoprotein carrier for triglycerides synthesized in the liver and destined for use in the heart and muscle, has a complement of five apoproteins. Among them are apoB-100, a protein performing a structural role in the complex, and apoC-I, -II, and -III. The first two of these activate the enzymes lecithin cholesterol acyltransferase (LCAT) and lipoprotein lipase. Curiously, apoC-III, a minor component of both chylomicrons and VLDL, inhibits lipoprotein lipase. Following discharge of the triglycerides, the remnants of VLDL return to the liver.

LDL contains a single apoprotein and is the principal carrier of cholesterol to the peripheral tissue as both the free sterol and esters. The discharge of the lipid contents of this complex requires the recognition of the LDL B-100 apoprotein by a receptor located on the surface of recipient cells. When the protein is bound to the receptor, the receptor-LDL complex is engulfed by the cell in a process known as endocytosis. The endocytosed LDL discharges its contents within the cell, and B-100 is degraded to free amino acids that are used to synthesize new proteins or are metabolized as an energy source. The elucidation of the process of cellular uptake of LDL by Michael S. Brown and Joseph L. Goldstein earned them the Nobel Prize for Physiology or Medicine in 1985.

Michael S. Brown

(b. April 13, 1941, New York, N.Y., U.S.)

American molecular geneticist Michael S. Brown contributed to the elucidation of a key link in the metabolism of cholesterol in the human body. He shared the 1985 Nobel Prize for Physiology or Medicine with Joseph L. Goldstein.

Brown graduated from the University of Pennsylvania, Philadelphia, in 1962 and received his M.D. from that university's medical school in 1966. He became friends with Goldstein when they were both working as interns at Massachusetts General Hospital in Boston during 1966–68. After conducting research at the National Institutes of Health from 1968 to 1971, he became an assistant professor at the Southwestern Medical School in Dallas, Texas, where he was reunited with his colleague Goldstein.

In Dallas the two men began their collaborative research on the genetic factors that are responsible for high levels of cholesterol in the bloodstream. They compared the cells of normal persons with those of persons having familial hypercholesterolemia, which is an inherited tendency to get abnormally high blood cholesterol levels and, as a result, atherosclerosis and other circulatory ailments.

Brown and Goldstein were able to trace a genetic defect in the afflicted persons that resulted in their lacking or being deficient in cell receptors for low-density lipoproteins (LDL), which are the primary cholesterol-carrying particles. Their research established that these cell receptors draw the LDL particles into the cells as a prelude to breaking them down, and thus remove them from the bloodstream. The two men also discovered that the cell capture of such lipoproteins inhibits the further production of new LDL receptors by the cells, thus explaining how high-cholesterol diets overwhelm the body's natural capacity for withdrawing cholesterol from the bloodstream.

Brown later collaborated with Goldstein in research to develop new drugs effective in lowering blood cholesterol levels and in researching the basic genetic code behind the LDL receptor. From 1977 he was professor and director of the Center for Genetic Diseases at the Southwestern Medical School, where in 1985 he was elevated to regental professor. In 1984 Brown and Goldstein were awarded the Louisa Gross Horowitz Prize for Biology or Biochemistry, and in 1988 Brown was awarded the National Medal of Science.

In the 1990s Brown and Goldstein discovered sterol regulatory element binding proteins (SREBPs), transcription factors that control the uptake and synthesis of cholesterol and fatty acids. In their follow-up studies they uncovered the mechanism by which SREBPs are activated to regulate the metabolism of lipids. In 2003 they were awarded the Albany Medical Prize. Brown and Goldstein shared a laboratory, where they conducted their research jointly.

The primary function of HDL with its complement of apoproteins is to take up cholesterol from the cells of the body and deliver it to the liver for its ultimate excretion as bile acids and salts. The major apoproteins are A-I, an LCAT activator, and A-II. All of the HDL apoproteins have their biosynthetic origin in the liver. When HDL is secreted by this organ, it is a small, flattened discoid devoid of cholesterol but containing phospholipids and the apoproteins. In the peripheral tissues, HDL picks up cholesterol from the surface membranes of cells and, through the agency LCAT, converts it into esters using acyl chains from phosphatidylcholine.

Joseph L. Goldstein

(b. April 18, 1940, Sumter, S.C., U.S.)

American molecular geneticist Joseph L. Goldstein contributed to the discovery of the process by which cholesterol is metabolized in the human body. He shared the 1985 Nobel Prize for Physiology or Medicine with Michael S. Brown.

Goldstein received his B.S. degree from Washington and Lee University, Lexington, Va., in 1962 and obtained his medical degree from the Southwestern Medical School of the University of Texas at Dallas in 1966. Goldstein became friends with Brown when they were both working as interns at Massachusetts General Hospital from 1966 to 1968. Goldstein then conducted research under the auspices of the National Institutes of Health from 1968 to 1972, studying genetically predisposing factors that caused the accumulation of blood cholesterol in people prone to heart attacks. He returned to teach at the Southwestern Medical School in Dallas in 1972 and was there reunited with his colleague Brown.

The two men then began a concerted study of the processes affecting the accumulation of cholesterol in the bloodstream. In the course of their research they discovered that low-density lipoproteins (LDLs), which are primary cholesterol-carrying particles, are withdrawn from the bloodstream into the body's cells by receptors on the cells' surface. The genetic absence of these LDL receptors was found to be the cause of familial hypercholesterolemia, a disorder in which the body's tissues are incapable of removing cholesterol from the bloodstream. The new understanding of cells' receptors' role in the regulation of cholesterol levels in the bloodstream spurred the successful use of drugs and the manipulation of diet in lowering blood cholesterol levels.

From 1976 Goldstein was professor of medicine and from 1977 chairman of the department of molecular genetics at the University of Texas Health Science Center in Dallas; he was named regental professor of the University of Texas in 1985. In addition to the Nobel Prize, Goldstein and Brown have received numerous awards for their research on cholesterol and lipoproteins, including the Louisa Gross Horowitz Prize for Biology or Biochemistry (1984), the Albert Lasker Basic Medical Research Award (1985), and the National Medal of Science (1988).

In the 1990s the two scientists made another groundbreaking advance in cholesterol research when they discovered a new family of transcription factors called sterol regulatory element binding proteins (SREBPs). Goldstein and Brown found that SREBPs controlled the synthesis of cholesterol and fatty acids, and in subsequent studies they elucidated the mechanism of activation that enables SREBPs to regulate lipid metabolism. In 2003 Goldstein and Brown were honoured with an Albany Medical Center Prize for their work on SREBPs.

BIOLOGICAL FUNCTIONS OF LIPIDS

The majority of lipids in biological systems function either as a source of stored metabolic energy or as structural matrices and permeability barriers in biological membranes. Very small amounts of special lipids act as both intracellular messengers and extracellular messengers such as hormones and pheromones. Amphipathic lipids, the molecules that allow membranes to form compartments, must have been among the progenitors of living beings. This theory is supported by studies of several simple, single-cell organisms, in which up to one-third of the genome is thought to code for membrane proteins and the enzymes of membrane lipid biosynthesis.

CELLULAR ENERGY SOURCE

Fatty acids that are stored in adipose tissue as triglycerides are a major energy source in higher animals, as is glucose, a simple six-carbon carbohydrate. In healthy, well-fed humans only about 2 percent of the energy is derived from the metabolism of protein. Large amounts of lipids are stored in adipose tissue. In the average American male about 25 percent of body weight is fat, whereas only 1 percent is accounted for by glycogen (a polymer of glucose). In addition, the energy available to the body from oxidative metabolism of 1 gram of triglyceride is more than twice that produced by the oxidation of an equal weight of carbohydrate such as glycogen.

STORAGE OF TRIGLYCERIDE IN ADIPOSE CELLS

In higher animals and humans, adipose tissue consisting of adipocytes (fat cells) is widely distributed over the body—mainly under the skin, around deep blood vessels, and in the abdominal cavity and to a lesser degree in association with muscles. Bony fishes have adipose tissue mainly distributed among muscle fibres, but sharks and other cartilaginous fishes store lipids in the liver. The fat stored in adipose tissue arises from the dietary intake of fat or carbohydrate in excess of the energy requirements of the body. A dietary excess of 1 gram of triglyceride is stored as 1 gram of fat, but only about 0.3 gram of dietary excess carbohydrate can be stored as triglyceride. The reverse process, the conversion of excess fat to carbohydrate, is metabolically impossible. In humans, excessive dietary intake can make adipose tissue the largest mass in the body.

Excess triglyceride is delivered to the adipose tissue by lipoproteins in the blood. There the triglycerides are hydrolyzed to free fatty acids and glycerol through the action of the enzyme lipoprotein lipase, which is bound to the external surface of adipose cells. Apoprotein C-II activates this enzyme, as do the quantities of insulin that circulate in the blood following ingestion of food. The liberated free fatty acids are then taken up by the adipose cells and resynthesized into triglycerides, which accumulate in a fat droplet in each cell.

MOBILIZATION OF FATTY ACIDS

In times of stress when the body requires energy, fatty acids are released from adipose cells and mobilized for use. The process begins when levels of glucagon and

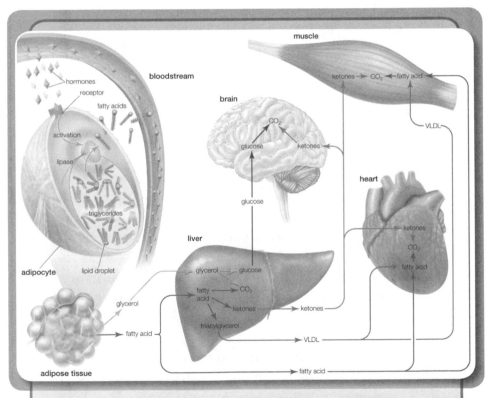

When hormones signal the need for energy, fatty acids and glycerol are released from triglycerides stored in fat cells (adipocytes) and are delivered to organs and tissues in the body. Encyclopædia Britannica, Inc.

adrenaline in the blood increase and these hormones bind to specific receptors on the surface of adipose cells. This binding action starts a cascade of reactions in the cell that results in the activation of yet another lipase that hydrolyzes triglyceride in the fat droplet to produce free fatty acids. These fatty acids are released into the circulatory system and delivered to skeletal and heart muscle as well as to the liver. In the blood the fatty acids are bound to a protein called serum albumin. In muscle tissue they are taken up by the cells and oxidized to carbon dioxide (CO_2) and water to produce energy. It is not clear whether a special transport mechanism is required for enabling free fatty acids to enter cells from the circulation.

The liver takes up a large fraction of the fatty acids. There they are in part resynthesized into triglycerides and are transported in VLDLs to muscle and other tissues. A fraction is also converted to small ketone molecules that are exported via the circulation to peripheral tissues, where they are metabolized to yield energy.

OXIDATION OF FATTY ACIDS

Inside the muscle cell, free fatty acids are converted to a thioester of a molecule called coenzyme A, or CoA. (A thioester is a compound in which the linking oxygen in an ester is replaced by a sulfur atom.) Oxidation of the fatty acid–CoA thioesters actually takes place in discrete vesicular bodies called mitochondria. Most cells contain many mitochondria, each roughly the size of a bacterium (7 to 10 μm, or millionths of a metre, in diameter), although in specialized cells they may be larger and have special shapes. The mitochondrion is surrounded by a double-membrane system enclosing a fluid interior space called the matrix. In the matrix are found the enzymes that convert the fatty acid–CoA thioesters into CO_2 and water (the chemical waste products of oxidation) and also adenosine triphosphate (ATP), the energy currency of living systems. The process consists of four sequential steps.

The first step is the transport of the fatty acid across the innermost of the two concentric mitochondrial membranes. The outer membrane is very porous so that the CoA thioesters freely permeate through it. The impermeable inner membrane is a different matter; here the fatty acid chains are transported across in the following way. On the cytoplasmic side of the membrane, an enzyme catalyzes the transfer of the fatty acid from CoA to a molecule of carnitine, a hydroxy amino acid. The carnitine ester is transported across the membrane by a transferase protein located in the membrane, and on the matrix side a second enzyme catalyzes the transfer of the fatty acid from carnitine back to CoA. The carnitine that is re-formed by loss of the attached fatty acid is transferred back to the cytoplasmic side of the mitochondrial membrane to be reused. The transfer of a fatty acid from the cytoplasm to the mitochondrial matrix thus occurs without the transfer of CoA itself from one compartment to the other. No energy is generated or consumed in this transport process, although energy is required for the initial formation of the fatty acid–CoA thioester in the cytoplasm.

The second step is the oxidation of the fatty acid to a set of two-carbon acetate fragments with thioester linkages to CoA. This series of reactions, known as β-oxidation, takes place in the matrix of the mitochondrion. Since most biological fatty acids have an even number of carbons, the number of acetyl-CoA fragments derived from a specific fatty acid is equal to half the number of carbons in the acyl chain. For example, palmitic acid (C_{16}) yields eight acetyl-CoA thioesters. In the case of rare unbranched fatty acids with an odd number of carbons, one three-carbon CoA ester is formed as well as the two-carbon acetyl-CoA thioesters. Thus, a C_{17} acid yields seven acetyl and one three-carbon CoA thioester. The energy in the successive oxidation steps is conserved by chemical reduction (the opposite of oxidation) of molecules that can subsequently be used to form ATP. ATP is the common fuel used in all the machinery of the cell (e.g., muscle, nerves, membrane transport systems, and biosynthetic systems for the formation of complex molecules such as DNA and proteins).

The two-carbon residues of acetyl-CoA are oxidized to CO_2 and water, with conservation of chemical energy in the form of $FADH_2$ and NADH and a small amount of ATP. This process is carried out in a series of nine enzymatically catalyzed reactions in the mitochondrial matrix space. The reactions form a closed cycle, often called the citric acid, tricarboxylic acid, or Krebs cycle (after its discoverer, Nobelist Sir Hans Krebs).

The final stage is the conversion of the chemical energy in NADH and $FADH_2$ formed in the second and third steps into ATP by a process known as oxidative phosphorylation. All the participating enzymes are located inside the mitochondrial inner membrane—except one, which is trapped in the space between the inner and outer membranes. In order for the process to produce ATP, the inner membrane must be impermeable to hydrogen ions (H^+). In the course of oxidative phosphorylation, molecules of NADH and $FADH_2$ are subjected to a series of linked oxidation-reduction reactions. NADH and $FADH_2$ are rich in electrons and give up these electrons to the first member of the reaction chain. The electrons then pass down the series of oxidation-reduction reactions and in the last reaction reduce molecular oxygen (O_2) to water (H_2O). This part of oxidative phosphorylation is called electron transport.

ATP

Adenosine triphosphate, or ATP, is the energy-carrying molecule found in the cells of all living things. ATP captures chemical energy obtained from the breakdown of food molecules and releases it to fuel other cellular processes. Cells require chemical energy for three general types of tasks: to drive metabolic reactions that would not occur automatically; to transport needed substances across membranes; and to do mechanical work, such as moving muscles. ATP is not a storage molecule for chemical energy (energy storage is the job of carbohydrates, such as glycogen, and fats). When energy is needed by the cell, it is converted from storage molecules into ATP. ATP then serves as a shuttle, delivering energy to places within the cell where energy-consuming activities are taking place.

ATP is a nucleotide that consists of three main structures: the nitrogenous base, adenine; the sugar, ribose; and a chain of three phosphate groups bound to ribose. The phosphate tail of ATP is the actual power source that the cell taps. Available energy is contained in the bonds between the phosphates and is released when they are broken, which occurs through the addition of a water molecule (a process called hydrolysis). Usually only the outer phosphate is removed from ATP to yield energy. When this occurs ATP is converted to adenosine diphosphate (ADP), the form of the nucleotide having only two phosphates.

ATP is able to power cellular processes by transferring a phosphate group to another molecule (a process called phosphorylation). This transfer is carried out by special enzymes that couple the release of energy from ATP to cellular activities that require energy. Although cells continuously break down ATP to obtain energy,

ATP also is constantly being synthesized from ADP and phosphate through the processes of cellular respiration. Most of the ATP in cells is produced by the enzyme ATP synthase, which converts ADP and phosphate to ATP. ATP synthase is located in the membrane of cellular structures called mitochondria. In plant cells, the enzyme also is found in chloroplasts. The central role of ATP in energy metabolism was discovered by biochemists Fritz Albert Lipmann and Herman Kalckar in 1941.

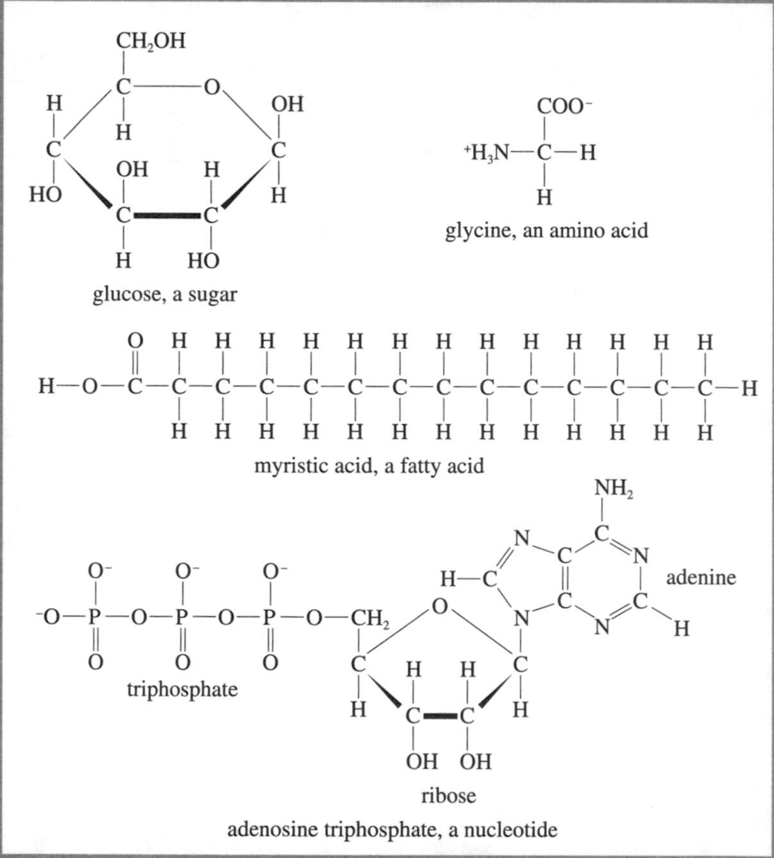

glucose, a sugar

glycine, an amino acid

myristic acid, a fatty acid

triphosphate

adenine

ribose

adenosine triphosphate, a nucleotide

Examples of members of the four families of small organic molecules: sugars (e.g., glucose), amino acids (e.g., glycine), fatty acids (e.g., myristic acid), and nucleotides (e.g., adenosine triphosphate, or ATP). Copyright Encyclopædia Britannica; rendering for this edition by Rosen Educational Services

The chemical energy available in these electron-transfer reactions is conserved by pumping H^+ across the mitochondrial inner membrane from matrix to cytoplasm. Essentially an electrical battery is created, with the cytoplasm acting as the positive pole and the mitochondrial matrix as the negative pole. The net effect of electron transport is thus to convert the chemical energy of oxidation into the electrical energy of the transmembrane "battery." The energy stored in this battery is in turn used to generate ATP from adenosine diphosphate (ADP) and inorganic phosphate by the action of a complex enzyme called ATP synthase, also located on the inner mitochondrial membrane. British chemist Peter Mitchell received the Nobel Prize for Chemistry in 1978 for his discovery of the conversion of electron transport energy into a transmembrane battery and the use of this battery to generate ATP. It is interesting that a similar process forms the basis of photosynthesis—the mechanism by which green plants convert light energy from the Sun into carbohydrates and fats, the basic foods of both plants and animals. Many of the molecular details of the oxidative phosphorylation system are now known, but there is still much to learn about it and the equally complex process of photosynthesis.

The β-oxidation also occurs to a minor extent within small subcellular organelles called peroxisomes in animals and glyoxysomes in plants. In these cases fatty acids are oxidized to CO_2 and water, but the energy is released as heat. The biochemical details and physiological functions of these organelles are not well understood.

REGULATION OF FATTY ACID OXIDATION

The rate of utilization of acetyl-CoA, the product of β-oxidation, and the availability of free fatty acids are the determining factors that control fatty acid oxidation. The concentrations of free fatty acids in the blood are hormone-regulated, with glucagon stimulating and insulin inhibiting fatty acid release from adipose tissue. The utilization in muscle of acetyl-CoA depends upon the activity of the citric acid cycle and oxidative phosphorylation—whose rates in turn reflect the demand for ATP.

In the liver the metabolism of free fatty acids reflects the metabolic state of the animal. In well-fed animals the liver converts excess carbohydrates to fatty acids, whereas in fasting animals fatty acid oxidation is the predominant activity, along with the formation of ketones. Although the details are not completely understood, it is clear that in the liver the metabolism of fatty acids is tightly linked to fatty acid synthesis so that a wasteful closed cycle of fatty acid synthesis from and metabolism back to acetyl-CoA is prevented.

Lipids in Biological Membranes

Biological membranes separate the cell from its environment and compartmentalize the cell interior. The various membranes playing these vital roles are composed of roughly equal weight percent protein and lipid, with carbohydrates constituting less than 10 percent in a few membranes. Although many hundreds of molecular species are present in any one membrane, the general organization of the generic components is known. All the lipids are amphipathic, with their hydrophilic (polar) and hydrophobic (nonpolar) portions located at separate parts of each molecule. As a result, the lipid components of membranes are arranged in what may be called a continuous bimolecular leaflet, or bilayer. The polar portions of the constituent molecules lie in the two

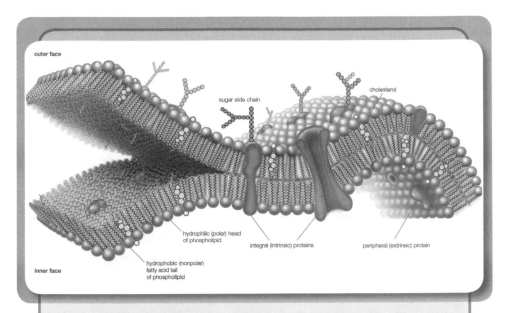

Intrinsic proteins penetrate and bind tightly to the lipid bilayer, which is made up largely of phospholipids and cholesterol. Extrinsic proteins are loosely bound to the hydrophilic (polar) surfaces, which face the watery medium both inside and outside the cell. Some intrinsic proteins present sugar side chains on the cell's outer surface. Encyclopædia Britannica, Inc.

bilayer faces, while the nonpolar portions constitute the interior of the bilayer. This structure forms an impermeable barrier for essential, water-soluble substances in the cell and provides the basis for the compartmentalizing function of biological membranes.

Some protein components are inserted into the bilayer, and most span this structure. These so-called integral, or intrinsic, membrane proteins have amino acids with nonpolar side chains at the interface between the protein and the nonpolar central region of the lipid bilayer. A second class of proteins is associated with the polar surfaces of the bilayer and with the intrinsic membrane proteins. The protein components are specific for each type of membrane and determine their predominant physiological functions. The lipid component, apart from its critical barrier function, is for the most part physiologically silent, although derivatives of certain membrane lipids can serve as intracellular messengers.

The most remarkable feature of the general biomembrane structure is that the lipid and the protein components are not covalently bonded to one another or to molecules of the other group. This sheetlike structure, formed only by molecular associations, is less than 10 nm in thickness but many orders of magnitude larger in its other two dimensions. Membranes are surprisingly strong mechanically, yet they exhibit fluidlike properties. Although the surfaces of membranes contain polar units, they act as an electric insulator and can withstand several hundred thousand volts without breakdown. Experimental and theoretical studies have established that the structure and these unusual properties are conferred on biological membranes by the lipid bilayer.

COMPOSITION OF THE LIPID BILAYER

Most biological membranes contain a variety of lipids, including the various glycerophospholipids such as phosphatidyl-choline, -ethanolamine, -serine, -inositol, and -glycerol, as well as sphingomyelin and, in some membranes, glycosphingolipids. Cholesterol, ergosterol, and sitosterol are sterols found in many membranes. The relative amounts of these lipids differ even in the same type of cell in different organisms. Even in a single cell, the lipid compositions of the membrane surrounding the cell (the plasma membrane) and the membranes of the various organelles within the cell (such as the microsomes, mitochondria, and nucleus) are different.

On the other hand, the lipid compositions of all the cells of a specific type in a specific organism at a given time in its life are identical and thus characteristic. During the life of an organism, there may be changes in the lipid composition of some membranes; the physiological significance of these age-related changes is unknown, however.

PHYSICAL CHARACTERISTICS OF MEMBRANES

One of the most surprising characteristics of biological membranes is the fact that both the lipid and the protein molecules, like molecules in any viscous liquid, are constantly in motion. Indeed, the membrane can be considered a two-dimensional liquid in which the protein components ride like boats. However, the lipid molecules in the bilayer must always be oriented with their polar ends at the surface and their nonpolar parts in the central region of the bilayer. The bilayer structure thus has the molecular orientation of a crystal and the fluidity of a liquid. In this liquid-crystalline state, thermal energy causes both lipid and protein molecules to diffuse laterally and also to rotate about an axis perpendicular to the membrane plane. In addition, the lipids occasionally flip from one face of the membrane bilayer to the other and attach and detach from the surface of the bilayer at very slow but measurable rates. Although these latter motions are forbidden to intrinsic proteins, both lipids and proteins can exhibit limited bobbing motions.

Within this seemingly random, dynamic mixture of components, however, there is considerable order in the plane of the membrane. This order takes the form of a "fluid mosaic" of molecular association complexes of both lipids and proteins in the membrane plane. The plane of the biological membrane is thus compartmentalized by domain structures much as the three-dimensional space of the cell is compartmentalized by the membranes themselves. The domain mosaics run in size from tens of nanometres (billionths of a metre) to micrometres (millionths of a metre) and are stable over time intervals of nanoseconds to minutes. In addition to this in-plane domain structure, the two lipid monolayers making up the membrane bilayer frequently have different compositions. This asymmetry, combined with the fact that intrinsic membrane proteins do not rotate about an axis in the membrane plane, makes the two halves of the bilayer into separate domains.

An interesting class of proteins is attached to biological membranes by a lipid that is chemically linked to the protein. Many of these proteins are involved in intra- and intercellular signaling. In some cases defects in their structure render the cells cancerous, presumably because growth-limiting signals are blocked by the structural error.

INTRACELLULAR AND EXTRACELLULAR MESSENGERS

In multicellular organisms (eukaryotes), the internal mechanisms that control and coordinate basic biochemical reactions are connected to other cells by means of nerves and chemical "messengers." The overall process of receiving these messages and converting the information they contain into metabolic and physiological effects is known as signal transduction. Many of the chemical messengers are lipids and are thus of special interest here. There are several types of external messengers. The first of these are hormones such as insulin and glucagon and the lipids known collectively as steroid hormones. A second class of lipid molecules is eicosanoids, which are produced in tissues and elicit cellular responses close to their site of origin. They are produced in very low levels and are turned over very rapidly (in seconds). Hormones have sites of action that are remote from their cells of origin and remain in the circulation for long periods (minutes to hours).

Steroid Hormones and Gene Expression

Lipid hormones invoke changes in gene expression. In other words, their action is to turn on or off the instructions issued by DNA to produce proteins that regulate the biosynthesis of other important proteins. Steroids are carried in the circulation bound singly to specific carrier proteins that target them to the cells in particular organs. After permeating the external membranes of these cells, the steroid interacts with a specific carrier protein in the cytoplasm. This soluble complex migrates into the cell nucleus, where it interacts with the DNA to activate or repress transcription, the first step in protein biosynthesis.

Eicosanoids

Three types of locally acting signaling molecules are derived biosynthetically from C_{20} polyunsaturated fatty acids, principally arachidonic acid. Twenty-carbon fatty acids are all known collectively as eicosanoic acids. The three chemically similar classes are prostaglandins, thromboxanes, and leukotrienes. The eicosanoids interact with specific cell surface receptors to produce a variety of different effects on different tissues, but generally they cause inflammatory responses and changes in blood pressure, and they also affect the clotting of blood. Little is known about how these effects are produced within the cells of target tissues. However, it is known that aspirin and other anti-inflammatory drugs inhibit either an enzyme in the biosynthesis pathway or the eicosanoid receptor on the cell surface.

Intracellular Second Messengers

With the exception of the steroid hormones, most hormones such as insulin and glucagon interact with a receptor on the cell surface. The activated receptor then generates so-called second messengers within the cell that transmit the information to the biochemical systems whose activities must be altered to produce a particular physiological effect. The magnitude of the end effect is generally proportional to the concentration of the second messengers.

An important intracellular second-messenger signaling system, the phosphatidylinositol system, employs two second-messenger lipids, both of which are derived from phosphatidylinositol. One is diacylglycerol (diglyceride), the other is triphosphoinositol. In this system a membrane receptor acts upon an enzyme, phospholipase C, located on the inner surface of the cell membrane. Activation of this enzyme causes the hydrolysis of a minor membrane phospholipid, phosphatidylinositol bisphosphate. Without leaving the membrane bilayer, the diacylglycerol next activates a membrane-bound enzyme, protein kinase C, that in turn catalyzes the addition of phosphate groups to a soluble protein. This soluble protein is the first member of a reaction sequence leading to the appropriate physiological response in the cell. The other hydrolysis product of phospholipase C, triphosphoinositol, causes the release of calcium from intracellular stores. Calcium is required, in addition to triacylglycerol, for the activation of protein kinase C.

CHAPTER 6

I n the early part of the 19th century, substances such as wood, starch, and linen were found to be composed mainly of molecules containing atoms of carbon (C), hydrogen (H), and oxygen (O), and to have the general formula $C_6H_{12}O_6$. Other organic molecules with similar formulas were found to have a similar ratio of hydrogen to oxygen. The general formula $C_x(H_2O)_x$ is commonly used to represent many carbohydrates, which means "watered carbon."

Carbohydrates are probably the most abundant and widespread organic substances in nature, and they are essential constituents of all living things. Carbohydrates are formed by green plants from carbon dioxide and water during the process of photosynthesis. Carbohydrates serve organisms as energy sources and as essential structural components. In addition, part of the structure of nucleic acids, which contain genetic information, consists of carbohydrate.

CLASSIFICATION AND NOMENCLATURE

Although a number of classification schemes have been devised for carbohydrates, the division into four major groups—monosaccharides, disaccharides, oligosaccharides, and polysaccharides—used here is among the most common. Most monosaccharides, or simple sugars, are found in grapes, other fruits, and honey. Although they can contain from three to nine carbon atoms, the most common representatives consist of five or six joined together to form a chainlike molecule. Three of the most important simple sugars, glucose—also known as dextrose, grape sugar, and corn sugar—fructose (fruit sugar), and galactose, have the same molecular formula, $(C_6H_{12}O_6)$, but because their atoms have different structural arrangements, the sugars have different characteristics (i.e., they are isomers). Slight changes in structural arrangements are detectable by living things and influence the biological significance of isomeric compounds. It is known, for example, that the degree of sweetness of various sugars differs according to the arrangement of the hydroxyl groups (-OH) that compose part of the molecular structure. A direct correlation that may exist between taste and any specific structural arrangement, however, has not yet been established—it is not yet possible to predict the taste of a sugar by knowing its specific structural arrangement. The energy in the chemical bonds of glucose indirectly supplies most living things with a major part of the energy that is necessary for them to carry on their activities. Galactose, which is rarely found as a simple sugar, is usually combined with other simple sugars in order to form larger molecules.

Two molecules of a simple sugar that are linked to each other form a disaccharide, or double sugar. The disaccharide sucrose, or table sugar, consists of one molecule of glucose and one molecule of fructose; the most familiar sources of sucrose are sugar beets and cane sugar. Milk sugar, or lactose, and maltose are also disaccharides. Before the energy in disaccharides can be utilized by living things, the molecules must be broken down into their respective monosaccharides.

Oligosaccharides, which consist of three to six monosaccharide units, are rather infrequently found in natural sources, although a few plant derivatives have been identified. Polysaccharides (the term means many sugars) represent most of the structural and energy-reserve carbohydrates found in nature. Large molecules that may consist of as many as 10,000 monosaccharide units linked together, polysaccharides vary considerably in size, in structural complexity, and in sugar content. Several hundred distinct types have thus far been identified. Cellulose, the principal structural component of plants, is a complex polysaccharide comprising many glucose units linked together. Cellulose is the most common polysaccharide. The starch found in plants and the glycogen found in animals also are complex glucose polysaccharides. Starch (from the old English word *stercan* meaning "to stiffen") is found mostly in seeds, roots, and stems, where it is stored as an available energy source for plants. Plant starch may be processed into such foods as bread, or it may be consumed directly—as potatoes, for instance. Glycogen, which consists of branching chains of glucose molecules, is formed in the liver and muscles of higher animals and is stored as an energy source.

The generic nomenclature ending for the monosaccharides is -ose. Thus, the term pentose (pent = five) is used for monosaccharides containing five carbon atoms, and hexose (hex = six) is used for those containing six. In addition, because the monosaccharides contain a chemically reactive group that is either an aldehyde group or a keto group, they are frequently referred to as aldopentoses or ketopentoses or aldohexoses or ketohexoses. In the examples that follow, the aldehyde group is at position 1 of the aldopentose, and the keto group is at position 2 of the ketohexose. Glucose is an aldohexose—it contains six carbon atoms, and the chemically reactive group is an aldehyde group.

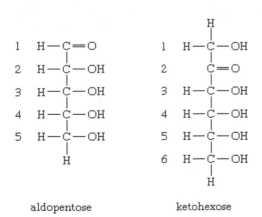

aldopentose   ketohexose

BIOLOGICAL SIGNIFICANCE

The importance of carbohydrates to living things can hardly be overemphasized. The energy stores of most animals and plants are both carbohydrate and lipid in nature. Carbohydrates are generally available as an immediate energy source, whereas lipids act as a long-term energy resource and tend to be utilized at a slower rate. Glucose, the prevalent uncombined, or free, sugar circulating in the blood of higher animals, is essential to cell function. The proper regulation of glucose metabolism is of paramount importance to survival.

Sugar Beet

The sugar beet (*Beta vulgaris*) is a biennial plant of the Amaranthaceae family. It is cultivated for its juice, from which sugar is processed. The sugar beet is second only to sugarcane as the major source of the world's sugar.

Sugar was produced experimentally from beets in Germany in 1747 by the chemist Andreas Marggraf, but the first beet-sugar factory was built in Silesia in 1802. Napoleon became interested in the process in 1811 because the British blockade had cut off the French Empire's raw sugar supply from the West Indies, and under his influence 40 factories to process beet sugar were established in France. The industry temporarily collapsed after Napoleon's fall but recovered in the 1840s. Beet-sugar production then increased rapidly throughout Europe, and by 1880 the tonnage had overtaken that of cane sugar. Beet sugar now accounts for almost all sugar production in continental Europe and for almost one-third of total world production. The top 12 sugar-beet producing countries are France, the United States, Russia, Germany, Ukraine, Turkey, Poland, China, Belgium, Egypt, the Netherlands, and Iran.

The sugar beet has long been grown as a summer crop in relatively cool northern parts of the temperate zones of the world and thus within the densely populated, well-developed areas where much of the product is consumed. More recently it has been grown as a winter crop in the southern parts of the temperate zones: South America, Africa, the Middle East, and southern Europe. In contrast, sugarcane can be grown only in tropical or subtropical regions.

The growing period from sowing to harvesting is 170 to 200 days. A good yield of beet roots is obtained when the climate has been mild throughout the growing period. A good sucrose content in the beet roots is secured when the last

Sugar beet (Beta vulgaris). Grant Heilman

period of growth has been cold. In the case of a winter crop, the ripening period is in the warm season, and ripening of the beet is promoted by withholding water to the beet.

Sucrose, a product of photosynthesis, is stored in the root, which can grow to 1 to 2 kg (2.2 to 4.4 pounds) and can contain 8 to 22 percent sucrose by weight. Sugar-beet harvesting usually starts late in September or early October and is performed rapidly so as to finish before the soil freezes. There are two methods of harvesting. In the Pommritzer method the topping and the lifting of the roots are performed by two separate machines. In the other method the two operations are carried out by one machine.

The beet plant is subject to many diseases and insect pests. Black root rot, a fungus disease characterized by lesions in the stem near the soil surface, and *Cercospora* leaf spot, a fungus infection in which the leaves become greenish yellow and root weight and sugar content are reduced, are most serious and can cause great damage if not controlled. Precautions must also be taken against damage by worms, beetles, and nematodes.

Disease-resistant beets of higher sucrose content and heavier root weight are constantly sought. Sugar beet is a cross-pollinated plant, and commercial varieties are hybrid plants. Superior polyploid varieties (varieties having multiple sets of chromosomes) have been developed.

The ability of ruminants, such as cattle, sheep, and goats, to convert the polysaccharides present in grass and similar feeds into protein provides a major source of protein for humans. A number of medically important antibiotics, such as streptomycin, are carbohydrate derivatives. The cellulose in plants is used to manufacture paper, wood for construction, and fabrics.

ROLE IN THE BIOSPHERE

The essential process in the biosphere, the portion of Earth in which life can occur, that has permitted the evolution of life as it now exists is the conversion by green plants of carbon dioxide from the atmosphere into carbohydrates, using light energy from the Sun. This process, called photosynthesis, results in both the release of oxygen gas into the atmosphere and the transformation of light energy into the chemical energy of carbohydrates. The energy stored by plants during the formation of carbohydrates is used by animals to carry out mechanical work and to perform biosynthetic activities. All green plants apparently photosynthesize in the same way, yielding as an immediate product the compound 3-phosphoglyceric acid.

$$
\begin{array}{c}
\quad\ \ \text{O} \\
\quad\ \ \|\\
\text{C}-\text{OH} \\
\quad\ \ | \\
\text{H}-\text{C}-\text{OH} \\
\quad\ \ | \\
\text{H}-\text{C}-\text{PO}_3\text{H}_2 \\
\quad\ \ | \\
\quad\ \ \text{H}
\end{array}
$$

3-phosphoglyceric acid

This compound then is transformed into cell-wall components such as cellulose, varying amounts of sucrose, and starch—depending on the plant type—and a wide variety of polysaccharides, other than cellulose and starch, that function as essential structural components.

ROLE IN HUMAN NUTRITION

The total caloric, or energy, requirement for an individual depends on age, occupation, and other factors but generally ranges between 2,000 and 4,000 calories per 24-hour period (one calorie, as this term is used in nutrition, is the amount of heat necessary to raise the temperature of 1,000 grams (35 oz) of water from 15 to 16 °C [59 to 61 °F]; in other contexts this amount of heat is called the kilocalorie). Carbohydrate that can be used by humans produces four calories per gram as opposed to nine calories per gram of fat and four per gram of protein. In areas of the world where nutrition is marginal, a high proportion (approximately 1 to 2 pounds [0.45 to 0.91 kg]) of an individual's daily energy requirement may be supplied by carbohydrate, with most of the remainder coming from a variety of fat sources.

Although carbohydrates may compose as much as 80 percent of the total caloric intake in the human diet, for a given diet, the proportion of starch to total carbohydrate is quite variable, depending upon the prevailing customs. In the Far East and in areas of Africa, for example, where rice or tubers such as manioc provide a major food source, starch may account for as much as 80 percent of the total carbohydrate intake. In a typical Western diet, 33 to 50 percent of the caloric intake is in the form of carbohydrate. Approximately half (i.e., 17 to 25 percent) is represented by starch; another third by table sugar (sucrose) and milk sugar (lactose); and smaller percentages by monosaccharides such as glucose and fructose, which are common in fruits, honey, syrups, and certain vegetables such as artichokes, onions, and sugar beets. The small remainder consists of bulk, or indigestible carbohydrate, which comprises primarily the cellulosic outer covering of seeds and the stalks and leaves of vegetables.

ROLE IN ENERGY STORAGE

Starches, the major plant-energy-reserve polysaccharides used by humans, are stored in plants in the form of nearly spherical granules that vary in diameter from about 3 to 100 μm (about .0001 to .004 inch). Most plant starches consist of a mixture of two components, amylose and amylopectin. The glucose molecules composing amylose have a straight-chain, or linear, structure. In contrast, amylopectin has a branched-chain structure and is a somewhat more compact molecule. Several thousand glucose units may be present in a single starch molecule (in the following diagram, each small circle represents one glucose molecule).

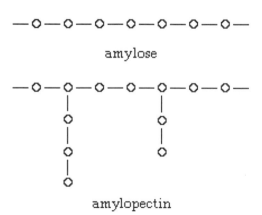

In addition to granules, many plants have large numbers of specialized cells, called parenchymatous cells, the principal function of which is the storage of starch. Examples of plants with these cells include root vegetables and tubers. The starch content of plants varies considerably. The highest concentrations are found in seeds and in cereal grains, which contain up to 80 percent of their total carbohydrate as starch. The amylose and amylopectin components of starch occur in variable proportions. Most plant species store approximately 25 percent of their starch as amylose and 75 percent as amylopectin. This proportion can be altered, however, by selective-breeding techniques, and some varieties of corn have been developed that produce up to 70 percent of their starch as amylose, which is more easily digested by humans than is amylopectin.

In addition to the starches, some plants (e.g., the Jerusalem artichoke and the leaves of certain grasses, particularly rye grass) form storage polysaccharides composed of fructose units rather than glucose. Although the fructose polysaccharides can be broken down and used to prepare syrups, they cannot be digested by higher animals.

Starches are not formed by animals. Instead, they form a closely related polysaccharide, glycogen. Virtually all vertebrate and invertebrate animal cells, as well as those of numerous fungi and protozoans, contain some glycogen. Particularly high concentrations of this substance are found in the liver and muscle cells of higher animals. The overall structure of glycogen, which is a highly branched molecule consisting of glucose units, has a superficial resemblance to that of the amylopectin component of starch, although the structural details of glycogen are significantly different. Under conditions of stress or muscular activity in animals, glycogen is rapidly broken down to glucose, which is subsequently used as an energy source. In this manner, glycogen acts as an immediate carbohydrate reserve. Furthermore, the amount of glycogen present at any given time, especially in the liver, directly reflects an animal's nutritional state—when adequate food supplies are available, both glycogen and fat reserves of the body increase, but when food supplies decrease or when the food intake falls below the minimum energy requirements, the glycogen reserves are depleted quite rapidly, while those of fat are used at a slower rate.

ROLE IN PLANT AND ANIMAL STRUCTURE

Whereas starches and glycogen represent the major reserve polysaccharides of living things, most of the carbohydrate found in nature occurs as structural components in the cell walls of plants. Carbohydrates in plant cell walls generally consist of several distinct layers, one of which contains a higher concentration of cellulose than the others. The physical and chemical properties of cellulose are strikingly different from those of the amylose component of starch.

In most plants, the cell wall is about 0.5 μm (2×10^{-5} inches) thick and contains a mixture of cellulose, pentose-containing polysaccharides (pentosans), and an inert (chemically unreactive) plasticlike material called lignin. The amounts of cellulose and pentosan may vary. Most plants contain between 40 and 60 percent cellulose, although higher amounts are present in the cotton fibre.

Polysaccharides also function as major structural components in animals. Chitin, which is similar to cellulose, is found in insects and other arthropods. Other complex polysaccharides predominate in the structural tissues of higher animals.

STRUCTURAL ARRANGEMENTS AND PROPERTIES

Carbohydrates contain various combinations of carbon and hydrogen atoms, hydroxyl groups, and carbonyl groups. The many different orders and geometric arrangements of these combinations produce a large number of isomers with the same chemical formula but different properties. In addition, each isomer has various derivatives, and each derivative is unique in its structural and chemical characteristics.

STEREOISOMERISM

Studies by Emil Fischer in the late 19th century showed that carbohydrates, such as fructose and glucose, with the same molecular formulas but with different structural arrangements and properties (i.e., isomers) can be formed by relatively simple variations of their spatial, or geometric, arrangements. This type of isomerism, which is called stereoisomerism, exists in all biological systems. Among carbohydrates, the simplest example is provided by the three-carbon aldose sugar glyceraldehyde. There is no way by which the structures of the two isomers of glyceraldehyde can be made identical, excluding breaking and re-forming the linkages, or bonds, of the hydrogen (-H) and hydroxyl (-OH) groups attached to the carbon at position 2. The isomers are, in fact, mirror images akin to right and left hands. The term *enantiomorphism* is frequently employed for such isomerism. The chemical and physical properties of enantiomers are identical except for the property of optical rotation.

Optical rotation is the rotation of the plane of polarized light. Polarized light is light that has been separated into two beams that vibrate at right angles to each other.

Solutions of substances that rotate the plane of polarization are said to be optically active, and the degree of rotation is called the optical rotation of the solution. In the case of the isomers of glyceraldehyde, the magnitudes of the optical rotation are the same, but the direction in which the light is rotated—generally designated as plus, or *d* for dextrorotatory (to the right), or as minus, or *l* for levorotatory (to the left)—is opposite. For example, a solution of D-(*d*)-glyceraldehyde causes the plane of polarized light to rotate to the right, and a solution of L-(*l*)-glyceraldehyde rotates the plane of polarized light to the left.

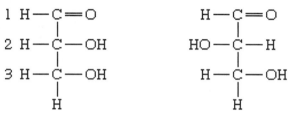

D-(*d*)-glyceraldehyde   L-(*l*)-glyceraldehyde

CONFIGURATION

Molecules, such as the isomers of glyceraldehyde—the atoms of which can have different structural arrangements—are known as asymmetrical molecules. The number of possible structural arrangements for an asymmetrical molecule depends on the number of centres of asymmetry. For example, for n (any given number of) centres of asymmetry, 2^n different isomers of a molecule are possible. An asymmetrical centre in the case of carbon is defined as a carbon atom to which four different groups are attached. In the three-carbon aldose sugar, glyceraldehyde, the asymmetrical centre is located at the central carbon atom. The four different groups attached to the atom are

$$\text{(1) } H - \overset{\displaystyle |}{C} = O, \text{ (2) } H -, \text{ (3) } - OH, \text{ and (4) } H - \overset{\displaystyle |}{\underset{\displaystyle |}{C}} - OH.$$
$$H$$

The position of the hydroxyl group (-OH) attached to the central carbon atom—that is, whether -OH projects from the left or the right—determines whether the molecule rotates the plane of polarized light to the left, or to the right. Since glyceraldehyde has one asymmetrical centre, n is one in the relationship 2^n, and there thus are two possible glyceraldehyde isomers. Sugars containing four carbon atoms have two asymmetrical centres. Hence, there are four possible isomers (2^2). Similarly, sugars with five carbon atoms have three asymmetrical centres, and thus have eight possible isomers (2^3). Keto sugars have one less asymmetrical centre for a given number of carbon atoms than do aldehydo sugars.

A convention of nomenclature, devised in 1906, states that the form of glyceraldehyde whose asymmetrical carbon atom has a hydroxyl group projecting to the right is designated as the D-configuration. The form in which the asymmetrical carbon atom has a hydroxyl group projecting to the left is designated as L. All sugars that can be derived from D-glyceraldehyde—that is, hydroxyl group attached to the asymmetrical carbon atom most remote from the aldehyde or keto end of the molecule projects to the right—are said to be of the D-configuration. Those sugars derived from L-glyceraldehyde are said to be of the L-configuration.

The configurational notation D or L is independent of the sign of the optical rotation of a sugar in solution. It is common, therefore, to designate both, as, for example, D-(*l*)-fructose or D-(*d*)-glucose. Both have a D-configuration at the centre of asymmetry most remote from the aldehyde end (in glucose) or keto end (in fructose) of the molecule, but fructose is levorotatory, and glucose is dextrorotatory— hence the latter has been given the alternative name dextrose. Although the initial assignments of configuration for the glyceraldehydes were made on purely arbitrary grounds, studies that were carried out nearly half a century later established them as correct in an absolute spatial sense. In biological systems, only the D or L form may be utilized.

When more than one asymmetrical centre is present in a molecule, as is the case with sugars having four or more carbon atoms, a series of DL pairs exists, and they are functionally, physically, and chemically distinct. Thus, although D-xylose and D-lyxose both have five carbon atoms and are of the D-configuration, the spatial arrangement of the asymmetrical centres (at carbon atoms 2, 3, and 4) is such that they are not mirror images.

HEMIACETAL AND HEMIKETAL FORMS

Although optical rotation has been one of the most frequently determined characteristics of carbohydrates since its recognition in the late 19th century, the rotational behaviour of freshly prepared solutions of many sugars differs from that of solutions that have been allowed to stand. This phenomenon, called mutarotation, is demonstrable even with apparently identical sugars and is caused by a type of stereoisomerism involving formation of an asymmetrical centre at the first carbon atom (aldehyde carbon) in aldoses and the second one (keto carbon) in ketoses.

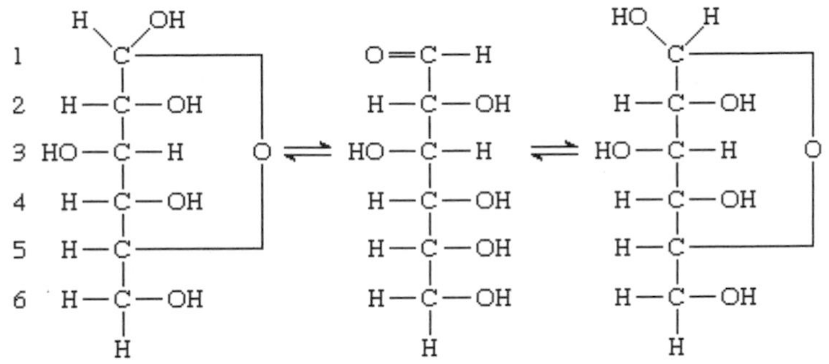

α-D-glucose
(hemiacetal form)

D-glucose
(linear, open-chain,
or free form)

β-D-glucose
(hemiacetal form)

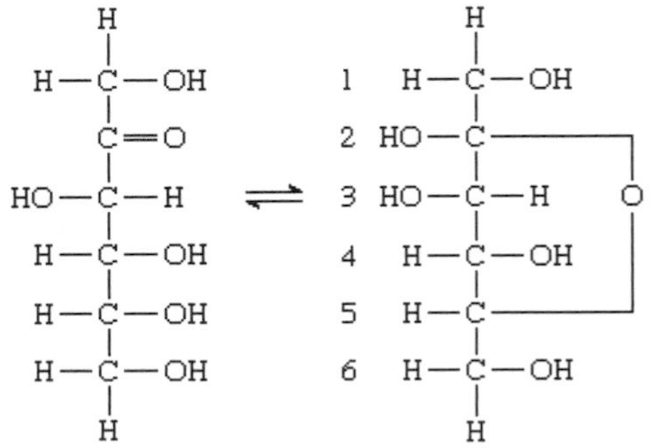

D-fructose
(linear, open-chain,
or free form)

α-D-fructose
(hemiketal form)

Most pentose and hexose sugars, therefore, do not exist as linear, or open-chain, structures in solution. Rather, they form cyclic, or ring, structures known as hemiacetal or hemiketal forms, respectively. These cyclic structures are formed by the addition of the hydroxyl group (-OH) from either the fourth, fifth, or sixth carbon atom (in the diagram, the numbers 1 through 6 represent the positions of the carbon atoms) to the carbonyl group at position 1 in glucose or 2 in fructose. A five-membered ring is illustrated for the ketohexose, fructose, and a six-membered ring is illustrated for the aldohexose, glucose. In either case, the cyclic forms are in equilibrium with (i.e., the rate of conversion from one form to another is stable) the open-chain structure—a free aldehyde if the solution contains glucose, a free ketone if it contains fructose. Each form has a different optical rotation value. Since the forms are in equilibrium with each other, a constant value of optical rotation is measurable. The two cyclic forms represent more than 99.9 percent of the sugar in the case of a glucose solution.

The carbon atom containing the aldehyde or keto group is defined as the anomeric carbon atom. Similarly, carbohydrate stereoisomers that differ in configuration only at this carbon atom are called anomers. When a cyclic hemiacetal or hemiketal structure forms, the structure with the new hydroxyl group projecting on the same side as that of the oxygen involved in forming the ring is called the alpha anomer, whereas that with the hydroxyl group projecting on the opposite side from that of the oxygen ring is called the beta anomer.

alpha anomer   beta anomer

The spatial arrangements of the atoms in these cyclic structures are better shown (glucose is used as an example) in the representation devised by the British organic chemist Walter Norman (later Sir Norman) Haworth about 1930. In the formulation the asterisk indicates the position of the anomeric carbon atom. The

Haworth formulation of β-D-glucose

carbon atoms, except at position 6' (top upper left), usually are not labelled.

The large number of asymmetrical carbon atoms and the consequent number of possible isomers considerably complicates the structural chemistry of carbohydrates.

Sir Walter Norman Haworth

(b. March 19, 1883, Chorley, Lancashire, Eng.—d. March 19, 1950, Birmingham)

British chemist Sir Walter Norman Haworth was known for his work in determining the chemical structures of carbohydrates and vitamin C. He was a cowinner, with the Swiss chemist Paul Karrer, of the 1937 Nobel Prize for Chemistry.

Haworth graduated from the University of Manchester in 1906 and received a Ph.D. degree from the University of Göttingen in 1910. He taught at the University of St. Andrews (1912–20) and the University of Durham (1920–25). Haworth joined the faculty of St. Andrews University in 1912. While at St. Andrews, he worked with the British chemists Sir James Irvine and Thomas Purdie in the study of carbohydrates, including sugars, starch, and cellulose. They found that sugars have a ringlike, rather than a straight-line, arrangement of their carbon atoms; these ringlike representations of sugar molecules have come to be known as Haworth formulas. Haworth's book *The Constitution of Sugars* (1929) became a standard text.

In 1925 Haworth became director of the chemistry department at the University of Birmingham, where he turned to the study of vitamin C, which is structurally similar to simple sugars. In 1934, with the British chemist Sir Edmund Hirst, he succeeded in synthesizing the vitamin, the first to be artificially produced. This accomplishment not only constituted a valuable addition to knowledge of organic chemistry but also made possible the cheap production of vitamin C (or ascorbic acid, as Haworth called it) for medical purposes. Haworth was knighted in 1947.

CLASSES OF CARBOHYDRATES

As noted above, carbohydrates are commonly classified as monosaccharides, disaccharides, oligosaccharides, and polysaccharides. Monosaccharides include simple sugars, such as glucose and fructose, while disaccharides are two-unit sugars, such as sucrose and lactose. Oligosaccharides consist of about three to 10 sugars. Polysaccharides, which are large molecules with up to 10,000 monosaccharide units, are by far the most complex of the carbohydrates. Examples of polysaccharides include cellulose, starch, and glycogen.

MONOSACCHARIDES

The most common naturally occurring monosaccharides are D-glucose, D-mannose, D-fructose, and D-galactose among the hexoses, and D-xylose and L-arabinose among the pentoses. In a special sense, D-ribose and 2-deoxy-D-ribose are ubiquitous because they form the carbohydrate component of RNA and DNA, respectively. These sugars are present in all cells as components of nucleic acids.

D-Xylose, found in most plants in the form of a polysaccharide called xylan, is prepared from corncobs, cottonseed hulls, or straw by chemical breakdown of xylan. D-galactose, a common constituent of both oligosaccharides and polysaccharides, also occurs in carbohydrate-containing lipids, called glycolipids, which are found in the brain and other nervous tissues of most animals. Galactose is generally prepared by acid hydrolysis (breakdown involving water) of lactose, which is composed of galactose and glucose. Since the biosynthesis of galactose in animals occurs through intermediate compounds derived directly from glucose, animals do not require galactose in the diet. In fact, in most human populations the majority of people do not retain the ability to manufacture the enzyme necessary to metabolize galactose after they reach the age of four, and many individuals possess a hereditary defect known as galactosemia and never have the ability to metabolize galactose.

D-Glucose (from the Greek word *glykys*, meaning "sweet"), the naturally occurring form, is found in fruits, honey, blood, and, under abnormal conditions, in urine. It is also a constituent of the two most common naturally found disaccharides, sucrose and lactose, as well as the exclusive structural unit of the polysaccharides cellulose, starch, and glycogen. Generally, D-glucose is prepared from either potato starch or cornstarch.

D-Fructose, a ketohexose, is one of the constituents of the disaccharide sucrose and is also found in uncombined form in honey, apples, and tomatoes. Fructose, generally considered the sweetest monosaccharide, is prepared by sucrose hydrolysis and is metabolized by humans.

Bees make honey at an apiary in the Gaza Strip , The Emerging Palestinian Autonomous Areas. Mohammed Abed/AFP/Getty Images

The reactions of the monosaccharides can be conveniently subdivided into those associated with the aldehyde or keto group and those associated with the hydroxyl groups. The relative ease with which sugars containing a free or potentially free aldehyde or keto group can be oxidized to form products has been known for a considerable time and once was the basis for the detection of these so-called reducing sugars in a variety of sources. For many years, analyses of blood glucose and urinary glucose were carried out by a procedure involving the use of an alkaline copper compound. Because the reaction has undesirable features— extensive destruction of carbohydrate structure occurs, and the reaction is not very specific (i.e., sugars other than glucose give similar results) and does not result in the formation of readily identifiable products—blood and urinary glucose now are analyzed by using the enzyme glucose oxidase, which catalyzes the oxidation of glucose to products that include hydrogen peroxide. The hydrogen peroxide then is used to oxidize a dye present in the reaction mixture. The intensity of the colour is directly proportional to the amount of glucose initially present. The enzyme, glucose oxidase, is highly specific for β-D-glucose.

In another reaction, the aldehyde group of glucose reacts with alkaline iodine to form a class of compounds called aldonic acids. One important aldonic acid is ascorbic acid (vitamin C), an essential dietary component for humans and guinea pigs. The formation of similar acid derivatives does not occur with the keto sugars.

$$
\begin{array}{c}
O \\
\parallel \\
C-\! \\
\mid \qquad\quad\ \rceil \\
HO-C \quad O \\
\parallel \quad\ \mid \\
HO-C \quad\ \mid \\
\mid \qquad\quad\ \mid \\
H-C-\! \\
\mid \\
HO-C-H \\
\mid \\
CH_2OH
\end{array}
$$

ascorbic acid,
vitamin C
(L-gulonolactone-
2, 3-enediol)

Either the aldehyde or the keto group of a sugar may be reduced (i.e., hydrogen added) to form an alcohol. Compounds formed in this way are called alditols, or sugar alcohols. The product formed as a result of the reduction of the aldehydo carbon of D-glucose is called sorbitol (D-glucitol). D-glucitol also is formed when L-sorbose is reduced. The reduction of mannose results in mannitol, that of galactose in dulcitol.

Sugar alcohols that are of commercial importance include sorbitol (D-glucitol), which is commonly used as a sweetening agent, and D-mannitol, which is also used as a sweetener, particularly in chewing gums, because it has a limited water solubility and remains powdery and granular on long storage. The hydroxyl group that is attached to the anomeric carbon atom (i.e., the carbon containing the aldehydo or keto group) of carbohydrates in solution has unusual reactivity, and derivatives, called glycosides, can be formed. Glycosides formed from glucose are called glucosides. It is not possible for equilibration between the α- and β-anomers of a glycoside in solution (i.e., mutarotation) to occur. The reaction by which a glycoside is formed involves the hydroxyl group of the anomeric carbon atom (numbered 1) of both α and β forms of D-glucose—α and β forms of D-glucose are shown in equilibrium in the reaction sequence—and the hydroxyl group of an alcohol (methyl alcohol in the reaction sequence). Methyl α-D-glucosides and β-D-glucosides are formed as products, as is water.

Among the wide variety of naturally occurring glycosides are a number of plant pigments, particularly those red, violet, and blue in colour. These pigments are found in flowers and consist of a pigment molecule attached to a sugar molecule, frequently glucose. Plant indican (from *Indigofera* species), composed of glucose and the pigment

α-D-glucose $\rightleftharpoons$ β-D-glucose + CH$_3$OH

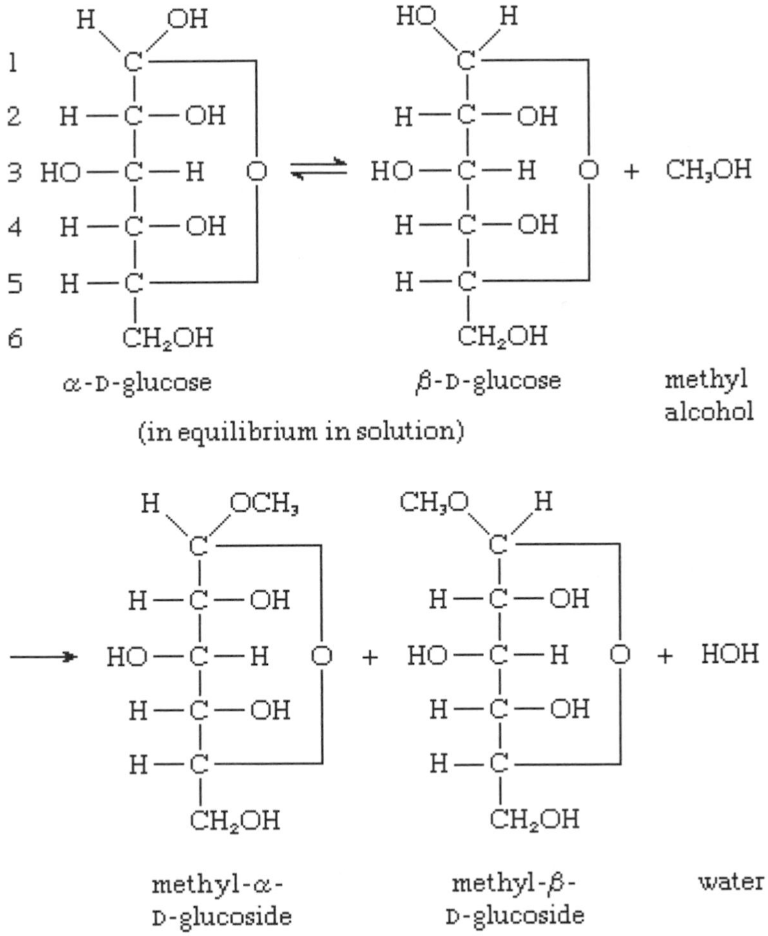

(in equilibrium in solution)

methyl-α-
D-glucoside + methyl-β-
D-glucoside + water

indoxyl, was important in the preparation of indigo dye before synthetic dyes became prevalent. Of a number of heart-muscle stimulants that occur as glycosides, digitalis is still used. Other naturally occurring glycosides include vanillin, which is found in the vanilla bean, and amygdalin (oil of bitter almonds). A variety of glycosides found in mustard have a sulfur atom at position 1 rather than oxygen.

A number of important antibiotics are glycosides. The best known are streptomycin and erythromycin. Glucosides—that is, glycosides formed from glucose—in which the anomeric carbon atom (at position 1) has phosphoric acid linked to it, are extremely important biological compounds. For example, α-D-glucose-1-phosphate, is an intermediate product in the biosynthesis of cellulose, starch, and glycogen. Similar glycosidic phosphate derivatives of other monosaccharides participate in the formation of naturally occurring glycosides and polysaccharides.

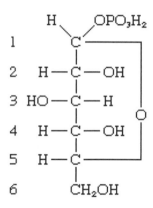

α-D-glucose-1-phosphate

The hydroxyl groups other than the one at the anomeric carbon atom can undergo a variety of reactions, several of which deserve mention. Esterification, which consists of reacting the hydroxyl groups with an appropriate acidic compound, results in the formation of a class of compounds called sugar esters. Among the common ones are the sugar acetates, in which the acid is acetic acid. Esters of phosphoric acid and sulfuric acid are important biological compounds. Glucose-6-phosphate,

for example, plays a central role in the energy metabolism of most living cells, and D-ribulose 1,5-diphosphate
is important in photosynthesis.

Treatment of a carbohydrate with methyl iodide
or similar agents under appropriate conditions results
in the formation of compounds in which the hydroxyl
groups are converted to methyl groups (-CH$_3$). Called
methyl ethers, these compounds are employed in structural studies of oligosaccharides and polysaccharides
because their formation does not break the bonds,
called glycosidic bonds, that link adjacent monosaccharide units. When complete etherification of the starch
molecule is carried out, using methyl iodide, methyl
groups become attached to the glucose molecules at the
three positions shown in the starch molecule (the glycosidic bonds are not broken by the reaction with methyl
iodide). When the methylated starch molecule then is
broken down (hydrolyzed), hydroxyl groups are located
at the positions in the molecule previously involved in
linking one sugar molecule to another, and a methylated
glucose, in this case named 2,3,6 tri-O-methyl-D-glucose,
forms. The linkage positions, which are not methylated, in a complex carbohydrate can be established
by analyzing the locations of the methyl groups in the
monosaccharides. This technique is useful in determining the structural details of polysaccharides, particularly
since the various methylated sugars are easily separated
by techniques involving gas chromatography, in which a
moving gas stream carries a mixture through a column
of a stationary liquid or solid, the components thus
being resolved.

When the terminal group (CH$_2$OH) of a monosaccharide is oxidized chemically or biologically, a
product called a uronic acid is formed. Glycosides that

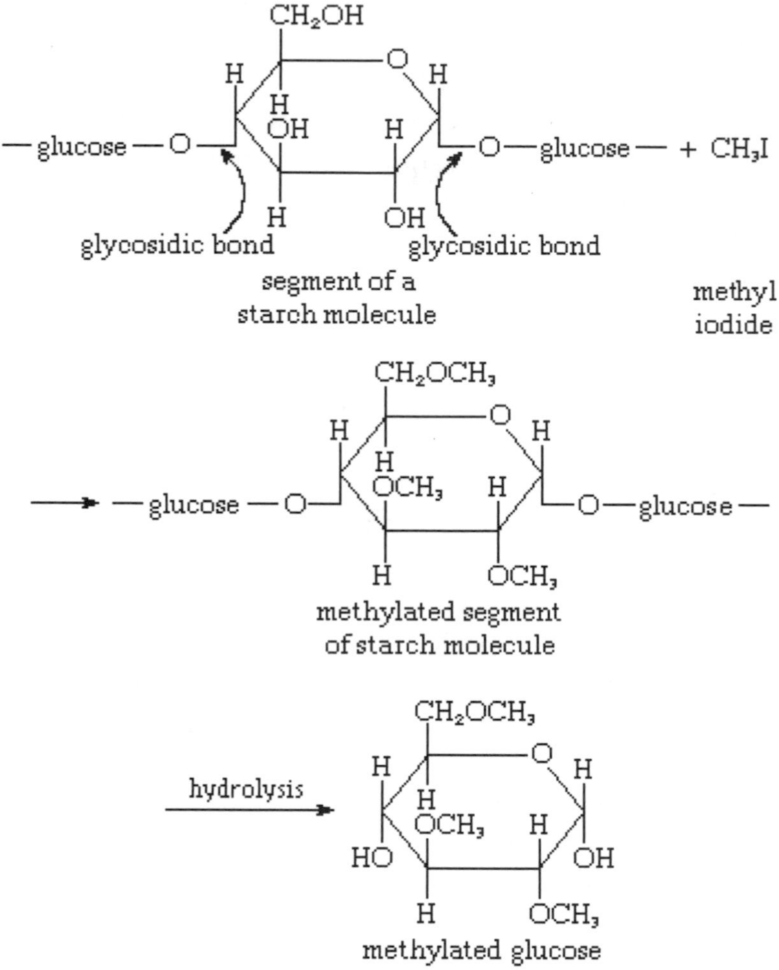

CH₂OH

H

H
OH

H

— glucose — O —

glycosidic bond

O

H

H

O — glucose — + CH₃I

glycosidic bond

OH

segment of a
starch molecule

methyl
iodide

CH₂OCH₃

H

H
OCH₃

H

→ — glucose — O —

O

H

H

O — glucose —

H

OCH₃

methylated segment
of starch molecule

CH₂OCH₃

H

H
OCH₃

H

HO

hydrolysis ⟶

O

H

H

OH

H

OCH₃

methylated glucose

are derived from D-glucuronic acid (the uronic acid formed from D-glucose) and fatty substances called steroids appear in the urine of animals as normal metabolic products. In addition, foreign toxic substances are frequently converted in the liver to glucuronides before excretion in the urine. D-glucuronic acid also is a major component of connective tissue polysaccharides, and D-galacturonic acid and D-mannuronic acid, formed from D-galactose and D-mannose, respectively, are found in several plant sources.

Other compounds formed from monosaccharides include those in which one hydroxyl group, usually at the carbon at position 2, is replaced by an amino group (-NH_2). These compounds, called amino sugars, are widely distributed in nature. The two most important ones are glucosamine (2-amino-2-deoxy-D-glucose) and galactosamine (2-amino-2-deoxy-D-galactose).

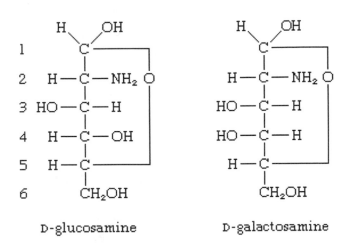

D-glucosamine   D-galactosamine

Neither amino sugar is found in the uncombined form. Both occur in animals as components of glycolipids or polysaccharides; e.g., the primary structural polysaccharide (chitin) of insect outer skeletons and various blood-group substances.

In a number of naturally occurring sugars, known as deoxy sugars, the hydroxyl group at a particular position is replaced by a hydrogen atom. By far the most important representative is 2-deoxy-D-ribose, the pentose sugar found in DNA. The hydroxyl group at the carbon atom at position 2 has been replaced by a hydrogen atom.

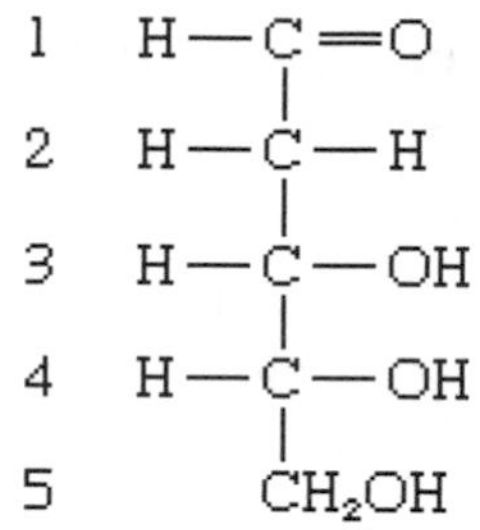

$$1 \quad H-C=O$$
$$2 \quad H-C-H$$
$$3 \quad H-C-OH$$
$$4 \quad H-C-OH$$
$$5 \quad CH_2OH$$

2-deoxy-D-ribose

Other naturally occurring deoxy sugars are hexoses, of which L-rhamnose (6-deoxy-L-mannose) and L-fucose (6-deoxy-L-galactose) are the most common. The latter, for example, is present in the carbohydrate portion of blood-group substances and in red-blood-cell membranes.

DISACCHARIDES AND OLIGOSACCHARIDES

Disaccharides are a specialized type of glycoside in which the anomeric hydroxyl group of one sugar has combined with the hydroxyl group of a second sugar with the elimination of the elements of water. Although an enormous number of disaccharide structures are possible, only a limited number are of commercial or biological significance.

SUCROSE AND TREHALOSE

Sucrose, or common table sugar, has a world production amounting to well over 10,000,000 tons annually. The unusual type of linkage between the two anomeric hydroxyl groups of glucose and fructose means that neither a free aldehyde group (on the glucose moiety) nor a free keto group (on the fructose moiety) is available to react unless the linkage between the monosaccharides is destroyed. For this reason, sucrose is known as a nonreducing sugar. Sucrose solutions do not exhibit mutarotation, which involves formation of an asymmetrical centre at the aldehyde or keto group. If the linkage between the monosaccharides composing sucrose is broken, the optical rotation value of sucrose changes from positive to negative. The new value reflects the composite rotation values for D-glucose, which is dextrorotatory (+52°), and D-fructose, which is levorotatory (-92°). The change in the sign of optical rotation from positive to negative is the reason sucrose is sometimes called invert sugar.

sucrose

The commercial preparation of sucrose takes advantage of the alkaline stability of the sugar, and a variety of impurities are removed from crude sugarcane extracts by treatment with alkali. After this step, syrup preparations are crystallized to form table sugar. Successive "crops" of sucrose crystals are "harvested," and the later ones are known as brown sugar. The residual syrupy material is called either cane final molasses or blackstrap molasses. Both are used in the preparation of antibiotics, as sweetening agents, and in the production of alcohol by yeast fermentation.

Sucrose is formed following photosynthesis in plants by a reaction in which sucrose phosphate first is formed. The disaccharide trehalose is similar in many respects to sucrose but is much less widely distributed. It is composed of two molecules of α-D-glucose and is also a nonreducing sugar. Trehalose is present in young mushrooms and in the resurrection plant (*Selaginella*). It is of considerable biological interest because it is also found in the circulating fluid (hemolymph) of many insects. Since trehalose can be converted to a glucose phosphate compound by an enzyme-catalyzed reaction that does not require energy, its function in hemolymph may be to provide an immediate energy source, a role similar to that of the carbohydrate storage forms (i.e., glycogen) found in higher animals.

LACTOSE AND MALTOSE

Lactose is one of the sugars (sucrose is another) found most commonly in human diets throughout the world. It composes about 5 percent or more of the milk of all mammals. Lactose consists of two aldohexoses—β-D-galactose and glucose—linked so that the aldehyde group at the anomeric carbon of glucose is free to react (i.e., lactose is a reducing sugar).

A variety of metabolic disorders related to lactose may occur in infants. In some cases, they are the result of a failure to metabolize properly the galactose portion of the molecule.

Although not found in uncombined form in nature, the disaccharide maltose is biologically important because it is a product of the enzymatic breakdown of starches during digestion. Maltose consists of α-D-glucose linked

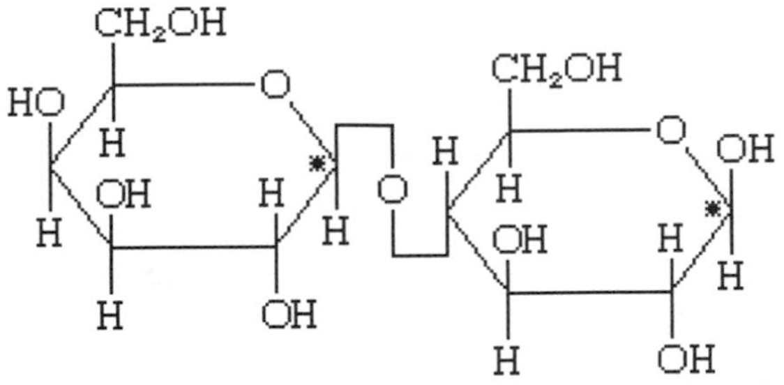

β-lactose

to a second glucose unit in such a way that maltose is a reducing sugar. Maltose, which is readily hydrolyzed to glucose and can be metabolized by animals, is employed as a sweetening agent and as a food for infants whose tolerance for lactose is limited.

POLYSACCHARIDES

Polysaccharides, or glycans, may be classified in a number of ways. The following scheme is frequently used. Homopolysaccharides are defined as polysaccharides formed from only one type of monosaccharide. Homopolysaccharides may be further subdivided into straight-chain and branched-chain representatives, depending upon the arrangement of the monosaccharide units. Heteropolysaccharides are defined as polysaccharides containing two or more different types of monosaccharides. They may also occur in both straight-chain and branched-chain forms. In general, extensive variation of linkage types does not occur within a polysaccharide structure, nor are there many polysaccharides composed of more than three or four different monosaccharides. In fact, most contain one or two.

HOMOPOLYSACCHARIDES

In general, homopolysaccharides have a well-defined chemical structure, although the molecular weight of an individual amylose or xylan molecule may vary within a particular range, depending on the source. Molecules from a single source also may vary in size, because most polysaccharides are formed biologically by an enzyme-catalyzed process lacking genetic information regarding size.

The basic structural component of most plants, cellulose, is widely distributed in nature. It has been estimated that nearly 10,000,000,000 tons of cellulose are synthesized yearly as a result of photosynthesis by higher plants. The proportion of cellulose to total carbohydrate found in plants may vary in various types of woods from 30 to 40 percent, and to more than 98 percent in the seed hair of the cotton plant. Cellulose, a large, linear molecule composed of 3,000 or more β-D-glucose molecules, is insoluble in water.

The chains of glucose units composing cellulose molecules are frequently aligned within the cell-wall structure of a plant to form fibrelike or crystalline arrangements. This alignment permits very tight packing of the chains and promotes their structural stability but also makes structural analysis difficult. The relationships between cellulose and other polysaccharides present in the cell wall are not well established. In addition, the presence of unusual chemical linkages or nonglucose units within the cellulose structure has not yet been established with certainty.

During the preparation of cellulose, raw plant material is treated with hot alkali. This treatment removes most of the lignin, the hemicelluloses, and the mucilaginous components. The cellulose then is processed to produce papers and fibres. The high resistance of cellulose to chemical or enzymatic breakdown is important in the manufacture of paper and cloth. Cellulose also is modified chemically for other purposes. For example, compounds such as cellulose acetate are used in the plastics industry, in the production of photographic film, and in the rayon-fibre industry. Viscose rayon is produced from an ester of cellulose, and cellulose nitrate is employed in the lacquer and explosives industries.

The noteworthy biological stability of cellulose is dramatically illustrated by trees, the life span of which may be several thousand years. Enzymes capable of breaking down cellulose are generally found only among several species of bacteria and molds. The apparent ability of termites to utilize cellulose as an energy source depends on the presence in their intestinal tracts of protozoans that can break it down. Similarly, the single-celled organisms present in the rumina of sheep and cattle are responsible for the ability of these animals to utilize the cellulose present in typical grasses and other feeds.

Xylans are almost as ubiquitous as cellulose in plant-cell walls and contain predominantly β-D-xylose units linked as in cellulose. Some xylans contain other sugars, such as L-arabinose, but they form branches and are not part of the main chain. Xylans are of little commercial importance.

The term *starch* refers to a group of plant reserve polysaccharides consisting almost exclusively of a linear component (amylose) and a branched component (amylopectin). The use of starch as an energy source by humans depends on the ability to convert it completely to individual glucose units. The process is initiated by the action of enzymes called amylases, synthesized by the salivary glands in the mouth, and continues in the intestinal tract. The primary product of amylase action is maltose, which is hydrolyzed to two component glucose units as it is absorbed through the walls of the intestine.

A characteristic reaction of the amylose component of starch is the formation with iodine of a complex compound with a characteristic blue colour. About one iodine molecule is bound for each seven or eight glucose units, and at least five times that many glucose units are needed in an amylose chain to permit the effective development of the colour.

The amylopectin component of starch is structurally similar to glycogen in that both are composed of glucose units linked together in the same way, but the distance between branch points (in the following schematic diagrams, -O- represents one glucose unit) is greater in amylopectin than in glycogen, and the former may be thought of as occupying more space per unit weight.

The applications of starches other than as foods are limited. Starches are employed in adhesive manufacture, and starch nitrate has some utility as an explosive.

Glycogen, which is found in all animal tissues, is the primary animal storage form of carbohydrate and, indirectly, of rapidly available energy. The distance between branch points in a glycogen molecule is only five or six units, which results in a compact treelike structure. The ability of higher animals to form and break down this extensively branched structure is essential to their well-being. In conditions known as glycogen storage diseases, these activities are abnormal, and the asymmetrical glycogen molecules that are formed have severe, often fatal, consequences. Glycogen synthesis and breakdown are controlled by substances called hormones.

Large molecules—for example, pectins and agars—composed of galactose or its uronic-acid derivative

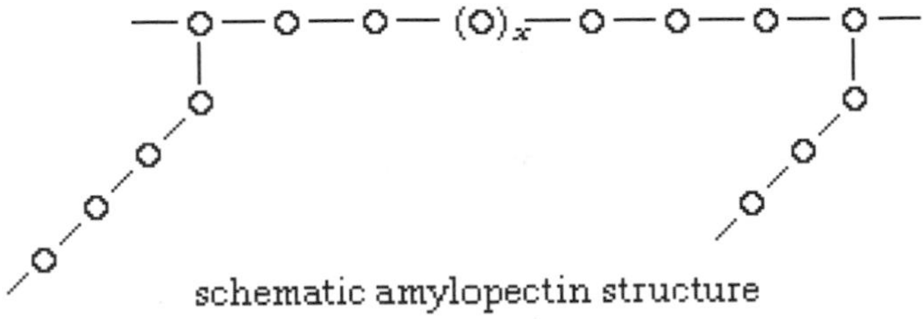

schematic amylopectin structure

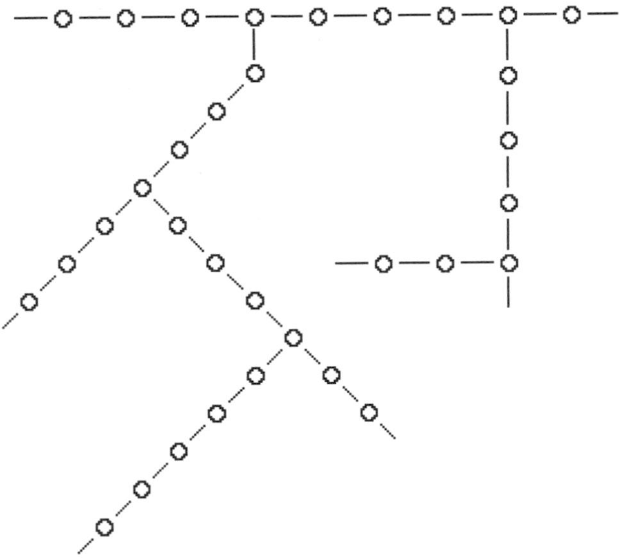

schematic glycogen structure

(galacturonic acid) are important because they can form gels. Pectins, which are predominantly galacturonans, are produced from citrus fruit rinds. They are used commercially in the preparation of jellies and jams. Agar is widely employed in biological laboratories as a solidifying agent for growth media for microorganisms and in the bakery industry as a gelling agent. It forms a part of the human diet in the form of seaweed.

Dextrans, a group of polysaccharides composed of glucose, are secreted by certain strains of bacteria as slimes. The structure of an individual dextran varies with the strain of microorganism. Dextrans can be used as plasma expanders (substitutes for whole blood) in cases of severe shock. In addition, a dextran derivative compound is employed medically as an anticoagulant for blood.

Chitin is structurally similar to cellulose, but the repeating sugar is 2-deoxy-2-acetamido-D-glucose (N-acetyl-D-glucosamine) rather than glucose.

N-acetyl-D-glucosamine

Sometimes referred to as animal cellulose, chitin is the major component of the outer skeletons of insects, crustaceans, and other arthropods, as well as annelid and nematode worms, mollusks, and coelenterates. The cell walls of most fungi also are predominantly chitin, which comprises nearly 50 percent of the dry weight of some species. Since chitin is nearly as chemically inactive as cellulose and easily obtained, numerous attempts, none of which has thus far been successful, have been made to develop it commercially. The nitrogen content of the biosphere, however, is stabilized by the ability of soil microorganisms to degrade nitrogen-containing compounds such as those found in insect skeletons. These microorganisms convert the nitrogen in complex molecules to a form usable by plants. If such microorganisms did not exist, much of the organic nitrogen present in natural materials would be unavailable to plants.

HETEROPOLYSACCHARIDES

In general, heteropolysaccharides (heteroglycans) contain two or more different monosaccharide units. Although a few representatives contain three or more different monosaccharides, most naturally occurring heteroglycans contain only two different ones and are closely associated with lipid or protein. The complex nature of these substances has made detailed structural studies extremely difficult. The major heteropolysaccharides include the connective-tissue polysaccharides, the blood-group substances, glycoproteins (combinations of carbohydrates and proteins) such as gamma-globulin, and glycolipids (combinations of carbohydrates and lipids), particularly those found in the central nervous system of animals and in a wide variety of plant gums.

The most important heteropolysaccharides are found in the connective tissues of all animals and include a group of large molecules that vary in size, shape, and interaction with other body substances. They have a structural role, and the structures of individual connective-tissue polysaccharides are related to specific animal functions. Hyaluronic acid, for example, the major component of joint fluid in animals, functions as a lubricating agent and shock absorber.

The connective-tissue heteropolysaccharides contain acidic groups (uronic acids or sulfate groups) and can bind both water and inorganic metal ions. They can also play a role in other physiological functions, such as in the accumulation of calcium before bone formation. Ion-binding ability also appears to be related to the anticoagulant activity of the heteropolysaccharide heparin.

The size of the carbohydrate portion of glycoproteins such as gamma-globulin or hen-egg albumin is usually between five and 10 monosaccharide units. Several such units occur in some glycoprotein molecules. The function of the carbohydrate component has not yet been established except for glycoproteins associated with cell surfaces. In this case, they appear to act as antigenic determinants—that is, they are capable of inducing the formation of specific antibodies.

PREPARATION AND ANALYSIS OF CARBOHYDRATES

In general, monosaccharides are prepared by breakdown with acids of the polysaccharides in which they occur. Sugars usually are difficult to obtain in crystalline form, and the crystallization process usually is begun by "seeding" a concentrated solution of the sugar with crystals. The techniques employed for separation of monosaccharides depend to some extent on their physical and chemical properties. Chromatographic procedures are often used in the study of carbohydrate components.

Oligosaccharides and polysaccharides are prepared from natural sources by techniques that take advantage of size, alkaline stability, or some combination of these and other properties of the molecule of interest. It should be noted that preparation of an oligosaccharide or polysaccharide usually results in a range of molecular sizes of the desired molecule. The purity of a carbohydrate preparation, which is frequently based on an analysis of its composition, is more easily established for monosaccharides and disaccharides than for large, insoluble molecules such as cellulose.

ANALYTICAL TECHNIQUES

A variety of organic chemical analytical techniques are generally applicable to studies involving carbohydrates. Optical rotation, for example, once was frequently used to characterize carbohydrates. The ability to measure the rotation of the plane of polarized light transmitted through a solution containing a carbohydrate depends on finding a suitable solvent; water usually is used, with light at a wavelength of 589 mμ (millimicrons). Optical rotation is no longer widely used to characterize mono-saccharides. The magnitude and sign of the optical rotation of glycosides, however, is useful in assigning configuration (α or β) to the hydroxyl group at the anomeric centre. Glycosides of the α-configuration gen-erally have rotations of higher magnitude than do the same glycosides of the β-configuration. Optical rotation is not a completely additive property. A trisaccharide composed of three glucose residues, for example, does not have a rotation three times that of one glucose molecule. Sugar alcohols cannot form ring structures. In fact, their rotation values are extremely small, sug-gesting a relationship between ring structure and the ability of a carbohydrate to rotate the plane of polar-ized light. Certain types of reactions (e.g., glycoside hydrolysis) can be monitored by measuring the change in optical rotation as a function of time. This technique is frequently used to examine the breakdown of disac-charides or oligosaccharides to monosaccharide units, especially if a large change in the net optical rotation may be expected, as occurs in the hydrolysis of sucrose.

SPECTROSCOPIC TECHNIQUES

Several other optical techniques used in chemistry have been applied to the analysis of carbohydrates. Infrared spectroscopy, used to measure vibrational and rotational excitation of molecules, and nuclear magnetic resonance spectroscopy, which measures the excitation of certain components of molecules in a magnetic field induced by radio-frequency radiation, are valuable, although the similarity of the functional groups (i.e., the hydroxyl groups) limits use of the former technique for most sugars. Proton magnetic resonance spectroscopy, nuclear magnetic resonance applied to protons (H atoms), is employed to identify the relative spatial arrangements of individual hydrogen atoms in a molecule. When they are precisely placed, the corresponding positions of the hydroxyl groups attached to the same carbon atom can be deduced. An extension of this technique utilizes the resonance spectroscopy of carbon-13, a nonradioactive isotope of carbon, so that ring structures can be established with great accuracy. Both the proton and carbon magnetic resonance methods are best applied to monosaccharides. These methods, however, are less valuable in studying polysaccharides because an individual hydrogen atom in a large molecule is too small for accurate detection.

IDENTIFICATION OF SUBUNITS

The study of polysaccharide structure usually focuses on the chemical composition, the linkage between the monosaccharide units, and the size and shape of the molecule. The size and shape of a polysaccharide can be ascertained by techniques that are usually applied to large molecules. For example, the most accurate molecular weight determination measures the sedimentation properties of the molecule in an applied gravitational field (e.g., the rate at which a solid material is deposited from a state of suspension or solution in a liquid). Indications of the shape of polysaccharide molecules in solution are obtained from viscosity measurements, in which the resistance of the molecules to flow (viscosity) is equated with the end-to-end length of the molecule. The viscosity of hyaluronic acid, for example, shows a marked dependence on both concentration of the acid and the salt content of the solution, and, under conditions approximating those found in biological systems, a hyaluronic acid molecule may be thought of as occupying a great deal of space. Alternatively, the compact nature of a glycogen molecule of molecular weight equal to that of a molecule of hyaluronic acid results in its accommodation to a much smaller space than the latter molecule.

The identification of sugars in a mixture resulting from the hydrolytic breakdown of a heteropolysaccharide is most often carried out by chromatography of the mixture on paper, silica gel, or cellulose. Ready separations can be achieved between pentoses, hexoses, and, for example, deoxy sugars. Closely related compounds such as D-glucose and D-galactose also can be separated using chromatographic techniques. The linkage positions in polysaccharides are usually determined using the methylation procedure described previously. The various monosaccharide methyl ethers produced by the methylation are separated by gas–liquid chromatography.

Detailed statements about polysaccharide structure and function are limited by the statistical nature of some measurements (e.g., branching frequency), the biological variability of parameters such as size and molecular weight, and incomplete information about associative interactions in living things.

CONCLUSION

Decades of research have shown that chemical components, from elements such as hydrogen and oxygen to compounds such as nucleic acids and carbohydrates, are vital to life on Earth. Because of the brilliant work of countless chemists and molecular biologists there now exists a substantial body of scientific literature on some of life's most fundamental processes. Much of the progress in scientific understanding of the components of life has come as a result of advancements in both basic research and technology. This progress is reflected in modern Nobel Prize-winning research. For example, in 2009 the Nobel Prize in Chemistry was awarded to three individuals—Venkatraman Ramakrishnan, Thomas Steitz, and Ada Yonath—for their discoveries concerning the atomic structure and function of ribosomes, the protein-synthesizing particles of cells. In addition to uncovering new details about the process of protein synthesis, the techniques developed by the researchers to determine the three-dimensional atomic arrangement of various parts of ribosomes have proven valuable in medicine. They have been particularly useful in investigations of antibiotic structure aimed at determining the role of antibiotic configuration in drug-cell interactions.

Studies of carbohydrates and lipids have also been crucial in furthering scientists' knowledge of human health and disease. The elucidation of lipid structure and improvements in the understanding of lipid metabolism have enabled researchers to characterize the role of specific lipids in conditions such as cardiovascular disease. This work has led to the development of new medicines to treat disease, has helped government agencies formulate useful nutritional guidelines, and has influenced how foods are processed and manufactured.

For all that is known about the components of life, however, there remains much to be discovered. Indeed, a steady stream of questions concerning the basic processes by which cells perform routine tasks flows from the continual identification and characterization of

Israeli professor Ada Yonath (left) receives the Nobel Prize in Chemistry from King Carl XVI Gustaf of Sweden in Stockholm, Sweden, on December 10, 2009. Pontus Lundahl/AFP/Getty Images

molecules. Thus, as scientists come to understand more about substances such as nucleic acids and proteins, there emerge new problems concerning the complexities of their compositions, functions, and interactions. Scientists anticipate, however, that further progress in the study of the components of life will ultimately lead to a synthesis of many of the seemingly unrelated pieces of biochemical information that are currently known. Such a unification of information would provide a far more complete picture of life, one illustrating in greater detail the processes driving the many diverse functions of the chemical components of living organisms.

adipose Fatty.

amino acids Any of 20 different kinds of tiny, basic molecules that link into long chains to form proteins.

bacteria A domain of prokaryotes, single-celled organisms that can live in such diverse environments as water, dirt, or living creatures. Bacteria often cause or carry infectious diseases, but can sometimes provide beneficial effects as well.

bacteriophage A bacteria-infecting virus.

calorie In nutrition, a measurement that is used to determine food energy, or the metabolizing value of a food.

carbohydrates An organic substance formed by green plants during the process of photosynthesis that serves as an important food source for animals. Carbohydrates also are part of the structure of the nucleic acids of all living things.

chloroplast A structure within a plant cell in which light energy is absorbed and converted into chemical energy, a process called photosynthesis.

chromatin Protein-coated genetic material made up of DNA that is contained in a cell's nucleus. When cells divide, chromatin changes shape to form chromosomes.

codons Set of three adjacent bases on a DNA or RNA chain that code for a special amino acid and allow the creation of a protein molecule.

cytoplasm A cell's interior.

denaturation Breaking bonds of hydrogen in DNA so that two strands separate.

DNA (Deoxyribonucleic acid) A complex molecule, made up of a string of tiny molecules that exists inside the nucleus of every cell and contains the genetic instructions for making living organisms.

enzyme A protein that works as a catalyst by changing the rate of chemical reactions in living organisms.

eukaryote An organism whose cells have a nucleus, such as an animal, plant, or fungus.

genome The complete genetic content of a living thing, including its full set of chromosomes and all the DNA in its mitochondria.

intron A section of DNA that does not contain code for making proteins, but instead serves to indicate the beginning or end of a piece of DNA.

lesion A change called by disease or a wound. The change can be structural or biochemical.

lipids Organic substances that resist interaction with water, such as fats and oils.

metabolism The process by which food is converted into energy through complex chemical reactions in the cells of living organisms.

mitochondrion An enclosed structure inside eukaryotic cells that produces energy for the cell.

mutagen Something that causes a permanent change, or mutation, in a cell.

organelles Structures surrounded with enclosed membranes that are contained in a cell's cytoplasm.

peptides Compounds that are made up of chains of amino acids. They are similar to proteins but are smaller.

plasmid A tiny, circle-shaped molecule.

polymer A compound made up of large, connected molecules, which are composed of small molecules called monomers.

prokaryote An organism made up of a cell without a nucleus, such as a bacterium.

protein An organic compound composed of chains of amino acids and arranged in a complex structure. A protein can contain special domains that bind sugar molecules.

ribosome Specialized particles in the cell that contain RNA and protein.

RNA (Ribonucleic acid) A nucleic acid that works as part of the process of converting information from DNA into proteins cells need.

telomere Repeating segments of DNA that appear at the ends of chromosomes in eukaryotic cells. Because some segments are lost every time a cell is replicated, the number of repeats determines how long a cell will live.

transposons Stretches of DNA that are unstable and able to move around, both on or between chromosomes. Also called "jumping DNA" or "jumping genes."

NUCLEIC ACIDS

A scholarly yet accessible description of DNA is Maxim D. Frank-Kamenetskii, *Unraveling DNA: The Most Important Molecule of Life*, 2nd ed. (1997). The standard text in the field of molecular biology is James D. Watson et al. (eds.), *Molecular Biology of the Gene*, 4th ed. (1987). A classic textbook that considers nucleic acids within the larger context of cellular metabolism is Lubert Stryer, *Biochemistry*, 4th ed. (1995).

Comprehensive texts devoted to nucleic acids are Roger L.P. Adams, John T. Knowler, and David P. Leader (eds.), *The Biochemistry of the Nucleic Acids* (1992); and Stephen Neidle, *Principles of Nucleic Acid Structure* (2008). A comprehensive text with excellent illustrations that looks at nucleic acids from a chemical perspective is G. Michael Blackburn et al. (eds.), *Nucleic Acids in Chemistry and Biology*, 3rd ed. (2006). The definitive reference work describing DNA replication is Arthur Kornberg and Tania A. Baker, *DNA Replication*, 2nd ed. (1992).

AMINO ACIDS

David S. Goodsell, *Our Molecular Nature: The Body's Motors, Machines and Messages* (1996), contains many vivid depictions and unique drawings of the molecules of life, including amino acids, proteins, DNA, and RNA. Eric R. Braverman, Carl C. Pfeiffer, Kenneth Blum, and Richard Smayda, *The Healing Nutrients Within: Facts, Findings and New Research on Amino Acids*, 3rd ed. (2003), includes recent research on the beneficial roles of amino acids in cancer, heart conditions, depression, and Alzheimer disease, among other diseases; it is comprehensive and easily understood.

Reginald H. Garrett and Charles M. Grisham, *Biochemistry*, 3rd ed. (2005); and David L. Nelson and

Michael M. Cox, *Lehninger Principles of Biochemistry*, 5th ed. (2008), are excellent biochemistry textbooks, both written at the introductory college level and each with a chapter on amino acids. G.C. Barrett and Donald T. Elmore, *Amino Acids and Peptides* (1998), is intended for undergraduate and beginning graduate students in bio-chemistry and concentrates on amino acids and peptides without detailed discussions of proteins.

PROTEINS

Works specifically on proteins include Engelbert Buxbaum, *Fundamentals of Protein Structure and Function* (2007); Johann Schaller et al., *Human Blood Plasma Proteins: Structure and Function* (2008); Arthur M. Lesk, *Introduction to Protein Science: Architecture, Function, and Genomics*, 2nd ed. (2010); and Murray P. Deutscher (ed.), *Guide to Protein Purification* (1990), a critical description of the principles and practice of the numerous methods used in preparing pure proteins.

LIPIDS

A well-written basic textbook that covers all aspects of lipid metabolism and function is Dennis E. Vance and Jean E. Vance (eds.), *Biochemistry of Lipids and Membranes* (1985). An advanced general biochemistry text with accessible material on lipids is Christopher K. Mathews, K.E. van Holde, and Kevin G. Ahern, *Biochemistry*, 3rd ed. (2000).

Lipid structures, properties, and metabolism are col-lected in Frank D. Gunstone, John L. Harwood, and Fred B. Padley (eds.), *The Lipid Handbook* (1994). The premier book on biological membranes is Robert B. Gennis, *Biomembranes: Molecular Structure and Function* (1989). A readable compendium of information about lipids is contained in Donald M. Small, *The Physical Chemistry of Lipids*, vol. 4 of *Handbook of Lipid Research* (1986). A readable discussion of the structure and metabolism of lipoproteins is contained in Charles R. Scriver, Arthur L. Beaudet, William S. Sly, and David Valle, *The Metabolic and Molecular Bases of Inherited Disease* (1995).

The discovery, biochemistry, and physical chemistry of sphingolipids are detailed in Julian N. Kanfer and Sen-itiroh Hakomori, *Sphingolipid Biochemistry*, vol. 3 of *Handbook of Lipid Research* (1983). A collection of scientific articles on lipids can be found in Robert M. Bell, John H. Exton, and Stephen M. Prescott (eds.), *Lipid Second Messengers*, vol. 8 of *Handbook of Lipid Research* (1996).

CARBOHYDRATES

Works primarily of historical interest are Frederick J. Bates et al., *Polarimetry, Saccarimetry and the Sugars* (1942), practical information on sucrose and other common sugars together with methods for analysis and preparation of simple derivatives — many of the data tables provide useful reference information; and Walter Norman Haworth, *The Constitution of the Sugars* (1929), a classic description of the knowledge of sugar chemistry at that time, particularly Haworth's work in defining the ring structure of the carbohydrates.

General information on carbohydrates is provided in Benjamin G. Davis and Antony J. Fairbanks, *Carbohydrate Chemistry* (2002); Thisbe K. Lindhorst, *Essentials of Carbohydrate Chemistry and Biochemistry*, 3rd ed. (2007); Karla L. Roehrig, *Carbohydrate Biochemistry and Metabolism* (1984); and Robert V. Stick, *Carbohydrates: The Sweet Molecules of Life* (2001). Methods of analysis are described in M.F. Chaplin and John F. Kennedy (eds.), *Carbohydrate Analysis: A Practical Approach*, 2nd ed. (2003). John F. Kennedy (ed.), *Carbohydrate Chemistry* (1988); and J. Thiem (ed.), *Carbohydrate Chemistry* (1990), include information on synthesis.

Index

A

B

P